THE SECRET PROPHECIES OF
NOSTRADAMUS

EDITED BY CYNTHIA STERNAU AND MARTIN H. GREENBERG

MJF BOOKS

NEW YORK

Published by MJF Books
Fine Communications
Two Lincoln Square
60 West 66th Street
New York, NY 10023

Library of Congress Catalog Card Number 96-78828
ISBN 1-56731-180-6

This edition published by arrangement with DAW Books

Manufactured in the United States of America on acid-free paper

MJF Books and the MJF colophon are trademarks of Fine Creative Media, Inc.

10   9   8   7   6   5   4   3   2   1

ACKNOWLEDGMENTS

To the Reader © 1995 by Cynthia Sternau.

Quatrain One; The Book of Sarah © 1995 by Karen Haber.

Not the German Mountains © 1995 by Hamilton.

Radical Chick © 1995 by Jack Nimersheim and Ralph Roberts.

S.T.O.P.—N.O.S. © 1995 by Tina L. Jens.

Last of the Red-Lead Fleet © 1995 by Nancy Holder.

Buckeye Jim in Egypt © 1995 by Mort Castle.

Twenty Years Later, by Separation Peak © 1995 by Kristine Kathryn Rusch.

Waging Peace © 1995 by Nina Kiriki Hoffman.

The Fire of the Dark © 1995 by Lawrence Greenberg.

Playing in the Street © 1995 by Dean Wesley Smith.

The Apocalypse Quatrain © 1995 by Robert Weinberg.

CONTENTS

TO THE READER:

I wrote these words more than four hundred years ago, and they must be read and interpreted until the Day of Judgment, when the human race accounts for its actions, and all darkness is obliterated by the light of God.

These are my dreams, my prophecies. I give them to you in this form so that you may choose the way for yourself—and for everyone and everything on this planet. Choose not in the shadow of ignorance, but illuminated by the bright light of knowledge, which is all.

Many are the voices who have interpreted me. Each generation of humankind has found new meanings, and new examples, from my Truth. For just as truth is often stranger than fiction, so is this Truth, my Truth, now expressed through fiction. The eleven voices interpreting my prophecies, and these words in my own voice, the twelfth, point to one end only. This, then, you must read and unveil for yourself. Here is the medium, I offer the message. Let there be an end to ignorance and an end to violence. Let calm and beauty and greenness prevail on Earth. Prosper, love, and create, for there is little time left for us before the Light comes. Go, then, in peace.

—Michel de Nostredame

QUATRAIN ONE: THE BOOK OF SARAH

by *Karen Haber*

Century I, #1

Gathered at night in deep study I sit
Alone, upon the tripod stool of brass
Exiguous flame comes out of solitude
Promise of magic that may be believed

Two faces peered in the window. Strange faces, staring past the scalloped lace curtains and the blue-and-white delft pitcher, at Sarah Osgood, sitting in her gleaming kitchen with the blue backsplash above the white stove.

Almond-shaped purple eyes, with pupils that caught the light and reflected it in odd coruscating bursts, watched her. Long triangular noses, moist and velvety, quivered in the warm summer air. Sleek and graceful shorthaired bodies, one orange, the other lavender, perched easily upon the outer sill. They stared as though they had never before seen anything like a seventy-eight-year-old woman in a faded blue house-dress.

For a moment she didn't move, caught by their gaze. *How strange,* she thought. *Strange and kind of pretty.* Could they be cats?

3

A shudder passed through her body and, blinking hard, she sat up even straighter.

Don't be ridiculous, she told herself. Of course they were cats. What else could they be? Probably belonged to that new family down the block.

They had narrow tails neatly tucked by their feet, iridescent whiskers, small rounded ears atop their heads, and four limbs ending in soft paws. Sarah had never heard of cats with purple eyes and whiskers that looked like antennae sprouting from the back of their heads, but maybe they were a new breed. She didn't know cats, really, She had always liked dogs.

"Hello," she said. "Where did you come from?"

The eyes widened. One of them made a pawing motion at the window glass. Did they hear her? Understand?

She felt an absurd urge to coo and spout baby talk. Sarah had never really had any pets—her late husband, Frank, wouldn't tolerate them. Remembering his aversion to all things that weren't formulaic—and therefore solvable—she felt vaguely irritated, and said sharply, "What are you doing here? Are you lost? Shoo. Go home, kitties."

The timer on her oven hummed, building swiftly toward the buzz which meant the ginger cookies for the church bake sale were ready. Three dozen tawny, aromatic cookies had to be cooled and wrapped. Sarah bent to the task and when, later, she remembered to look back through the window, the little faces were gone.

She shrugged and thought no more of it.

That night she had a light dinner of pea soup and bread, brushed and braided her long salt-and-pepper

4

hair, and put on her quilted blue robe. With a sigh she settled down in her corduroy recliner with the brass feet, peppermint tea sending up fragrant steam from her Haviland porcelain cup with the lucky cloverleafs, and set up the ouija board.

It was a habit. Every night, for the past year. Ever since she had found Frank in the backyard, slumped over the azalea bush he had been pruning.

After the funeral, after the first few horrible weeks, when she was beginning to feel more like herself and less like some automatic thing covered in flesh, she had bought the board at a garage sale. It was just a whim: a joke, really. And, at first, she had believed it, believed that she was just distracting herself, making an elaborate ceremony out of trying to contact Frank on the other side. Part of the mourning process. Without her noticing, the joke slowly hardened into ritual. Now, every night, without fail, she tried to reach her dead husband.

Sarah had a firm belief in an afterworld: didn't the Bible promise that the righteous would eat of the tree of life in the paradise of God? All of her married life she had tried to help Frank to see the way. "Pray with me," she had begged him. "Come to church."

For answer, he had laughed and told her that, as a man of science, it was impossible for him to put any trust in what was just some leftover medieval hoohah intended to pacify the serfs.

Well, Corinthians said: "The unbelieving husband is sanctified by the wife." So, every night, Sarah prayed for the deliverance of her husband's soul, and tried to tell him so. To tell him that if, as she feared, he was writhing now in the never-ending fires of Hell, he should take heart. She was praying, working day and night, to redeem and deliver him.

Of course, if anyone from the church had caught her ritually whispering "God bless!" as she lit the vanilla-scented candle which she always placed near the ouija board, or pressing her fingers hard against the heart-shaped plastic tripod as she waited for an answer, she would have blushed right down to the bottoms of her toes. But Sarah had lived long enough to know that certain things just couldn't be explained by logic. They required faith. Time and again she had said so to Frank, and he had laughed and laughed and laughed. Each time, she had forgiven him. It was the Christian thing to do.

"Frank?" she whispered. "Hello? Can you hear me?"

She asked the same questions every night, calmly waiting for an answer. An answer that hadn't come, yet.

Most nights she had patiently, devotedly, lit her candle and queried the spirit world. But tonight she found herself growing a bit restive. "Hello," she said flatly. "Is anybody out there? Anyone? Anyone at all?"

Listen to me, she thought. *I'm getting giddy. Must have put too much sugar in that tea. God works in ways we can't understand. I mustn't question them. Or Him.*

She got up, blew out the candle, took her cup to the kitchen, rinsed it, and set it on the drainboard by the sink. On her way upstairs she shut off the light in the den, not even bothering to put away the ouija board and pointer.

* * *

QUATRAIN ONE: THE BOOK OF SARAH

She dreamed, that night, of Frank. She often dreamed of him. But this time she was telling him that he must hurry, hurry up and write the letter she was waiting for. Was he listening? He kept smiling in an odd fixed way, like some old snapshot whose colors had begun to fade. No, he wasn't listening. He never listened. Why should he be one bit different in death than he had been in life? With sudden anger she tore him in half and threw the pieces into the wastebasket.

She awoke to the sound of gasping and thumping.

At first she thought it was her own heart beating and her lungs wheezing in the cool morning air. But, no. Those sounds were coming from outside of her body.

What was it? Someone in the house? An intruder? Now her heart was pounding indeed.

What on earth could be making that strange noise? She had never heard anything like it before, and yet it sounded so familiar, so terribly, terribly familiar.

Clutching her robe around her, one hand on the telephone, she peered out the window. And saw something, she wasn't quite sure what.

It seemed mechanical. It was silvery and had moving parts, sort of. Flashing yellow lights and strange rubbery-looking appendages. The wheezing sound came from the great bellows which seemed to power the thing. The thumping came as it tried—and failed—to mount the porch steps.

What could it be? Was it a street cleaner? Some kind of new postal machine? If so, why was it out so early, and with no one to tend it? No, no, it couldn't be. She had no idea what it was.

"Go away," she said. "I'll call the police."

Thump! Bump!

The thing crashed up against the stairs again, turned, and went careening down the lawn toward the rose bushes at the edge of the yard. By the time Sarah had gotten downstairs, the machine was gone, leaving pink petals scattered across the grass.

Sarah peered out the front door for one moment longer, shook her head, and went back inside to get dressed. Her knees ached and, she climbed the stairs slowly, clinging to the carved mahogany banister. Her arthritis was certainly acting up. Maybe it was going to rain.

Sure enough, at ten o'clock, the skies darkened as blue-gray and ocher clouds shouldered up against one another to the accompaniment of ominous rumbling. Lightning slashed across the thunderheads. Rain began to thrum against the roof. The pleasant rhythm soon became a resounding downpour which drowned out the weather report on the radio.

At eleven-thirty, the strange cats were back, peering into her kitchen, wet and miserable-looking.

"Oh, all right," Sarah said. "Come in." She raised the window and with nimble grace they bounded over the sill, over the blue and white delft, and into the room. "I can't leave you outside in the rain, can I? Come get dry."

They shook like dogs, scattering moisture everywhere in an ankle-high radius. Sarah retreated out of range until they were finished. Then, side by side, they hunkered down near the stove and regarded her with bright, expectant gazes.

"Are you hungry?" she asked. "I've got some tuna I could give you. Cats like tuna, don't they?" She got a small can of chunk light tuna from the cabinet next to the refrigerator, opened it, and emptied the contents into a yellow plastic dish which had originally held margarine.

Politely they sniffed the proffered fish, looked at one another, and settled back on the blue flowered linoleum, tucking their feet out of sight.

They don't really seem to be hungry, Sarah thought. *Maybe they caught some mice outside.*

The cats blinked, eyelids drooping, and suddenly they were asleep, curled sweetly one around the other.

They certainly are odd kitties, Sarah thought.

The storm grew worse. Rain pounded the roof and winds pummeled the trees in the front yard. The lights flickered, came back, faded again, and went out. Sarah reached under the sink and grabbed her extra vanilla candles and flashlight: Frank had taught her to be prepared for emergencies.

A high wind sent tree limbs flailing. No, that wasn't a tree limb. It was a figure, moving unsteadily across the window, backlit by sporadic flashes of lightning.

Sarah froze, too afraid even to breathe.

A knock at the kitchen door. A rattling of the knob.

Who in the world would be out in this weather, knocking at her door? She could understand pets, lost in a storm. But people?

"Hello?" she cried. "Who's there?" She hooked the security latch and cracked the door open so that she could peer out. "Yes? What is it?"

A figure stood on the threshold, barely visible in the storm's gloom. "Allo? Pardon. Au secours?" The voice was reedy, high, and strangely accented.

It's some foreigner, she thought. Oh, of course. Last Sunday Pastor Bronson had said something about a

9

visiting church group from Osaka. Or was it Orleans? Well, it didn't matter. This traveler must have gotten separated from the rest of his group.

"My goodness, come in," she said, and unhooked the latch. "You'll catch your death out there." And stopped, staring in wonder at the things to which she had opened her door.

Her flashlight beam played over the two individuals who stood dripping on her doormat. One was about her height, blue-green with rainbow teeth, no visible nose or eyebrows, and strange, colorless eyes. In place of hair it had crenellated green fronds which drooped down in a way that reminded her of a fern she had seen at the supermarket.

The other was taller, yellow-orange in hue, with what appeared to be two heads growing out of its narrow shoulders. Its eyes were also pale, and it, too, was noseless.

Sarah opened her mouth to scream, but all that came forth was a faint guttural cough.

Get hold of yourself, she thought. *There's an explanation for this, surely. Some neighborhood kids are playing a prank with rubber masks.* She cleared her throat, caught her breath, and said, "Isn't it a little bit early for Halloween?"

"Pardon?"

"All right, it's a good joke." Sarah forced a smile. "You had me going there, I admit it. What are you kids up to?"

"Kids?" said the blue-green one.

"Up?" said Yellow-orange.

Perhaps these weren't masks. But she refused to consider that possibility very deeply.

10

QUATRAIN ONE: THE BOOK OF SARAH

"What are you doing outside in a storm like this?" she asked.

The yellow-orange one seemed puzzled. "Ce n'est pas Transit Five? Rangoonville, Avril four, 3247?"

Was he asking for directions to a bus stop? "Where is Rangoonville? Is that where you're headed? I'm afraid I can't help you. This is Newton, Illinois. And it's June 4, 1997. The planet Earth," she added sharply. "In case you hadn't noticed. You *are* lost, aren't you?"

"Lost," Blue-green said.

"Ja." Yellow-orange nodded with both heads.

Sarah took a step backward and they followed her right into the house.

"Wait," she said, aware that she was sputtering like an overheated teapot. She knew that she had invited them in, but she wasn't certain she wanted such peculiar people in her kitchen. Especially with the lights out.

"No worry, we're future," said Blue-green, showing all of his rainbow teeth. "Oh, mayhap ne pas *your* future. Jahan, du dire. Su etude old Ameriglish."

The yellow-orange Jahan smiled with both mouths and said, "Please, missus, do not misoverstand us. No harm, we mean du. Calm. Calmforte."

"I beg your pardon," Sarah said.

"Nein, gentler missus. Du we beg. Trufully."

"No offense," Sarah said. "But I think you ought to let Mr. Green-blue here . . ."

"Am Lunoir."

". . . do the talking." Sarah was backed up against the refrigerator, helplessly waving her flashlight. Her gaze fell upon the two cats curled together. They had slept right through the arrival of Jahan and Lunoir.

11

Strange visitors, strange cats. A strange night. Very strange. "Um, are those your pets? Your cats?"

The blue-green Lunoir looked down at the two coiled, dormant felines and shook his head. "Not felis catus. How you call? Cats. Nein. Is Occipus. No seule animal. Conglom. Scouts por hive, perhapment. Je regret that je not engineered por transgenetics learning or to satisfy query."

"Transgenetics? Is that like physics? My husband was a physicist, you know." Sarah warmed to the topic. She always enjoyed discussing Frank, especially with anyone who hadn't known him.

"Physicist?" Jahan began to chortle.

"Physics!" Lunoir laughed outright, great honking guffaws.

"What's so funny about physics?" Sarah demanded.

"Pardon," Lunoir choked out. "Is, what you dit? Alchemy. False. Mal belief. Ersatz. Man into Gott. Argent de lead. Schwarz matter. Le field unifier."

"Jawohl, false," Jahan said.

"Heaven," Lunoir added, chuckling.

"Hell!" Jahan shrieked, giggling out of both mouths.

"Eine kleine sine waves," they both howled, practically falling over. "Les quarks."

Sarah watched them with growing irritation. She felt strangely insulted. "Excuse me, but I don't see the joke. And aren't you confusing religion with science?"

"Confusing. Yes!" They grinned, both of them seemingly delighted that she understood so well.

"What, may I ask, do you folks believe in?"

"Magique," Jahan announced proudly. "Geisteswissenschaften."

QUATRAIN ONE: THE BOOK OF SARAH

"Spirits," Lunoir said, nodding until its tendrils were dancing to and fro.

Sarah drew herself up indignantly. "I'm not going to sit here in my own kitchen," she said, "and be told that religion and science are silly piffle, but that magic is real. You people are really odd. I'm half tempted to call the police." For emphasis she picked up the telephone receiver and shook it like a weapon.

Jahan and Lunoir wilted, fronds and tendrils drooping pathetically.

"Non, non, pardon."

"Please, we lost. Etranger."

"Yes, so you said. Well, I'm not the Traveler's Aid Society." She put the receiver to her ear. Instead of a dial tone, she heard a flat whine. Some wires must have come down in the storm. "Damn!" She flung the receiver back into its cradle.

A fresh crack of thunder split the air. Sarah looked out the window. If anything, it was raining harder than before. She gazed back at her unwelcome visitors. They seemed to have no intention of leaving, and now she couldn't summon help, even if she wanted to. What was she supposed to do, leave her own house?

Calm down, she told herself. *After all, you invited them in. They seem harmless. Just strange. Extremely strange. Frank might even have enjoyed meeting them.*

Goosebumps prickled across her skin at the thought: *Perhaps Frank has already met them.*

With her next breath, she wondered if she could be losing her mind. Quickly, she needed to say something, anything, to distract herself.

"Um, your kitties, here," she said. "They didn't like the tuna fish I gave them. What do they eat?"

13

"Eat?" Lunoir seemed puzzled.

Jahan shrugged, his petals waving in delicate arcs. "Not alimentation. Le soleil."

"You mean they're sun-powered cats, like those water heaters I read about?"

"Nein bin cats."

"All right, whatever you say they are." Sarah decided to play along. "And if they eat sunshine, what do you eat? Stardust?"

"Le soleil."

"Hmmph. Then what do you do on a day like today?"

"Supplementaire." Jahan held out a pale green palm and revealed several faceted, shimmering gems.

"I suppose those are your vitamins."

Lunoir beamed. "Ja!"

Sarah sat down heavily. Her head was spinning. Maybe it was a dream and she would awaken feeling vaguely silly, just as she did after her dreams of Frank. "But where do you come from? France? You're not with any church group. You can't be."

"Church group? Crèche?"

Of course they weren't with a church group, she realized. She might be trying to tell herself that she was sitting around a candle in a darkened house with two cats and an atheistic French couple wearing silly rubber masks. But no masks—or costumes—could be that convincing. And these people weren't from France. In fact, they surely weren't from any place that Sarah had ever heard of. Still, whatever they might be, they were lost travelers, and they seemed harmless. She couldn't in good conscience turn them out into the storm, could she? Nor could she turn away the cats—the noncats. Oh, whatever they were.

She felt slightly ridiculous playing hostess to such odd guests. How to entertain them? Perhaps she should suggest a card game, gin rummy, say. Or they could sing—that was always cheering.

Just around the time she thought she might start giggling aloud from nervous hysteria, the rain eased, the thrumming lessening to a plink, plank, plunk against the roof. The clouds lightened and rolled away, propelled by a stiff wind, as the sun came out, making the lawn sparkle.

The cats opened their purple eyes, stood up, and walked to the door where, politely, they waited.

Jahan and Lunoir were right behind them.

"Soleil," they said in unison.

"Good luck," Sarah said, as she opened the door. "I hope you find that bus you were looking for, or whatever it was." With considerable relief, she watched them scamper down the walk.

Lunoir turned to smile and wave. Rainbows were radiating from his mouth. His face was glowing with unearthly light.

". . . And I saw a mighty angel come down from heaven, clothed with a cloud and a rainbow was upon his head and his face was as it were the sun . . ."

Sarah gasped, understanding coming full upon her and nearly hammering her to her knees.

She had been visited by angels. The cats were not cats, the people were not people, the eerie machine thumping through her garden was not some street cleaning device run amok. Harbingers of paradise. Tokens of the end of all things. The kingdom of God was at hand. Yes, yes, it must be. It must!

Grateful and awed, Sarah bent her head in prayer, giving thanks for this wondrous sign. Tears coursed down her cheeks and she wept for joy. "Glory to God," she whispered. "Hallelujah." As if in further confirmation, the lights in her kitchen sprang back to life. With a full heart, Sarah blew out her candle.

That night, as rain pattered across her roof, she made her evening ouija call.

"Frank," she said. "I had some wondrous visitors today. They said they were from the future. And they didn't believe in physics, Frank. Or religion. What do you think of that?

"At first I didn't understand them. But now I do. I think I was being tested. Frank, my darling. I hope I proved worthy. Perhaps I'll be seeing you again, soon. Very soon. Don't worry."

Predictably, Frank was silent. But Sarah understood.

The next day, she awoke to the usual cheerful neighborhood noises: the buzz of a lawn mower, the whisper of leaves in the wind, the chirp of robins questing for worms. It all seemed perfectly normal out there. But deep inside, at the center of her being, Sarah felt an unusual hollow feeling. What's more, her knees and elbows hurt: most of her joints felt swollen and sore.

All the long day and on into early twilight she had a sense of anticipation, as though something unexpected and amazing might happen. As dusk brought down its purple curtain, a sudden rainstorm blew in, rattling the eaves and shutters. Sarah welcomed it with a sigh of relief, wondering if it would bring any strange visitors to her door.

But the rain stopped quickly and the clouds parted, letting the cold white stars peek through. And there was no strangeness at all. Not even one cloud-borne heavenly messenger. Sarah's one-sided conversation with Frank that evening was brief and dispirited.

She awoke the following morning to a peculiar sound, a sort of whirr-chirp, which seemed oddly familiar, although she knew she had never heard it before, outside of her dreams.

On the green and sparkling dew-fresh lawn, a purple metal barrel girdled by a strip of blinking blue lights was rolling around, apparently self-propelled, muttering aloud.

Sarah felt a sense of vindication at the sight. Hadn't she expected something unusual? Another sacred sign? Of course, it might just be some sort of remote-controlled toy, like those small cars she had seen on television. Just as those occipusses could have been fancy pedigreed cats, and Jahan and Lunoir could have been wearing rubber masks. But Sarah didn't think so.

Whatever the thing on the lawn was, it was tearing up the rye grass which had been Frank's pride and joy.

She threw on her housedress, hurried downstairs, and got out onto the porch just as the barrel made another pass at the azalea bushes. It was a narrow miss.

How did one address a piece of machinery? Sarah felt a pang of fear. The Good Book said, "... beasts full of eyes before and behind ..." She stared at the ring of blue lights blinking all along the barrel's girth and wondered if they were eyes. Could this barrel destroying her lawn be a special emissary from God?"

"Excuse me," she said. "Hello?"

"Morning, ma'am." The voice out of the machine was a touch mechanical, but a pleasant enough baritone. Sarah had heard worse out of human throats. Especially at choir practice.

"What are you doing?" she said. "You're ruining my grass."

"Can't be helped. Gotta find the misalignment."

"I see," she said, although she didn't. "Can't you be more careful about where you look?"

"I'm not the usual linemech for this sector," the barrel said. "But your regular mech is downtime in the seventeenth century trying to unfreeze a bad coupling under the Uffizi Palace. When we got a call that one of the transit joiners here was out of whack, the boys in the shop gave me a quick vernacular implant and, bingo, I was back on the milk run to the twentieth century. Haven't been down here in three or four hundred years. Looks like I got here just in time, too, if you'll excuse the pun."

"What do you mean?"

"This's an important convergence point for the entire sector. Never had much trouble with it before, but some of the polarity is reversed. Probably some deep seismic activity. Already been some slippage. Without servicing, pretty soon you'd be looking at some real bad discontinuities. Even a chance of a major erosion between eras. Scary stuff."

Sarah thought suddenly of Revelation: "The third part of the sun was smitten and the third part of the moon, and the third part of the stars. And I beheld and heard an angel flying through the midst of heaven, saying with a loud voice, 'Woe, woe, woe to the inhabiters of the earth . . .' "

She tried to sound calm. "Would it happen right here?"

"For starters. But don't worry, ma'am. See this magnetic pylon I'm sinking down yonder?"

Sarah peered closely and saw a thin gray metal rod which was slowly disappearing into the ground near her basement window. "That pole? Yes."

"This should take care of the problem."

"Oh," she said. She wasn't really certain whether she understood what he was talking about.

"In fact, this baby could take considerable shocks, even some dislocation, and still function. You might get the odd juxtaposition now and again, travelers missing their connections and suchlike, but nothing serious."

"Serious? You mean, dangerous?" Awesome visions out of the Good Book swam before her eyes: a woman clothed with the sun, standing upon the moon, crying out in childbirth. A red dragon with ten horns and seven heads wearing seven golden crowns.

"There's nothing to worry about, ma'am. We make it our business to take care of the past. But tell you what. If you have any trouble, any little thing at all, you just call me. Ask for Blue Seven." A shimmering silver card popped out of the barrel's side and floated down slowly into Sarah's hand.

"Thank you," Sarah said.

The barrel emitted a twanging three-chord chime and vanished from sight.

"Holy, holy, holy," she whispered, and tucked the card into her purse.

I don't really believe it, Sarah thought. *I must be in shock.*

But it was a pleasant sort of shock, oddly peaceful, and so she set off for her afternoon Bible class, watching the world around her peaceably, with eyes which had already beheld miracles.

Class was held weekly in the basement of the First Congregational Church, a neat red brick building church. It was the same church in which, after much pleading and tears from Sarah, Frank had agreed to be married.

The classroom smelled of freshly washed chalkboards and old erasers. The usual crowd had assembled: Lucy Hogan, Edith O'Neal, Ruth Ann Johnson, and Betty Wilson. Betty looked as though she might be suffering from another of her migraines, poor thing. And Lucy could do with a fresh dye job: her roots were showing white against the reddish-brown teased mass that sat atop her head like last year's hat.

The small wooden chairs were not the most comfortable seats, and Sarah had always felt a little silly sitting behind the children's desks while the minister grandly presided from the front of the room. But she liked Dr. Bronson. He was a nice boy with a round, open face.

The minister rushed in, late as usual. His brown hair needed to be combed and his clerical collar was slightly askew. As he peered at the assembled group, his pale, watery blue eyes were magnified by the rimless lenses of his glasses, giving him a slightly bug-eyed appearance.

"Sorry, ladies," he said. "A parishioner with an

emergency needed my attention. Now, what were we studying?"

"St. Luke," said Ruth Ann.

Sarah thought, rather uncharitably, that Ruth Ann was always rushing to answer the pastor's questions, never giving anyone else a chance. Nevertheless, she enjoyed the discussion of the loaves and the fishes, and an impromptu question about John the Baptist and Salome produced much lively give and take, not to mention some laughter.

When Dr. Bronson asked for other comments, Sarah stood up eagerly.

"I had a thought about Heaven," she said. "About the coming Kingdom."

Dr. Bronson smiled. The incandescent classroom lights reflected off of his lenses, momentarily obscuring his eyes. "Go on, Mrs. Osgood. What about Heaven?"

"Well, we'll be entering it soon, won't we? The Kingdom? Its time is almost upon us."

The wattage of the minister's smile dimmed slightly. "I'm afraid I don't understand . . ."

Sarah persevered. "What I mean is, I know it exists. I've seen the signs. They've been coming thick and fast. Maybe you've been seeing them, too. I didn't understand them right off, I admit. But now I do."

Somebody gasped. Someone else—it sounded like Lucy—giggled nervously.

Father Bronson looked at her in an indulgent way which, in the past, Sarah had always taken for fondness. Today, for some reason, it reminded her of Frank in one of his condescending moods. Just before he began one of his interminable lectures about whatever it was he thought she didn't understand.

"Signs?" he said. "The coming Kingdom of God? Well, these are all very interesting topics, Sarah. Very interesting. I'm sure we'll all want to discuss them fully next week." He made a great show of looking at his watch. "Unfortunately, we're out of time, just now. Thanks for coming, ladies."

Ruth Ann popped up out of her seat like a puppet. "Good-bye, Dr. Bronson," she trilled.

Lucy brushed past Sarah and whispered, "Are you sure you feel all right?"

"Hurry up, Edith," Betty called. "Our ride's waiting."

As the chattering group filed out, the minister motioned for Sarah to stay.

She had always enjoyed being singled out by Dr. Bronson for special attention. In fact, her heart was beating harder than usual, but then, she wasn't accustomed to speaking before a group of people, especially about such important, wonderful things. Sarah couldn't wait to hear what the pastor would have to say privately about her exciting news.

When they were alone, Dr. Bronson took her hand and asked, "Now what's all this about seeing signs of Heaven? I've never heard you say anything like that before."

"Because I have seen them," Sarah said proudly. "*Today*. Outside of my house, just before I came here. I just wondered if other people had seen anything, too."

He squeezed her fingers and released them, leaning back. "I'm sure that we would all like to see them, Sarah."

"Yes, and—"

"Could you describe these signs for me?"

Sarah told him as carefully as she could what she had seen. When she was done, Father Bronson had a curious little frown etching lines between his eyebrows.

"And when did you start noticing these signs?"

"Day before yesterday."

"Aha. So it's been fairly recent."

Sarah couldn't restrain herself any longer. "Dr. Bronson," she said. "Remember, last Sunday, when you read from Revelation? 'Behold, I stand at the door, and knock, if any man hear my voice and open the door, I will come in to him.' Remember?"

"Of course, Sarah, of course."

"Well, that door has opened for me! Oh, isn't it wonderful?"

He patted her shoulder and when he spoke, his voice was very, very tender. "Sarah, I'm sure that the Kingdom of God will come, perhaps even in our lifetime. I certainly hope so. But when the first signs of it occur, we should see them all together. Everyone will see the wonders at the same moment. Do you understand? That's the way it's written."

"But—"

"So perhaps the Day of Judgment is not right upon us."

Sarah stared at him. "But I saw them."

"I know you did."

"Then what do all these portents mean?" she asked.

"Well, let's explore that for just a minute." He gave her an earnest, searching look. "What else could these things be a sign of?"

23

She shook her head, stumped and speechless.

"I know you've had a difficult transition to make," Dr. Bronson said. "You were devoted to your husband."

"We were very close."

"He was a fine man. And it takes time to come to terms with such a big change, such a huge loss. Have you been getting out? Seeing friends? Keeping in touch?"

"Well, yes. A bit." She didn't want to tell him that most of her friends were dead. Young people were so easily upset by comments like that.

"Hmmm. There's somebody I think I'd like you to meet." The pastor rooted around in the pocket of his tweed jacket and finally pulled out a slightly tattered brown card which he handed to Sarah. On it, in precise black letters, was printed: "Ellen Whiteside, MSW, gerontological therapy."

Sarah was so shocked she didn't know what to say. Dr. Bronson thought she needed a therapist. He didn't believe what she had told him, not a word of it.

The minister smiled wryly. "I've upset you, haven't I?"

"Well, I hardly expected *this*."

"Please, Sarah," he said. "Forgive me. I mean no offense. Just take the card home and think about it. If you don't want to see Ellen Whiteside, that's perfectly okay. I just think you might enjoy having a supportive listener to talk to. And, of course, I want you to tell me whenever you think you've seen any holy signs. Let's keep track of them together, shall we?"

Sarah nodded. She felt confused and hurt. All of her

elation had trickled away. Dr. Bronson didn't believe her.

"Do you want me to walk you home?" he asked.

He thought she was some helpless old woman! Sarah drew herself up haughtily. "No, thank you. I can do fine by myself."

"Of course you can. But I want you to promise to come and see me early next week so we can talk about this some more. In fact, I'm going to give you a call, Sarah. And I want you to remember that my door is always open."

Smiling gently, Dr. Bronson helped her up as though she might break at any moment. Sarah nodded her thanks and, head held high, walked out.

At home Sarah felt disjointed and edgy, half-distracted and very irritable. She forgot to defrost the peas, then burned the veal chop.

Well, she wasn't really very hungry anyway. She threw the whole thing out. A little cottage cheese on toast filled the empty place inside. Afterward she brewed some peppermint tea and sat, sipping it from her Haviland cup, trying to feel more cheerful.

"R-i-ing!"

"Oh!" At the unexpected sound of the phone Sarah jumped up, knocking the cup from its saucer to the floor where it shattered as though made of eggshell.

"R-i-ing!"

Flustered and horrified, she couldn't move. A moment later, the phone stopped ringing. Only then did Sarah sink, deflated, into her chair.

I'm a fool, she thought. *A foolish old woman frightened by a ringing telephone, sitting around alone near the end of her life, staring at the ruin of her favorite teacup. Dreaming of angels on the front lawn.*

The room blurred as her eyes filled with tears. She hadn't felt so unhappy in ages. What was wrong with her? Maybe Dr. Bronson had been correct after all. Maybe she did need to go see that therapist woman. Perhaps she had been hallucinating. Perhaps she was losing her mind. The end of the world! The coming Kingdom! What had gotten into her?

She reached for her white leather purse, unsnapped the catch, and pulled out the card with the therapist's phone number on it. But wait, this wasn't the worn brown card with the black lettering from Dr. Bronson. No, it was the silver card that she had received from that funny little barrel with the blinking lights which had been rolling around her yard that morning.

Had it really been just that morning? It seemed like so long ago.

The card shimmered in her hand.

Sarah looked at it. The longer she stared at it, the better she felt. Slowly, she smiled.

She swept up the mess on the floor, brewed another cup of tea, and poured it into a trim blue mug. Then she reached for a fresh vanilla candle, lit it, and went into the den to have a talk with Frank.

Once she was settled in her chair with the ouija board in her lap, she placed her hands against the plastic tripod and said gently, "Frank? Honey, can you hear me?"

"I just wanted to tell you. I understand now. I thought you weren't listening. You have to admit, you haven't exactly been responsive. Of course, you never did listen to me very much.

QUATRAIN ONE: THE BOOK OF SARAH

"Well, this afternoon I even doubted my own faith. Made a fool of myself in Bible class. Now Dr. Bronson thinks I'm crazy, poor man.

"But I realize that these strange creatures have all been sent by God as emissaries. Messengers. They're proof of the afterlife. And I know you must be there, waiting. So I finally understand, darling, and I'll be ready. I promise."

She tapped the tripod once, affectionately, folded up the board, and put both pieces back into the blue cardboard box where they belonged.

Sarah slept deeply that night and dreamed not of Frank but of small electric cars with flashing blue lights racing up and down her front walk.

In the morning she awoke with a smile on her face, feeling younger than she had in a very long time. Her knees didn't hurt. Her fingers weren't swollen. She washed, dressed, and even took some time to make up her face. Then she went out into the front yard.

The lawn looked perfect: no sign of the damage from that crazy barrel yesterday. What had it said to her?

"... *pretty soon you'd be looking at some real bad discontinuities. Even a chance of a major erosion between eras. Scary stuff.*"

She remembered Dr. Bronson last Sunday, intoning from the Book of Revelation: "And behold, a door was opened in heaven: and the first voice was as it were of a trumpet talking with me; which said, Come up hither, and I will shew thee things which must be hereafter."

A door was opened ...

Humming, Sarah picked up a spade from the potting

27

table, and, bending down carefully, began to dig in the damp soil by the basement window.

It took her all morning to find the long, thin rod that the barrel had buried yesterday. What had it called it? A magnetic pylon? Whatever. Because of the arthritis her hands weren't very strong and she could only manage to budge the pole a couple of inches. Well, that would have to do, at least for now.

She covered the rod with soil. The sky, formerly so sunny and blue, was clouding up and there was a chill in the air. The newspaper had promised rain that evening.

Sarah went inside to wash her hands. She had a light lunch, then settled in a chair by the window.

The sky darkened and the first faint rumbles of thunder could be heard in the distance.

And, behold, a door was opened in heaven.

Outside, the first drops of rain were beginning to fall, plink, plank, plunk, upon the roof.

Sarah sipped her tea and waited for the coming Apocalypse, and Frank.

NOT THE GERMAN MOUNTAINS

by Hamilton

Century III, #67

There shall be a new race of Philosophers
Who despise death, gold, honors, and wealth
They shall be near the German mountains
To ensure them support and followers

BOOK I

"Where are we, Sam?"

"*I* don't know. What do you think—*I* know every-thing? Do you think *I* know everything, Megan? What! Why is it assumed that *I* know everything around here? What time is it, Hershel?"

"We gave up the watches. Remember?"

"Did I ask you, Megan? Did I ask *you?* I asked Hershel here what time is it, and you pipe in with the give-up-the-watches routine. Of course I remember we gave up the watches."

"Sam, Sam, oh, best of boys, why such an unmiti-gated show of temper this morning?"

"This afternoon. It has to be at least two o'clock. Look at the sun, Megan. Why *did* we give up watches?"

"You know why, Sam. Shall I recite the versent?"

"I know, I know:

29

> *"Time PASSES, Future gained*
> *Watch not, want naught"*

See?"

"Not *that* versent, Sam. Listen:

> *"Ornaments Off*
> *Lest GOODNESS retreat"*

"Yeah, yeah, yeah. Hershel, you're uncommonly quiet. Psychonavigating? Hershel? Hershel!"

"Yes ... Sam ... sorry ... psychonavigating."

"And?"

"Our presentation goes well despite our age. There will be dissension only among the United Culturists."

"If we alter a versent, will they comply? We probably still have seventeen minutes to make changes ..."

All laugh and simultaneously snicker the word "seventeen."

"... what did they object to? Versent 362, I bet."

"No, Sam, dear friend, Versent 396:

> *"Currency binds the SOCIAL tank*
> *Our delivery, our justice, our thanks."*

"Because it implies system?"

"The opposite, Sam, the opposite. I must say, good boy, for being a genetically engineered philosopher, you *do* miss the mark at times."

"For every problem there exist several different ways of approach, Hershel."

"Pray tell, Sam. Enlighten us, our entire twelve years."

NOT THE GERMAN MOUNTAINS

"Very well. It is not true that Versent 362, as stated during our sixth year of philosophic inquiry and enrichment, reads:

"How damagingly PURE the trophy display
A young heart grave weeps and sighs?"

"You quote with precision, Sam. Go on."
"Thank you."
I ask you, Megan, for the benefit of enlightening Hershel—bestowing honor upon the events of human behavior requires systems, right?"
"Yes."
"Ethical systems, dear comrade?"
"Certainly not, as evidenced by line two, what about those not honored whose potential floats dead."
"But a system, nevertheless. Right, Megan? Hershel?"
"Yes, of course, a system. I see, Sam. The United Culturists would deny the system, but embrace the issue. Good point. How should we alter 362?"
"Megan?"
"I would suggest beginning the versent, *why* damagingly PURE."
"To elevate the despise to interrogative?"
"Yes."
"Question outweighs fact . . ."
". . . And negates system. Brilliant, Sam."
"Resurrected?"
"Resurrected, Sam. Back in the saddle, but why so obsessed with time today? The watch incident, the outburst."
"Hershel, Megan, have you forgotten where we are

31

going; how important this day is; how challenging the task ahead?"

Laughter, amazement and palpable resolve fill the still vehicle air.

From the driver's front window perspective, Mounts Chryslar, Empire, Zeckendorf, AT&T, WTC, MetLife, and Tyrannosaurs Trump appear as black and white protons and neutrons nestled and presumably, yet undetectably pulsating in an exceptionally stable fresh atom.

The Neutral philosophers, Megan, Hershel, and Samantha exude the confidence of universal nature as the vehicle thunders toward the rooftop of the United Cultures building.

FADE IN: SCRATCHING SOUNDS. FIRELIGHT FLICKERING IN A CAVE.

Things change little. Things change majestically. The day goes fast. Century *question mark,* (here documented as question mark because civilization stopped counting somewhere in the twenty-third C), inhabited by Megan, Hershel, Sam, and billions of other chemically combined results of carbon, hydrogen, oxygen, and nitrogen mixed together, differs technologically. Cities, states, countries, factions, politics, MYTH, sociology, anthropology, salsiology, fratricide, suicide, nephocide . . . and on and on and more and more technically sophisticated, exist, but with a markedly different foundation.

Humankind must evolve to something, right? The mind matures slowly, like everything else, over billions of years—what if, though, what if the process of evolution strictly adhered to the principles observed by the Studiously Affluent Consortium of Biotechnicians? What if, through DNA manipulation, a new human being, designed with the greatest of intention to solve humankind's diabolical need to aggress, transgress, intergress, blossomed in laboratory perfect wombs, jumped into the arena of the unwell world, and actually answered difficult questions, finger-pointing the way to Absolute Understanding?

They exist.

They walk this day from copter pad to United Cultures podium.

Megan, Hershel, Sam. Known mentally as the MHS project these past seven years, I have, through extraordinary means and stealthy methods, obtained documents that substantiate a valiantly guarded trade secret—hundreds of superior brains were sacrificed for the benefit of the MHS project fulfillment.

I found out about the zenith top-secret project site via a friend of a friend of a relative of a surprisingly weak operative of the Sub-Limestone Intelligence Alley (a circular, tubular facility several thousand feet below Central Landfill, the midpoint eyesore of the good ol' Newer York City-State, the principal political gathering point in these United States' of Municipality Cooperatives). Being a responsible journalist, I immediately informed everyone in the world I knew of this most coveted covert cavernous community known to post-modern times—an act that, in present times, could hypothetically happen, but given the overwhelmingly tenacious versent driven following of MHS, would not affect the Population At Large, for:

"Expose narrowly the pattern's web
Nestle in SOFT pairs, tranquil, quiet"

In our world, ironically brought breathlessly close to destruction by Ready Access Military Involving Tension (affectionately referred to as global warming) NewsWatchmen no longer exist. We all remember the minute RAMIT formed, however—that instantaneous compulsory network born simultaneously with Essence Extraction Capability.

Why am I documenting this you might ask, you . . . post you . . . whomever, whatever follows in the next phase, as predicted by MHS versent number 706:

"Bend, INEVITABLE, the thinking flesh tree
Bosom in uncontrolled movement"

Essence Extraction Capability, a direct result of humankind's awareness of a sixth sense organ, the steen, located in subcutaneous tissue adjacent to the brain stem, made this world a better place to live, but not necessarily a better place to live in, as living in a world requires certain . . . definitions of place and purpose. True, the steen enables any person to rationalize paradox and transcend observation, but that sense, even when combined with the talents of eye, ear, nose, skin, and tongue, cannot promote happiness, goodness, honesty, faith, or any other Most Important Tenet. What promotes MITs and harmonious attributes has to come from mindful decisions patterned in the sociological global framework.

Not.

We need a philosophy. Badly.

Since every multisensory being has EEC, violence, as we knew it, has disappeared. Shortly after violence disappeared, the web of social-driven myth began to shiver in subtle yet not decidedly definite ways. *R*eligion, *P*olitics, and *M*oney still held the society together—but the individual knew better—knew intrinsically, painfully, that the strong RPM forces were nearing breakdown. Global awareness of this nervous activity prompted the cocooning operation referred to earlier as a location—the Sub-Limestone Intelligence Alley. (Please note: when society scales down to the authentic power of the individual units, group nomenclature evolves to points in space-time as opposed to relative points of reference.)

By now, blessed creatures of distant time, you may want to know the definition of EEC. I beg your pardon, and quote:

> *"What OBVIOUSNESS denies*
> *The marched pride conceals."*

EEC/eek!/acronym Also written Eec or eec:

Short for essence extraction capability, a name for either one or two retropsychokinetic steen-induced manipulations (properly called EEC-1 and EEC-2) which cause a breakdown of the whatness of subatomic particles, leading in most all cases to the development of Nuclear Events Spontaneously Tactical. EEC-1, a triggering phase, alerts one's steen to the acute seriousness of a potential NEST disease. EEC-2 stages full-blown NEST. The USMC Center for Violence Control was the first agency to identify the ramifications of an all out EEC-2 epidemic. Their findings, substantiated by a bizarre controlled experiment on planet Unsafe, indicate that it would take only forty-seven NESTs to destroy a world. With a population of eleven billion that means that a truly negligible percentage of people have the power to completely destroy our world. Luckily, the steen, an extremely fragile sense apparatus, equips an individual with the ability to distinguish between self and society as one paradoxically relates to the other. RAMIT (Ready Access Military Involving Tension—briefly stated, a universal agreement between individuals that any tense act can and will be immediately retaliated in military style) formed as a result of this remarkable, universal sense. There have been twelve reported NESTs (eleven physically impaired individuals; one anomaly) in the last four hundred years, the last one occurring over two hundred years ago. The individual as society paradox drove various SIT (Socially Interested Terrestrials) groups to initiate project MHS.

This definition resides here. Only here. There are no dictionaries on this planet because:

> *"Trap the versent lyre and*
> *Doubly dense in WORD habit flat"*

I scratch onto walls of this cave as evidence that language still exists. O fellow spelunkers, have at it. Read what you will into my writing. I am a journalist in a world where no journalism exists.

NOT THE GERMAN MOUNTAINS

When society, as we had become accustomed to defining it, shifted to individuality, and with the aspect of violence more or less flushed out, a strange dilemma lay at the seat of humankind's linear throne—how do you spend your day? With no need to compete, (competition quickly fell into the realm of violence subscript, hence unacceptable on the individual level as EEC could kick to NEST in even innocent forms of the WORD POTENTIAL), why work? Why wear the suit? Who makes the suit? Suddenly there are no suits.

But there are suits. People do not walk around nude, even in this century. People make their own suits. Suits of every kind. Elaborate, sequined, robelike apparel. Pleated pants. Pajama pants. Cardigan and blazer jackets. Dirndl skirts with elasticized waistbands, for big bang sake. Ties—bow, string, neck. Ascots! Who brought those back? You see them, though, but with no media, no photographs, who's to know? You. You will know, because you are standing there with a light source reading about it. You understand the words you are reading because you took the trouble to engage your mind with vocabulary. You are amused. By the way, my name ... Parl/4'e. What a hoot, eh? Dates back to late twentieth century.

And the accoutrements—cuff links, necklaces, shining golden metal dangling from homemade thread, homemade design, homemade illusion ... The Individual Cut, the model buried deeply within DNA, encoded since the beginning of life.

Currency stopped being minted. The barter system has prevailed for quite some time. Funny thing though: those materials responsible for the foundation of ersatz mediums of exchange became the most desirable elements of that peculiarly human spondulicks obsession. So what happened? Gold, silver, platinum, titanium accelerated to the peak word of most all civilizations: *M*oney. Not coin, not bill—*M*oney. Raw, unaltered, dirt-on-the-hands *M*oney. Still around. After all these years, that than which nothing greater can be conceived, the transaction basic to the trading imperative, probably something genetic in source, however irritating a building block bug, continues to dictate everything from the disposal of waste to the raising of architectural behemoths. Even stripped of myth, *M*oney rules.

Entertainment as it had been known died less than a minute after RAMIT. Too much violence and sex. And the big question you ask yourself, if you have any knowledge of oral history, or have taken the trouble to access COME (Computer Organization of Matriculation Education), and if you subscribe to Lam5/32'd's theory that sex equals violence, the question relating to entertainment and sex hugely matters. Before RAMIT, sex. After RAMIT, no sex. So how do we reproduce, you may wonder? That is if you are not of this planet or if you have devolved. The steen. The female steen sends messages that miraculously transform bacteria lining the vagina walls into spermatozoa. These little swimmers can be activated at will in order to impregnate fertile eggs.

Testosterone took a dive in the male of the species. Androgen suicide. Men still grow beards, deepen their voices in the teen steen years and develop impressive muscles. What good any of this does remains as unknown as ancient man's appendix. Yet females continue to produce men. Men who involve large and small groups in *R*eligion and *P*olitics, two unfortunate webs you may assume rendered obsolete in a system such as the one I am describing. I know, I know. What about all the violence associated with these two words *R*eligion and *P*olitics. Well, quite frankly, once the violence was extracted, *R*eligion and *P*olitics grew in intensity and individual compliance. When boredom as manifest in violence ceased, boredom with a capital "B" loomed in the fabric psyche like a dry capellini around extra virgin oil, as,

> *"Boredom outlet without,*
> *UNITS decline, rigid, unctuous"*

The former driving rationalization that *R*eligion and *P*olitics exist merely to pacify the masses does not seem to stop the purveyors of said disciplines in peremptorily peaceful times. Everywhere I look, cults, cliques, Argus-eyed civil engineers cook up group activities and mythical blankets for brethren and common political prisoners to hold onto. Mostly men, I add. I add because a particular gender should not dictate such powerful restraints in societies based on individual freedom, especially in light of the hermaphroditic talents of one over the other. Clearly, the absence of role in the continuation of the species led males to utter desperate depths unparalleled in the grand historical perspective. Yet how adroitly they pivot unshaved minds and dribble the heads of engendered states; how ridiculously entangled in the mythical and directional gulfs; how sadly lost in a maze of linguistic theological roots and proportionate gnarly weeds of justice. Systems of right and wrong, good and bad, *R*eligion and

*P*olitics, governed by man, confuse the participants of civilization most when formalized for reasons other than violence. Suicide can happen, and that's dangerous. Hence, and I scratch BIG HENCE, a select group of individuals, men and women, bigender operatives who reinvented pen and paper (I saw the documents) signed a Declaration of Intention in order to establish a more perfect USMC. I need to mention right now that prior to RAMIT, computer technology had reached an extremely literate self-learning level light-years ahead of monitor/keystroke commands. Virtual interaction with heuristically enhanced software mutated and selected, patterned and embellished human learning curves. Now, not only can anyone plug in, anyone, subject to their predetermined cerebral cortex capacity, of course, with a human brain has the ability to solve problems utilizing the electronic sophistication of an impartial, impersonal mate, the computer. Members congregating at the Sub-Limestone Intelligence Alley, all oddly enough exceptional specimens of cerebral cortex capacity, plugged in seven years ago. The answer to the question took three minutes to assimilate in the minds of the congregation.

After signing the Declaration of Intention and inserting their thumbs into BERTHA (not an acronym, just a one-of-a-kind giant computer with thousands of inputs), several hundred men and women committed suicide in response to a growing concern amongst higher minds (both biological and electronic) that the significance of falsity inherent in RPM would eventually result in global NESTing and the ultimate destruction of the entire universe. As the documents I read illustrated, and may I inform the lucky reader that knowing how to read, but existing in a society without the written word available must be likened to the unwakable nightmare. Reading intoxicates me. Not a bad thing. Where was I? Oh, as the documents I read illustrated, part of the congregation committed suicide, not as an act of violence, for this would have resulted in our extinction, but as an act of deliberate, unconditional compassion. You see, the computer, driven by collective intellectual hysteria, prompted a solution completely outside the RPM structure. It predicted that only a philosophy could overcome the predictable effects of RPM. A philosophy with universal implication. A philosophy within the grasp of every conscious steen-born individual. A foe to boredom. A paragon mental citadel in which to pursue happiness and individual satisfaction. "To leap tall buildings with a single bound." In essence, to change the inner light from red to green.

You wonder about the intellectual suicides, don't you? Well, even if you don't I'll tell you. I alluded to it before. You see, BERTHA decided that a philosophy had to be formulated and then embraced by all. It also sensed that neither the people plugged in nor itself possessed the knowledge necessary to orchestrate such a mammoth project, therefore, the only logical answer to the collective question nestled in "being." A new "being" would have to evolve in order to solve the problem. The genetic technology necessary to address the task rested deep within the memory banks of the computer. Volunteers' brains would be needed for research and development. Quite simple really. Sacrifice a few hundred higher brains for the safety of the universe *and* acquisition of human happiness on a global scale. Reason enough to join the Sub-Limestone Intelligence

Alley as spokesperson. You could almost elevate my role to journalist.

ENTER: Megan, Hershel, Samantha, seven-year-old philosophers. The United Cultures building.

"Good afternoon. My name is Par1/4'e. I am your host this afternoon for a most auspicious occasion. Joining us today are three philosophers who have an awesome message to convey. Before listening to their speech, I feel compelled to once again state the problem we face as individuals . . . the problem that led to the search for philosophical help.

We suffer from boredom. The kind of boredom that only comes from not being able to interact with violent intent. Damn the Steen! The sense that robbed us of our urges and gave us an individual freedom incapable of dealing with society.

We have managed to pull away enough of the former social format in the areas of religion, politics, and money in order to function.

We foster the oral traditions of religion that teach afterlife as an antidote to chasing the finite, a lie we hate and despise.

We look to politics for judgment, standards, and honorable discourse. We see through the verbal gauze. There is no honor.

We trade with each other. We use money to adorn ourselves. We sicken when we reflect on such petty mercantile thoughts.

We know we are above all this and we are bored. We know that boredom is the most subtly vicious catalyst for internal violence. Our steens are heavy with pain.

NOT THE GERMAN MOUNTAINS

We are ready to implode. With the collective power of a trillion supernovas we know we have the NESTing ability to obliterate all that is."

A PREGNANT PAUSE.

"You are all familiar with some of the versents going around, the two-line medications that have kept our steens occupied these past few years. What most of you do not know is the source of these verbal pills. They sit behind the curtain in back of me. Before I introduce you to the authors, please put on your helmets, plug into BERTHA, and access MHS in the menu. There you will find the complete list of 666 versents. You can take these back to your cultural constituencies.

A BEE BUSY HALF HOUR ENSUES. SMILING FACES ABOUND AS THE INFORMATION IS DISSEMINATED.

"Ladies and gentlemen, I present Megan, Hershel, Samantha. Project MHS."

CURTAIN OPENS. AN AUDIBLE HUSH STAMPEDES THE GREAT HALL AS THE THREE SEVEN-YEAR-OLD PHILOSOPHERS WAVE TO THE AUDIENCE.

"Ladies and gentlemen, let me assure you, the philosopher children sitting before you possess fully mature steens. They have been genetically engineered with one purpose in mind—to squelch our nauseating boredom by philosophical means."

ANOTHER PREGNANT PAUSE. A SNEEZE, A COUGH, OTHERWISE SILENCE.

"I have been told that the 666 versents are mere teasers designed to stimulate an interest level for this afternoon's paramount message. Megan, Hershel, and Samantha have informed me that their speech is short, but that our steens should be prepared to grapple with acres of thought.

"Now, I think we are ready, therefore . . . Philosophers?"

MEGAN, HERSHEL, AND SAMANTHA RUSH TO THE MICROPHONE. ANTICIPATORY TEARS RACE DOWN EVERY FACE IN THE ENORMOUS ROOM. THERE IS SOME FEEDACK AS THE TRIO TEST THEIR PERFECT HARMONY. THEN THEY SING:

"Above all else, avoid RPM."

AND WITH THE SONG CAME SHOWERS OF HUMAN RELIEF AND YEARS OF AFFECTION FOR THE PHILOSOPHER CHILDREN.

RADICAL CHICK

by Jack Nimersheim and Ralph Roberts

Century VI, #8

Those who serve in the kingdom of Knowledge
Upon political change shall become impoverished
Once exiled, without support, having no money
Literacy and learning will not be of great value

Felicity's career at the Academy started badly. A staff counselor ultimately diagnosed her as being "creatively challenged." In those initial days and weeks, however, no one knew what to make of her aberrant behavior.

In the first month of her freshman year—it being only a partial month, at that—Felicity discovered an entirely new and novel solution to an old and almost forgotten mathematical mystery. That she would even attempt such a feat should have alerted the Academy's administrative staff to the problems that lay ahead. It didn't.

Few people remembered Pierre Fermat's "unsolvable problem," which the French mathematician proposed and then enigmatically professed to have solved within the margins of a book he wrote in the mid-seventeenth century. In this same note, Fermat claimed that lack of space prevented him from presenting his proof. Consequently, the so-called Last Theorem remained an enigma for more than three centuries, until 1993. That's when an English mathematician named Andrew Wiles resolved the matter, at least for most cases. Wiles' solution, itself now almost a century old, consumed hundreds of pages filled with oblique prose and cryptic calculations. Felicity's proof, which worked in *all* cases, required a mere three paragraphs to elucidate.

Had she been satisfied with this single accomplishment, Felicity might have saved herself and her family a lot of grief. But she wasn't; and she didn't.

The night before turning in her paper on Fermat's proof, Felicity hacked her way into the school's super computer and loaded into its memory a deceptively sophisticated little program of her own devising. Once again, her actions raised no red flags. In hindsight, it's easy to chide the Academy for such gross negligence. This condemnation, however, ignores two critical facts. For one thing, Felicity designed her program to run in background processing mode, making its execution virtually impossible to detect. Even more to the point, the system to which she uploaded this elegant code was vastly underutilized, as were all of the school's computers. Not a single person capable of recognizing the significance of a few million surplus CPU cycles appearing within the system's audit report signed on, during the three-day period of her unauthorized access.

Thus was Felicity able to announce proudly, on the last Friday of September during her first year at the Academy, that she had determined the value of *pi* to over six-hundred million decimal places. Furthermore, she revealed, this incredible cipher, which for centuries had been considered a nonreiterative value through infinity, did indeed repeat. She then explained, with just a touch of condescension, how it shouldn't surprise anyone that this pattern avoided detection for so long. After all, the pattern of the repetition only emerged after the initial two-hundred million decimal places had been calculated.

Several academic anachronisms—aging recipients of the Nobel Prize, the Hawking Award, and such—praised Felicity's achievements. Two or three went so far as to petition an audience with her. Neither the Academy authorities nor Felicity's parents, who were called in for a special conference, responded to these requests. Instead, they agreed that the most judicious action they could take was to issue the precocious young girl fourteen demerits and confine her to her room for two weeks.

"How could she do this to us, Arthur? Didn't she listen to none of that stuff we said, before we sent her off to the Academy?"

"Now, now, darling," Felicity's father was trying his best to comfort his wife. "This is only a phase she be passing through. It ain't nothing more. Have you already forgot how, when I was her age, I done formulated an accurate mathematical model of the event horizon surrounding unstable singularities? But look at me now. I ain't such a bad guy, considering my youthful indiscretions."

"Of course not. Still, you gotta admit, it wasn't all that easy for you to drop them radical roots. I doubt you'd a done it without the genetic treatments," Felicity's mother replied. "Oh, don't be gettin' yourself all offended, dear. You can't deny that what I said is gospel! I done prayed—against hope, it now appears—that our daughter would be spared that same trauma."

Arthur and Grace Levine loved their daughter, a short but perky girl with merrily flashing brown eyes and raven hair. But they also admitted openly her faults. When she was younger, they wondered about the creamy skin that seemed immune to the blemishes which often afflicted her contemporaries. And they worried about her vivacious intelligence. They tried to brush this off as nothing more than a childish manifestation that would fade with time. Time's passing, however, failed to produce the desired results.

Their concerns turned to consternation when Felicity's impressive intellect started alienating her friends and classmates. Knowing what such seemingly innocent rebuffs could eventually lead to, they decided to stave off these potential problems before they began. This decision led directly to their enrolling Felicity in the Academy, her father's alma mater, where they hoped their daughter would learn to behave more like her peers.

"You better be wising up, girl," Sudie MacCready said. By the time both girls were seniors, Sudie was one of the few people in Felicity's class who even pretended to be friends with her. A plump, unpopular girl, her sardonic personality limited Sudie's social contact to those few who could tolerate her for a few minutes, at most.

"I refuse to be something I'm not," Felicity replied, brushing black hair away from her face in a charming gesture. A passing young man in the hallway showed interest until he recognized her. Slightly embarrassed, he turned away, his face dull.

"Your name turned up on the on-line news network last night," Sudie said, sniffing in disdain. "You are . . ." she paused, shuddering before completing the obscenity, then lowering her voice to a hiss, "making history."

Felicity glanced over at her coyly as they strolled between classes. "Why, Sudie, I didn't know you could still read."

"I can't. My little brother tol' me about it." Sudie was not in the least bit embarrassed by this admission. "You better slow down, Felicity, or they won't be letting you graduate."

This gave Felicity pause, hammering home, as it did, the full depths of her dilemma. To not graduate from the Academy was to be declared unfit for society. Based on this declaration, she could be institutionalized for the rest of her days, leaving her parents forever tainted by her failure.

"I'll try," she said quietly, as much to herself as to Sudie. "Yes, I'll try."

"You is taking all of your Homework, ain't you?" Sudie asked suspiciously.

"Of course," Felicity assured her. "Every night."

She wondered, however, as she had many times before, whether the series of drugs called Homework might prove ineffective on her. They certainly worked for her classmates, who over the course of a few days could forget entire subjects. In her case, all they seemed to produce was a minor headache that faded as quickly as it came.

Further analysis of the situation would have to await

another time, however. The bell signaling the start of her advanced mathematics class rang, just as she and Sudie entered the room.

"Today we'll continue our exercises in unlearning the multiplication tables," Mrs. Garvey, Felicity's third-period teacher, announced. "Remember, class, this subject contributes 30% to your senior grade. Passing it is mandatory, if you expect to advance to the finals."

Mrs. Garvey was old—over forty, Felicity guessed. She had sunken, intense eyes, which she focused like a laser cannon at a student near the back of the second row.

"Marvin, what's seven times three?"

Felicity felt sorry for her classmate as he proudly declared: "Twenty-one, Mrs. Garvey."

Mrs. Garvey consulted a book sitting atop her desk. "That's right," she said, making no effort to hide her contempt. "Try harder next time, young man."

Next, the cannon eyes ratcheted around toward Felicity. She imagined the clicks as range adjustments were made and two armor-piercing shells loaded. "How much is two times eight, Ms. Levine?"

The correct answer, sixteen, was about to tumble instinctively from her lips. She caught herself just in time.

"Er . . . um . . . I afraid I have no idea, Mrs. Garvey."

"A very good answer, my dear. I'm glad to see *someone* in this class is taking their Homework seriously."

Felicity smiled in response to Mrs. Garvey's compliment. *I really will do better,* she vowed to herself. *I*

RADICAL CHICK

will graduate. I will. I will! I'll make the Academy—and my parents—proud.

The Academy comprised a sprawling warren of marble buildings, many of which now displayed crumbling facades. Still, it was a pleasant enough place, possessing as it did tree-lined streets and quiet shaded spots where students were encouraged to sit and stare blankly at creation in the approved manner.

At one time, its name had been Harvard, and the institution had been of the type for higher education once called *universities*. Now, over thirty years after the triumph of the New Luddite Church and the world's conversion to the True Peace of Ignorance, the Academy served a loftier purpose. For several years after its realignment, it had been named the Academy for Gifted Students. Political correctness soon prevailed, however, and its name was changed once again—this time to the Academy for Conformity and Standardized Performance. In both cases, most people simply referred to it as the Academy.

The Academy maintained a special place in the educational scheme of things. The world's public schools handled the vast majority of students well enough. Administering the drugs called Homework reinforced a global transition to Holy Mediocrity. In such a state of grace, the world attained true peace for the first time in human history. The explanation for this impressive accomplishment was simple. If one cannot conceive of conquering his enemies, he starts no wars. If one does not possess the intellect required to scheme and manipulate, she does not cheat her friends or neighbors.

Many people initially rebelled against the Luddite

philosophy. Although they might disagree with some of its underlying tenets, however, they could not argue with its success. Over time, the wars and economic collapses that engendered its initial popularity became less numerous. The differences that previously set one person or nation against another first dwindled and then disappeared completely. As the world became a gray, quiet place, a new era—a Golden Age—materialized.

Even in this idyllic environment, however, aberrations occurred. The most devout parents sometimes produced children handicapped by extraordinary intelligence. Properly training these children for placid adulthood, even with the help of mind-numbing pharmaceuticals, proved beyond the scope of more traditional schools. Thus were institutions like the Academy reluctantly established. They were equivalent, in the old style, to a high school or, perhaps more correctly, a junior high. They specialized in converting potential troublemakers, introducing them to the rigid precepts of the True Peace of Ignorance.

So must it be, said the Prophets.

I *will* succeed. I *will* graduate, Felicity vowed yet again on the golden afternoon of a Native American Summer. She walked alone across the quad, Sudie having sought a less sparkling conversation elsewhere.

"Hiya, stupid," a passing freshman said, not knowing her and thus being polite.

Felicity paused and looked around the crowded campus. She saw hundreds of students relaxing after class, their blank faces gazing without understanding at the dappled shadows under the spreading elms. The uncomprehending stares reflected, as was the norm, the blessed peace of the nonthinking.

I shall *be like them,* she both admonished and instructed herself, then caught her error. No, she corrected herself, I'll *done be* like them, afore I'm done.

Deciding against returning to her dorm before supper, she wandered off in no particular direction, toward no specific goal. As she walked, Felicity practiced placidity of expression and turgidity of thought. It seemed to be working! For a few moments her mind drifted as aimlessly as her body did; the scenes she passed were as nothing to her. Could this herald the beginning of a successful transformation?

The distant strains of muffled music interrupted her speculation. She sighed and sought out the sound, which filtered through the open door of a run-down bar located in a seedy neighborhood bordering the Academy's property. It was a haunting but simple melody, a classic from the Late Manilow era—this being both the preferred and authorized structure of the currently popular music. Most of her friends considered it a pleasant diversion. Felicity found it extremely boring.

Felicity spent much of the next week conceiving an entirely new form of musical expression, one that relied on contrapuntal rhythms to complement half-tone progressions within the framework of a twelve-note scale. Try as she might to ignore the voice of her personal muse, she could not help herself.

Felicity needed to create. And so, she did.

The snows came during the December of Felicity's senior year. That month also brought with it a chilly encounter between Felicity and her curriculum counselor, Mr. Simmons.

Samuel Simmons was in his late fifties. Thinning hair splayed in an unkempt halo around his balding head. The thin lapel of his simple gray suit sported a New Luddite pin—an empty circle symbolizing the ever-so-blessed True Peace of Ignorance. As he spoke, his thin index finger tapped incessantly the report that was sitting atop his desk.

"What is the meaning of this, Ms. Levine? What sort of unacceptable activities are you up to, now?"

"I don't know, sir," Felicity said demurely, her hands clasped in her lap.

"Of course you know, and that's the problem," Simmons said. "I may not understand everything about your latest efforts," he added virtuously, "but I don't doubt for a moment that *you* do."

Felicity chose to remain silent, creating an extremely awkward pause.

"I remember your freshman year, here at the Academy," Simmons continued, no longer attempting to hide his scorn. "After the Fermat flap and your adventure with *pi,* you created a tensor calculus that even graduates could use. We suppressed it, of course, and tried doubling your drug dosage. You repaid our kindness by discovering previously hidden correlations between the Chaos Theory and atmospheric perturbations, a discovery that led directly to reliable long-range weather forecasting on a global scale. This forced us to increase your Homework load yet again.

"Oh, you were extremely cooperative. You consumed the pills like candy—after which you became fluent in seventeen languages and wrote what I have been told is the definitive history of the Egyptian dynasties, explaining away the mysteries of the pyramids within a brief sidebar.

"And we, we gave you even stronger pills. You then invented what is, if not a true perpetual-motion machine, a pretty darn impressive imitation of one. It's been chugging along on its own accord for the past three years."

" 'Not to worry,' I told Headmaster Quarm, 'she is just a bit immature for her age. I'm certain she'll soon outgrow this genius stuff . . .' "

Felicity gasped.

Simmons slammed his hand down on the desk. His naturally red face grew even more sanguine.

"I'm sorry, Ms. Levine, but your actions over the past three and a half years have moved me to a crassness of language I usually refuse to employ." Simmons paused for a moment to regain his composure. "And you is making me use all them big words, too," he finally added, employing the popular vernacular.

Felicity waved aside his apology. After all, she also displayed a tendency to fall back upon a crass, erudite mode of speech, rather than the simplicity of the Holy Vernacular, to utter "I do not have any," when a more educated and cultured person would correctly say, "I ain't got none."

Simmons was wringing his hands in agitation. He seemed to be truly concerned about her.

Maybe the old goat is not so bad after all, Felicity thought. *Maybe he really is only looking out for my best interests!*

"I think I need help, Mr. Simmons," she said.

"*Thinking* is your problem!" Simmons shouted. He

quickly followed this outburst with an apologetic gesture. "Forgive me, again. Concerning your comment, though, I may just have an answer.

"Yours is an extreme case, certainly the most extreme I've ever seen. Almost beyond remedy. There is a therapy, however, that may allow you to graduate with the rest of your class this spring, as I believe you wish to do. Keep in mind, however, that what I'm about to propose will sound quite radical."

Felicity unclasped her hands and leaned forward in her chair. "I don't care, Mr. Simmons. I'll try anything. *Anything!*"

"Okay. Now we know, Felicity, that you've been taking your Homework seriously since arriving here," Simmons continued. "We have ways of checking up on such things, you realize. In your case, though, the normal approaches don't seem to work. This doesn't mean we've given up hope. I have a feeling that you can still be helped. Doing so, however, requires the somewhat specialized skills of . . ." Simmons settled back into his chair. He sighed and looked around, almost furtively, before continuing. ". . . the Harvard Medical School," he uttered quietly.

Felicity found herself gasping again. She looked at him as if he had said something off-color, almost obscene. Indeed, that's exactly what he *had* done.

"But . . . But, Mr. Simmons . . . Sir. The Har . . . what you said . . . it no longer exists. It hasn't for decades. The Academy replaced it."

Simmons briefly consulted a reference book he had extracted from his desk. "You are half correct," he said tersely. "This Academy did supplant Harvard."

"But then, how . . . ?" Felicity sensed that his statement carried with it a caveat.

"The Harvard Medical School," Simmons said, moving hurriedly over the words so as not to soil his tongue any more than necessary, "was the single element of that which went before that we retained. Look, Felicity. The New Luddites are not so shortsighted that they would abandon the best in medical care, if for no other reason than to be able to provide such care for certain factions within the Church's leadership. Consequently, the medical school continues to train a variety of surgeons, clinicians, and other specialists—all clandestinely, I assure you."

Felicity was genuinely surprised to hear this news. It also shocked her that Simmons should call the Church of New Luddites "not so dumb." It was blasphemy. It was . . .

"Please, Ms. Levine, pay attention," the old man said. "In very rare cases like yours where the Academy fails to reduce . . . I'm sorry, but I must use this word . . . *intelligence,* we are permitted to seek solutions elsewhere. Do you understand what I'm saying?"

Felicity nodded. Obviously, old man Simmons was implying that her creative impulses—her bouts with genius—were simply too strong to eliminate with traditional treatments. The further implication was that she would not graduate if she did not bring those urges under control. The Har . . . this special program . . . promised a solution to her problems.

Felicity felt frightened, yet strangely excited, at the prospect of taking part in such forbidden activities.

"There really is nothing to worry about, Felicity. In fact, according to your file, your own father required this same therapy. And he came through it just fine. All I need is for you to sign the appropriate waiver forms. Then I can escort you over to the med . . . er . . . I'll accompany you to the clinic to begin your genetic treatments."

Taking the pen from the old man's outstretched hand, Felicity signed her name to several papers. Without thinking, she used the beautiful calligraphic script she had mastered in an idle five minutes, prior to breakfast last Tuesday.

Simmons looked at the fancy signature and groaned. "I hope they have their machines cranked up to full power. They're going to need it."

"What . . ." she started to ask, but Simmons waved her to silence as he came from behind his desk. He grabbed her arm and pulled it sharply. Rising to her feet, Felicity followed him meekly out of the office.

Every Saturday morning for three months, Felicity reported to the lab for her treatments. Finally, the winter snows surrendered to a spring thaw. As the world was reborn, so, too, was Felicity Levine. It wasn't an overnight metamorphosis, to be sure, but her progress was obvious. Most obvious.

To the mortification of Sudie MacCready, Felicity was soon doing better than she at forgetting her multiplication tables. By the end of February, even Mrs. Garvey was impressed. She remarked proudly to several of her fellow teachers that Felicity was, without a doubt, the dumbest student she had ever taught.

As Felicity's intelligence dropped, her popularity rose in equal measure. The boys were soon flocking around her. She was so stupid, she didn't understand what they wanted—which just made them admire and want her all the more.

Poor, plump Sudie MacCready grew incensed. Jealousy consumed her.

"Girl," she said one day between classes, "you can have any of them you want. Any of them! For God's sake, just be pickin' one. That way the rest of them can get back to noticing us other girls!"

"Pick one of what?" Felicity asked, a dull look in her eyes. "Flowers? Mr. Simmons says we are not allowed to pick . . . to pick . . . what was it we were going to pick?"

Sudie threw up her hands in disgust and stalked off.

At Easter break, Felicity was permitted to visit her parents. They were both ecstatic at the changes they saw in their daughter.

"All that money we done poured into the Academy," her father said, "it finally be paying off."

"Wonderful, dear, just wonderful," her mother said, hugging her close. "Ain't you just thrilled at how much the Academy is helping you?"

"What's the Academy?" Felicity asked, her eyes dull, her movements listless.

"Oh, baby!" her mother sobbed, a blissful smile on her face. "Oh, baby, baby, you done be gettin' *normal.*"

"Well," her father said, trying to hide a tear himself, "time to carve the Easter ham. It's terrific that we're a family again."

It was a wonderful, warm time. A week later, they came and took Felicity back to the Academy.

* * *

Samuel Simmons was especially glad to see her. She was, after all, his greatest success, an adolescent mind snatched from the brink of brilliance and delivered to a life of Holy Mediocrity.

"Just keep on like you are going," he told her, "and graduation is a sure thing."

"I ain't gonna fail ya now," Felicity slurred. She giggled. "I promise I won't . . . what was I talking about?"

Simmons brought his hands together in utter delight. "Of course not, dear Felicity, of course not. You have it made now."

Felicity stared at him uncomprehendingly.

"Oh, yes!" Simmons exclaimed, totally enthralled with his creation. "Yes, we've done it!"

And so, it seemed, they had. Felicity's achievement level sank beautifully and rapidly until she was soon judged to be the least intelligent student in the whole school. Each month when the Dean's List came out, her name held a place of honor at its lowest position!

In May, Felicity led her class in forgetting the alphabet, which they did in record time. Soon, high Church officials started coming around to sit in on her classes, to bask in this young woman's Holy Ignorance.

On the evening of the 31st of May, with only her final exam standing between Felicity and graduation, Simmons allowed himself to celebrate his success. He drank himself almost to oblivion, taking care to do so in the privacy of his own home, in the company of his darling wife.

After they had shared nearly a complete bottle of Jim Beam—well, not quite shared; the majority of it ended up in the proud counselor's bloodstream—Simmons made what he believed to be an almost lucid observation. "You know, Elaine ..." He paused to belch reflectively. "Felicity has become quite a *genius* at being dumb."

"Wash out your foul mouth," his wife said, just before surrendering to the bourbon and passing out in a most *un*ladylike manner on their living room floor.

"Hmmmm, yes," Simmons mumbled, a note of suspicion creeping into his voice. "She does display an almost unnatural brilliance for stupidity, doesn't she?"

Simmons himself then passed out, crumbling to the floor right next to his wife. When he awoke, he remembered nothing of the previous night's celebration.

Felicity not only failed her final exam with flying colors, she achieved the unheard of feat of *not getting a single answer right!* Not a single one!

Simmons, along with all the Academy's higher ups and most of the New Luddite Church's hierarchy, were present on graduation day to watch her give a short Valedictory speech:

"Mr. ... er ... um ... what's your name? Oh, heck. It don't matter. Honored guests and, well, the rest of you folks."

Applause interrupted her.

"Ah, shucks. Now you done made me forget what I was gonna say."

More applause.

"But ... it was fun and I ain't at all sorry ... that I did ... whatever it was we did."

The room erupted in sustained applause. Simmons leaped to his feet, but he was not the first. Cheers and accolades flew wildly on the wings of hard-clapping hands. Felicity was a paragon of virtue, the very epitome of the Holy True Peace of Ignorance. She was, in a word, a heroine—*their* heroine—the Dumbest of the Dumb.

"It don't get no better'n this," a happily sniffling Felicity Levine informed her parents, who had driven up for the celebration.

One short year later, Felicity sat in her plush office on the top floor of the newly and lavishly renovated John Hancock Building. It was but one of the many prominent skyscrapers that her recently formed holding company now owned—lock, stock, and potential lease income.

An electronic chime *pinged* softly.

"Enter," Felicity said.

The door opened and in walked Samuel Simmons.

"Felicity?" he whispered.

"Hi ya, Mr. S. Good to see you again. How have you been?"

"Oh, my God!" Simmons gasped. "It *is* you. I'd heard rumors, but I kept hoping that they were untrue."

"It is I, all right, Mr. S." Felicity threw her arms out and swirled in an impromptu pirouette. "So. What do you think of your prize student?"

"Then, it's true. You're smart again. Smart, heck. You're a genius!"

Felicity chuckled. Words like "smart" and "genius" no longer intimidated her. In fact, she spoke them freely and quite regularly, now. "Yes, I am a genius, aren't I? Actually, I always was—except in one area. I was dumb enough that it took me almost four years to figure out how to beat you at your own game."

RADICAL CHICK

"But ... but ... how did this happen?"

"Oh, please, Simmons! Did you really think I would believe all that rigmarole about 'Harvard Med' and 'genetic treatments?' I figured out your scam the very first day, less than five minutes after you hauled me over to that lab.

"What kind of fool did you take me for, old man. The virtual helmet. The soothing music. The camouflaged subtext. I experimented with all that stuff back in grade school.

"I understand full well how subliminals work. And once someone understands them, they don't work anymore.

"I may have been unable to finesse you, back then, but I sure as hell could outsmart you. After all, as you so regularly pointed out during our counseling sessions, *smart* was my forte.

"I ended up being so smart, in fact, that I knew the answer to every single question on the final exam. That knowledge made it easy to fake getting all of them wrong. As I stated earlier, it's all a game. And this time, it appears, you and your fellow Luddites have lost."

Simmons said nothing.

"Oh, c'mon, Simmons. Don't be such a sore loser. It's all quite logical, really. I couldn't beat you, and I certainly didn't want to join you. That left me with only one alternative: I had to do what you did, only *I* had to do it a whole lot better.

"I'll tell you what," Felicity said, grabbing the old man's arm and directing him toward the door. "Why don't the two of us have lunch together, my treat?

There's this little restaurant just off the lobby. I ate there last week and loved it. So, this morning, I bought it. We'll eat there. That way, I can be one of my own first customers."

S.T.O.P.—N.O.S.

by Tina L. Jens

Century VI, #44
By night at Nantes the rainbow shall appear
And the mountains of the sea shall raise up rain
The Gulf of Arabia shall bury a great tribe
A Monster shall be born in Saxony of a bear and a sow

"Japan wanted China. Italy wanted Ethiopia. And Germany wanted the world. Preoccupied with their faltering national economies, the major democracies took a myopic view of the territorial aggression. The U.S. adopted neutrality. The British sought appeasement. And the French tried to sandbag their homeland with the Maginot Line.

This left German Chancellor Adolf Hitler free to unilaterally tear up the Versailles Treaty in the face of an enfeebled League of Nations."

As the phone rang I shut my book with a sigh. With the way the week was going, I'd never get through my history of W.W. II.

"Sorry to bother you at home, Charlie, but you'll find a situation with academic principles in about three minutes on WJLA."

I wasn't scheduled to monitor anything tonight, but the work of a S.T.O.P.—N.O.S. agent is never done.

I clicked on the TV. My VCR was on the blink again, so I grabbed my Walkman out of my purse, threw a blank tape in it, and hit Record. The newscast was just coming out of the commercial break.

"Thousands of people are flooding into the town of Nantes, situated at the mouth of the Loire River in France. All because of a bizarre migration of glow-in-the-dark fish. These Scaleless Black Dragon Fish— which normally inhabit the deepest regions of the ocean—have caught the attention of marine biologists all over the world. Residents and scientists alike have been flocking to the riverbanks after dark to admire the rainbow of underwater color.

"In other news, the president says he intends to move ahead in his efforts to bring home the troops stationed in unified Germany."

The anchor's head was replaced by an image of the president.

"Fifty years ago, the world was faced with a dire fascist threat. America responded. Hitler was vanquished. And America vowed to prevent such an atrocity from ever recurring. Fifty years and billions of dollars later, America succeeded. Nazism is dead. Communism is dead. The Cold War is over. Russia, China, and unified Germany are all turning their eyes to freedom and democracy. True, some countries have farther to go than others. But America responded and America succeeded. Global domination is an obsolete threat.

"Now it is time to respond to the threats of a new age: Homelessness. Poverty. Drug abuse. World hunger. It is time to withdraw our troops from Europe and

S.T.O.P.—N.O.S.

Germany. It is time to deploy our forces against the new threats of a new age ..."

I clicked off the set.

A good S.T.O.P.—N.O.S. agent has to have a basic understanding of a broad range of topics, because you never know where one of your clues will come from. But it's a wide, wide world out there, so we each have our area of expertise. Mine's unusual phenomena in atmospheric conditions and the animal kingdom. Hence the call on my night off.

S.T.O.P.—N.O.S. is the Society To Oversee and Prevent Negative Oracle Scenarios. Our society was formed in the mid 1500s by a radical element in Catherine de' Medici's court who didn't like the amount of influence Nostradamus enjoyed with the Queen.

Over the centuries our organization has gone international and our goals have evolved away from your basic court intrigue. To quote our bylaws, "We're a global secret society dedicated to the covert management of sociopolitical situations as detected through prophetic and occult devices."

I replayed the tape. The story wasn't ringing any bells as far as prophecies went. But with more than 10,000 prophecies in our active database, that didn't mean anything. Still, by definition, deep-sea fish don't migrate up freshwater rivers. This one needed an on-site inspection.

I checked the clock. It was past Major Thom's bedtime. I thought about waiting another hour so I could rouse him out of a really deep sleep, but controlled the impulse. I didn't want him to be all grumpy for his first shot at field data collection.

Major Thom's not really a major and he's not in the

military. He's an ex-army brat of a three-star general. He'd traveled around the world twice by the time he was 15. After all that culture, he still favors the British. He claims he's a pacifist but boxes to keep fit. Worst of all, he's a David Bowie lookalike from the pre-glitter days. He's also a rookie agent in S.T.O.P.—N.O.S. and I was stuck playing nanny to him.

On the fourth ring his answering machine kicked in.

"So sorry, chap, but I'm afraid I can't make it to the phone just now. Leave a message and I'll ring you when I get in. Cheerio!"

I uttered a couple of loud obscenities to shock him awake and continued to grumble till he made it to the phone. "Sorry to drag you away from your beauty sleep, darling—but it's mission time. Plug into the database and get everything you can on Deep-sea Black Dragon Fish, the Loire River, and bioluminescence in aquatic species.

"Then book us on the earliest flight possible to Nantes, France, set up an interview with whichever scientist is in charge of studying this fish thing, find us some decent hotel rooms, get our field research gear, and pick me up an hour and a half before our flight. And remember to pack light. 'Night!"

I hung up. I figured Major Thom didn't have a clue as to what this fish thing was. But it was good training for him. You have to break the kids in right.

It was a quarter to six, I was half-packed, I hadn't even watered my plants yet, and Major Thom was leaning on the doorbell for the third time. I cranked "Exile On Main Street" up another notch, clicked my heels together three times, and fervently wished he'd go away. But I'm not Dorothy, this ain't Kansas, and Major Thom knows how to pick my front door lock.

"Charlie? Charlie? I know this may be presumptuous of me, but do you think you'll ever actually *open* the door for me?

"There you are . . . God this place is a mess!"

I shot him a dirty look as he leaned against my bedroom doorway in one of those casual poses he affects so well.

I continued to crawl around on my hands and knees sorting through the piles of clothing on the floor. I was trying to remember which piles were dirty and which were clean, but they'd gotten hopelessly muddled. I tried sniffing the armpits of the two black shirts in question. It didn't help. I figured if I couldn't tell, no one else could, and added them to the pile on the bed.

Major Thom maneuvered his way through the obstacle course on my floor and sat down on my bed. I leaned back on my heels and gave him yet another dirty look to let him know I thought that was being way too familiar for this hour of the morning. He didn't notice.

He was too busy sorting through my packing pile: two pairs of black stretch pants, a pair of ragged jeans, three black knit shirts, six pairs of socks with matching underwear, and a handful of jewelry.

He held up the Walkman, tape and book I had set out. "You're packing only the essentials I see."

" 'Sympathy For the Devil,' and a leather-bound, unexpurgated edition of *Ivanhoe,* are classified as essentials. Only a child such as yourself would fail to realize it. Now, why don't you stop sorting through my underwear and go do something useful, like water my plants."

Major Thom had done all right in the logistics department. We had a good flight and a rental car waiting for us. The rooms had been more difficult to get. Seems everything in town was booked up by the visiting fish scientists. That in itself was a phenomenon worth looking into.

As for the research, he hadn't been able to get much more than your basic city profile and a few stats on the river. The Loire is the longest river in France. It flows northwest, emptying out through the Bay of Biscay into the Atlantic Ocean. Nantes is the last stop the river makes before dumping into the ocean. Or the first stop a migrating fish would make coming in from the sea. We were pretty sure Deep-sea Black Dragon Fish didn't migrate there on a regular basis.

It was well past dusk by the time we reached the city. But finding the river wasn't a problem. We just followed the mob of people who had turned out to see the show. The crowd was held back from the riverbank by a human barricade of scientists. Young interns were wading into the river to collect water samples and net fish specimens. Teams of grad students, clad in hip boots and oversized sweatshirts, waded through the water weighing and measuring the fish. White-coated chemists analyzed the water at their portable labs. Ichthyologists, wearing much heavier protective bibs, worked behind their portable dissecting tables.

But the crowd of spectators and scientists were far outnumbered by the fish. Thousands of them churned the waters, illuminating the choppy waves with swirls of red, blue, green and yellow spots of neon light.

"Ms. Wats, what can I do for you?"

Major Thom had succeeded in locating Dr. Cynthia Hamlin, the marine biologist he'd conned into talking to us. The scientist was of the Amazon variety, tanned, athletic, and close enough to seven foot that I'd have a permanent crick in my neck if I talked to her for any length of time.

"Well, Doc, I don't know much about fish, but it doesn't take an expert to know something weird is going on here," I said.

"Your associate presented some impressive credentials, but I didn't quite follow what your interest in this matter is," she said. "I don't quite know where to begin."

I tried to set her at ease. "Basically, Doc, we monitor world events: social, political, religious; weather, fads, society marriages, natural disasters, and trends in the animal, mineral, and plant kingdoms. Just about anything that might be classified as Unusual Phenomenon," I said, trying not to sound too weird.

"Cynthia," Thom interrupted, "perhaps you could start by telling us something about the normal behavior of the fish."

"All right, Thom." The Amazon smiled at him and blushed.

Thom has that effect on women. All women. I gritted my teeth and tried to keep my trap shut.

"Even that's difficult," Hamlin said. "We don't know that much about the Melanostomidae Echiostoma Ctenobarba."

"Huh?" I said brilliantly. Thom, ever the hypocrite, nodded like he understood perfectly.

"That's a Deep-sea, Scaleless, Black Dragon Fish to you. But we don't know that much about its family or genus, much less this particular species."

She led us to a table, at water's edge, with a large aquarium set up on it. An unhappy specimen swam back and forth aquatically pacing its confines.

"We believe this is a typical male specimen: black, elongated, about a foot in length. You can see the bluish phosphores are distributed all across his body. The color varies over a spectrum of bluish white to green, depending on the individual specimen. Under certain handling conditions those phosphores will turn bright yellow. There's even a phosphore on the end of his barbels, or whiskers. What makes this species unique is the red phosphore on the cheek. Very few species exhibit a red color."

Thom practically had his nose pressed against the glass, he was so excited.

"I didn't know there was such a thing as a glow-in-the-dark fish!"

I rolled my eyes. The man was a true intellectual.

"Actually, Thom," Cindy was cooing, whether her passion was directed at the fish or my partner, I wasn't sure. ". . . of the twenty thousand living species of fish, approximately one thousand five hundred of the marine specimens are bioluminescent—glow-in-the-dark, as you say."

Important clue there. I broke in. "Let me get this straight, there are no fresh water fish with this talent?"

"That's correct, Ms. Wats. These fish can't live in

this river for long. They can't live in fresh water and they can't live at this depth."

I turned to watch the fish still prowling the aquarium. "Then why did they migrate here?"

"Why did they migrate at all?" she asked. "To the best of our knowledge, they have a limited, daily, *vertical* migration. They don't spawn. They don't even swim in schools. They're bottom-feeding loners. And if they stay here, they're going to die in a week—or less."

I looked at the river, lit up like an underwater carnival ride. "I guess we can classify this as an Official Unusual Phenomenon."

"Charlie? Charlie! Oh, crimeny!"

Coming from Major Thom, "Crimeny" was strong language. I took off my headphones and looked toward the passenger seat of my car to see what was wrong. He'd kicked over one of my coffee cups and it had splashed all over his chinos. Globs of curdled cream dotted his cuff.

"Haven't you ever heard of travel mugs?" he demanded, dabbing at his pants leg with a monogrammed handkerchief.

There were more than a dozen cups and saucers littering the floor of my little orange Pinto. Maybe it was time for a cleanup.

"While you've got the headphones off, do you suppose we could talk a bit?" he said.

"What about?" I asked.

"Anything! We've been working together for six months, carpooling every day, and the only thing I know about you is that you drink too much coffee, you're a lousy housekeeper, you have an amazing way with plants, and you're from the Midwest."

"How do you know I'm from the Midwest?" I said, suspiciously.

"Your accent."

"Look who's talking."

He sighed. "Is there anything you're prepared to tell me about yourself?"

"All right," I sighed. "I was born somewhere in the Heartland. I'm five foot two, thirty-five years old, a natural blonde, and my weight's none of your business."

"Charlie, I have eyes."

Yeah, and they're way too blue, I thought to myself.

"Tell me something about you I don't know," he coaxed.

"I've got a Bachelor's in Medieval Literature and a Master's in Occult Mythology. My bad habits include reading trashy novels—no more than two a month. I play the stereo too loud and dance naked in the living room at four a.m.—neighbors tell me I don't always remember to close the blinds."

He choked on that one, but I kept going.

"My pet peeves include Norman Mailer, David Bowie's 'Space Oddity,' the Grunge look, Call Waiting, and New Age tarot decks. I love Monty Python, hate Barry Manilow. Love incense, hate potpourri. Believe in ghosts, don't believe in reincarnation. And," I gulped a breath, "I have a hard and fast rule about dating men younger than me. So, tell me about yourself."

After a prolonged silence from the other side of the car, I checked to make sure he was still with me.

"I can't follow that," he said.

S.T.O.P.—N.O.S.

* * *

The phosphorescent Francophone fish had been nagging at me, but I hadn't been able to do anything about it since we'd pulled the field data recovery shift.

Our active seers feed their predictions in by computer. A couple of times a year we go out in the field to see if any new talent has surfaced. Major Thom and I had spent the last two weeks sitting in the parlors, on the window sills, or at the coffee shop tables of every new-age gypsy we could find in Minneapolis, Milwaukee, and Chicago.

Thankfully, us field agents just gather the prophecies. Besides the works of Nostradamus, our database includes the *Book of Revelations,* the predictions of Zolar, Edgar Cayce, and the handful of other prophets and seers who have proved to have a success rate above the statistical coincidence level. The data is presorted by the Central Computer, then analyzed by special agents. Even so, I was glad to get back to D.C., back at my desk and back to my regular duties. As I sorted though the reports in my computerized file basket, I decided it was time to look into our bioluminescent buddies.

I tapped into the Central Database. A cross-reference of Fish and France turned up too many entries to peruse. But Loire River, Bioluminescence, and the infinite variations of deep-sea, Scaleless, Black Dragon Fish, as well as the Latin version of their names, turned up nothing.

I pulled out a Polaroid Major Thom had snapped of the aquarium specimen, for inspiration.

On the bottom of the picture, Major Thom had scrawled, "Nantes, France, Cindy Hamlin" and a phone number. I was going to have to talk to that chap about our labeling system.

I plugged Nantes into the search parameters for lack of anything better to do.

A few seconds later I had a match staring me in the face.

I wasn't happy about the prophecy blinking on my computer screen. There are certain things one doesn't want to be successful at . . . such as discovering a doomsday prophecy is coming true.

By night at Nantes the Rainbow shall appear
And the mountains of the sea shall raise up rain
The Gulf of Arabia shall bury a great tribe
A Monster shall be born in Saxony of a bear and a sow

"By nishe Miss Nancy will appease the rainbow," I intoned. "Mountains and seahorses shall frolic in the rain. Arabian gold should be buried in deep sand. Sax'ny monsters . . ."

Major Thom leaned over and laid his head on my shoulder. "Give it a rest," he begged.

We were sitting side by side on the floor in my living room with our backs against my couch, so he didn't have far to lean.

"Only if yu'll pour me summore wine," I said, and burped.

We were back at my place, brainstorming on the prophecy and getting soused. Mainly getting soused. One should never face Nostradamus with a sober head. Major Thom was too young to know this. That's why I dragged him back to my place.

"My dear, I do beveeve, I mean be-lieve, you're out

of wine." He held the bottle upside down and shook it just to make sure.

"Oh no, no, no, no," I said, shaking my head. "Let us repair to the wine cell'ur."

He beamed. "Smashing idea!" he said. "Where's your wine cellar?"

That was classified information. I motioned him closer, then whispered in his ear, "Under my bed."

He nodded like that was a brilliant idea and followed behind me as I crawled across the living room floor into my bedroom.

It took me a few minutes to get to the stash. While I was working my way there, Major Thom cleared us some sitting room by dumping one pile of clothes on top of another. I had to push a lot of old shoe boxes, forgotten sweaters, and other camouflage out of the way. Then I crawled all the way under the bed.

"Charlie? Are you coming out?" Major Thom asked, peeking under the bedspread.

"Here it is!" I wriggled back out and fought to a sitting position. "A fine 1993 Lambrusco! April, I think." I turned the bottle, squinting at the label. "It was a very good month!"

Major Thom looked dubious.

"I have a September '92 Zinfandel under there," I offered.

"The present wine should be quite acceptable," Major Thom said with a burp. "Allow me to do the honors.

"So, ya wanna tell me what the prophecy means and why we're—oops, 'scuse me—getting royally plowed?"

"Thom, if we knew what the prophecy meant we wouldn't be here brainstorming it."

"That makes sense—far as it goes. Can't you tell me anything?"

I held my glass out for him to pour.

"I could tell you that you have beautiful blue eyes," I said. "I could tell you that out of all Bowie's periods, his preglitter phase was my favorite. I *could* tell you that when you grin like that, I get all weak-kneed. But I'm already weak-kneed, and none of those things help us right now."

Major Thom started to say something, but I rambled on.

"As for the prophecy, it's from Century VI, quatrain number forty-four of the Nostradamus canon. If you remember, the quatrains and the Centuries are not organized in any chronological order. A Nostradamus prophecy nearly always means disaster. No, make that—DISASTER—in a big, big way. We can't stop a prophecy from coming true, but through early recognition we can manage the repercussions of the event."

Thom brightened. "Is this a Phenomenal Situation of Magnitude?"

"A what?"

"A Phenomenal Situation of Magnitude—I read about it in our handbook. So what's the SOP?" He looked at me expectantly.

"The what?" I squeaked.

"You sound like a mouse when you get drunk. The Standard Operating Procedure, what is it?"

I looked at him, disgusted. "I wish you'd quit reading that damned CIA manual. I keep telling you we've got an English language translation."

Major Thom's face drooped.

"All right, we can talk in code if you want to."

Major Thom grinned again.

"Yes, this is a PSM. The SOP on a magnif— I mean, manifesting, prophecy varies depending on who the prophet is and how certain we are about the match up between the physical manifestation and the prediction in question.

"I mean, if it's a Jeanne Dixon prediction, all we do is call *The National Enquirer* or *People Magazine.* With a Nostradamus quatrain, you drop all mid-level— 'scuse me!—protocol and go straight to the top."

"Blimey!" Major Thom said. "This calls for a cup of tea!"

He pulled himself up on the side of the bed and stumbled off to the kitchen, talking all the way.

"I read in the manual that there are actually agents who spend their whole lives in the bureau without uncovering a PSM—and I've got one after just six months. This could be the start of a brilliant career!"

We were facing a disaster of biblical proportions and the kid was having delusions of grandeur. I figured I'd better go set him straight.

I staggered into the kitchen just in time to watch him pour perfectly good milk into a cup of industrial-strength hot tea. I considered visiting the "loo" for a good heave. But a good agent has to have a quick mind and an iron stomach.

"Look, Bucko, let's get something straight. A Phenomenal Situation of Magnitude is not your fast track to a position as Bureau CEO. Wrap your mind around the idea that we're facing a disaster of Nostradamic proportions—that should strike fear deep into your limey little heart. And if it doesn't, you've been reading all the wrong parts of that damned manual."

I swiveled one of the kitchen chairs around backward and tried to straddle it, and nearly fell on my face in the attempt.

"Let's talk tactics. As if we didn't have enough problems, Monica, the best Bureau Head S.T.O.P.—N.O.S. ever had, was forced into domestic retirement last year."

It was Thom's turn to act dumb.

"Huh?"

"She got preggies, so they forced her to quit."

"Why?" he asked wide-eyed.

His naivete was astounding. "Because our esteemed governmental leaders have profound paranoia of anyone who associates with citizens under the age of thirty."

"But I'm only twenty-fi—"

"Yeah, and they've got an open file on me," I told him. "Now listen up. Our new leader is a recent transfer from the CIA's domestic surveillance branch."

"The CIA doesn't spy on American citizens!" Thom protested.

"Yeah, and J. Edgar Hoover liked girls. Tell me another one."

I poured myself a cup of tea. This was going to take some time. I didn't want to cause the kid too much emotional trauma as I disillusioned him.

"Darlin', our relationship with the CIA's not quite as sweet as you think it is. Yes, we're a branch of the CIA—a highly secretive one. There're only about five people in the whole government who know we exist. Despite a former First Lady's predilection for personal astrologers, we're still very un-PC. So is the CIA for that matter," I said. "But the folks in the main branch of the CIA don't like us much either, because we have better toys, better computers, and more freedom than they have. There's nothing they would like better than to strip us of our operating budget. Normally, I wouldn't want you to worry your pretty little head about such things. But, we might be in trouble—I think our new Branch Head is a CIA mole."

"I surmise there's room for more than a singular interpretation of the phenomenon at hand," Branch Head said, after we had finished our presentation.

"What'd he say? I'm a little rusty in the Secret Agent dialect," I whispered to Major Thom.

It was okay, there wasn't a chance Mr. Mole could hear us. We were sitting at opposite ends of a huge oak table that would seat 20, easy. Mr. Mole had it transferred along with himself when he came to the bureau. The agency had to knock out a wall and combine two offices to find a room it would fit in. Never mind the fact that our bureau employed less than a dozen people, total.

"I think he's skeptical that glow-in-the-dark fish are the equivalent to a rainbow at night," Major Thom said.

"Hold on!" I said, jumping up. Mr. Mole continued to talk, so I pulled my shoe off and banged on the table Khrushchev-style. That got his attention. "I can count on my cat's paw—"

"You have a cat?" the Major asked, bewildered.

"Shut up, Thom! As I was saying, I can count on *a* cat's paw, the number of times Nantes has popped up in the news in the last several centuries. And it's bureau regulation to scrutinize any unusual activity occurring in cities specifically named in our canon of prophecies.

"Now, add to that a kamikaze migration of several thousand fish who *never* leave their happy homes at the bottom of the ocean, but suddenly decide to swim off into the waters of little ol' Nantes, where they can't breathe, mind you, all for the purpose of blinking their little old lights in Nantes Harbor. We got red lights. We got blue lights. We even got yellow and green lights. I know we're short a couple shades in the overall spectrum, but Nostradamus was writing in verse, for Pete's sake. It's hard to say, 'And a rainbow will appear in Nantes at nighttime, all except for the orange and purple colors' and still fit the quatrain meter!"

Major Thom was impressed with my speech. Mr. Mole wasn't. But then he hadn't heard most of it. He'd been talking most of the time.

". . . TO THAT END, WATS—we will not upgrade this to a Priority One Situation. You may continue to observe the possibilities and summarize them in a weekly memo to me, while continuing with your regular duties, of course. And, I suppose it wouldn't hurt for you to mention your suspicions to the rest of the department. Good-bye, Agent Wats, Agent Ronson."

"You know," I said, after we left his office, "when he transferred over here, I knew he was a mole—he just looked like it. And I suspected he was incredibly incompetent. But I had no idea he was an absolute imbecile. And stop calling him Sir!"

Major Thom was thoughtful. "This is all just an exercise in literary interpretation—on a cosmic scale of course. There's always the possibility that we're wrong."

I blew him a raspberry and left for my lunch break.

"There!" With a final screech of the pen and one last whiff of the fumes, I capped my red magic marker and taped the poster up on the wall beside our desks.

By night at Nantes the rainbow shall appear
And the mountains of the sea shall raise up rain
The Gulf of Arabia shall bury a great tribe
A Monster shall be born in Saxony of a bear and a sow

"We have to eat, sleep, dream, and think that prophecy until this thing is over," I told Thom.

"How long will that be?"

"Could be days, weeks, maybe months. But I doubt that. Nostradamus did a pretty good job of clumping his signs together."

I logged onto my computer as we talked.

"We've got to keep an open mind as we look for collaborating phenomenon. Remember, the big mistake most people make is trying to force the prophecy to fit the facts at hand. Interpreters have ignored specific names of people and places—even thrown out whole lines—trying to make interpretations fit."

"Yeah, I'm familiar with some of the old cases," Thom assured me. "Roberts' interpolation of the Jewish Holocaust from Century I, 59, for example."

He struck a vaguely Shakespearean pose and dropped his voice a couple octaves. "The exiles deported to the islands, at the advent of an even more cruel king, will be murdered. Two will be burnt who were not sparing in their speech."

I applauded briefly. "That was lovely, Olivier. But maybe you're being too hard on old Roberts."

"Possibly," the major agreed. "The casualty count is just off by five million, nine hundred, and ninety-nine thousand, nine hundred and ninety-eight, give or take few dead bodies."

I shrugged. "Nobody's perfect."

My computer beeped. I'd finally gotten Security Clearance. "I'll put in a request for a round-the-clock monitor on the Weather Channel to see if we can't get a line on the 'mountains of the sea raising up rain.' Meanwhile, why don't you start checking the day's news briefs?"

"Should we expand our search parameters?" Major Thom asked.

"Yeah. Gulf of Arabia suggests the Mediterranean area. Saxony could be any of the Euro-Germanic countries. And we've got no clue as to where the rain might happen."

After a couple of hours of expanding parameters and skimming news briefs, I had nothing but a case of ocular fatigue, medium severity. I sat back and groaned. "Whaddya got, Sherlock?"

Thom grunted. "Interested in increased volcanic activity in the Santorini Islands?"

"Should I be?"

"They're in the Mediterranean—more or less."

"I'll pass. What else?"

"I've got a Gen. Hugo Kurtz, who's not really a general, running for Chancellor on a neo-Nazi platform in the upcoming German elections."

"Anybody taking him seriously?"

"Not even his mother," Thom admitted.

"Next."

"I came across a possible explanation for the French fish migration."

"Yeah?"

"Well, it's highly speculative, but some scientists are linking it to increased geological activity caused by an increase in the subduction rate at the converging boundary of the African and Eurasian continental plates," Major Thom said.

That was helpful. "Are we speaking English today?" I asked him.

He smiled apologetically. "Okay. Are you familiar with the theory of plate tectonics?"

"Sure," I nodded. "Once upon a time the landmass was all joined together as one great supercontinent. Then for some unknown reason, it broke up and ever since then the continents have been floating around on the oceans, bumping into each other every few millennia."

"That's the rough concept, anyway," Thom was forced to agree. "They only move a few centimeters a year, but most of the continents are 'bumping' into each other, or scraping by each other, at one or more of their boundaries. And wherever that happens you get intense geological activity; earthquakes, volcanos, rising or falling mountain ranges."

He motioned me over to his side of the desk and tapped a command into his computer. Instantly, a multicolored world map formed. Another set of keystrokes set the continents in motion. Continents began sliding over each other, slipping past each other, drifting across oceans. With each movement, the boundaries were overlaid with shuddering lines of earthquakes rippling across the land, volcanos erupting, mountains heaving their way up through bedrock.

"Great graphics!" I pulled my chair closer to watch the geologic history lesson.

"Watch these two plates here," Thom said. "See how the African plate is sliding under the Eurasian plate? It's a bumpy process that triggers earthquakes not only on the continent, but on the ocean floor, too."

"Which, in turn, triggers a reaction by the fish." I got it now. Animals react in all sorts of ways to earthquakes. The theory was they could feel the shifts in the electronic fields caused by an earthquake. While the animals' reactions were not entirely understood, China was already using various species to predict earthquakes.

"But the fish have never reacted this way before, why now?" I tried to puzzle it out, as the continents continued to collide on the monitor in front of me.

I shook myself out of a daze and clicked the computer off. The major stood up to stretch. It was a pleasant sight. I decided to concentrate on that for a while.

"You know . . ."

Thom flexed his arms behind his head and executed a series of neck rolls that served to highlight his well-formed pectorals.

"The Persian Gulf is also known as the Gulf of Arabia. I wonder if Nostradamus was predicting the victor, or loser, of the Iran-Iraq conflict?"

"Did you say something?" I asked.

The major repeated his question and I gave it some thought.

"Let's do a little map work," I suggested.

Thom reached to turn his computer back on, but I stopped him.

"My eyes need a break."

I led the way to the maps and charts table. They might be old-fashioned, but they're a lot easier on the eyes.

Thom pulled out the sixteenth century blowups of Asia and the Mediterranean. After a few minutes of surveying, I shook my head.

"I don't think we can rely on that. That's relatively current usage," I said. "When Nostradamus was writing, there was no Gulf of Arabia."

"The whole Middle East was known as Arabia at one time or another," Thom said. "He could have been referring to the Persian Gulf, the Gulf of Aden, the Gulf of Oman, the Gulf of Kutch, the Gulf of Khambhat, or any of a dozen others. Where do we start?"

"Damus was always pretty accurate according to the geography of his time," I said. "If there wasn't a Gulf of Arabia at the time he was writing, then there must be a metaphor, a secret meaning, behind that name."

Six days later, we were still repeating the same exercise with about the same results. A British supply ship, which we'd sworn was doomed, made it safely across the Mediterranean Sea with a fresh supply of armaments for Syria. The neo-Nazi wannabe-general gave a couple of speeches that were trashed by the German media. The Santorini volcanos erupted a few more times. The French government declared the Nantes harbor a disaster site to qualify it for federal cleanup funds. And we discarded about a hundred hypotheses for lack of any substantiating phenomena.

It was sometime after midnight and I had just finished filling about my hundredth pitcher of water, when the phone rang. I dashed to get it.

"Hello, Charlie? It's Thom. Are you monitoring CNN?"

"No. I'm not scheduled to monitor anything tonight," I told him. "Neither are you."

Some people are fanatics. Me, I believe in conserving my energy.

"Well, switch it on, quick," he urged.

"Hang on, let me turn my tub off," I said, cradling the phone on my shoulder while I twisted the cold water knob off.

A heavy silence greeted that remark.

"Is that your way of telling me you're dripping wet and naked? . . . Are your curtains open?"

"Thomas," I said exasperated, "that's my way of telling you I'm watering my indoor rain forest. And *you* are a pervert. Now, what is it you're so hot and bothered for me to watch?" I asked, clicking on the TV.

"It's coming up again now," he told me.

"That's a lot more than I want to know about your—"

Major Thom was saved the trouble of dreaming up a snappy comeback—the news report shut me up.

"Three hundred French Foreign Legionnaires died in a freak accident last night, during an exhibition in the Sahara Desert. Military leaders from across the world were gathered at Rebiana, Libya, a desert oasis located in the southeastern corner of the country, to

witness an exhibition of desert survival techniques by the French Foreign Legion. The troops were on camelback doing overnight maneuvers about thirty miles west of Rebiana, when a freak sandstorm swallowed them up. We turn now to Wolf Blitzer for more on the story."

"Thanks, Bernard. Five camels wandered into the oasis this afternoon, battered and bleeding. They are believed to be the only survivors of this disaster ... "

We had spent the whole night watching the coverage, taking detailed notes and sleeping in two-hour shifts.

Anchorman, Bernard Shaw, did a satellite interview with a team of global meteorologists. The team theory was the sandstorm hadn't been a freak at all and had been perfectly predictable, if not in actual time, at least in theory. It could all be traced back to plate tectonics, again. For some unexplained reason, the African plate was subducting under the Eurasian plate at a much faster rate than normal. The subduction triggered more earthquakes and volcanic activity from the Santorini Islands and other Mediterranean volcanos. The airborne volcanic ash drifted over the ocean to North Africa, mixed with the sand whipped up by the normal wind patterns, and created a storm of monstrous proportions. The meteorologists went on to smugly conclude that weather patterns for most of the continent would be altered for years.

Of course, we summarized the events and presented the expert testimony in our report the next morning. Of course, the CIA rodent that we called "Boss" failed to appreciate the significance of the phenomenon.

"Sorry, Charlie, but it's not chronological," the mole said.

Now I understood why the rodent had imported the formal dining table with him. If he'd been within arm's length, I would have strangled him.

I tried one more time. "We realize that the lines of the quatrains usually occur chronologically, but there have been lots of exceptions to that rule. Prophesying centuries into the future is a tricky business. I think we ought to allow Damus some margin of error."

The mole's face registered no response to my impassioned plea.

"Perhaps we should take a look at the map," Major Thom suggested.

We spread the document out on the table.

I was uncertain whether CIA moles were required to study geography, so I decided to do a quick review. "See these Middle Eastern countries here: Saudi Arabia, Jordan, Israel, Iraq, etc? The countries have made it a full-time business to carve up the area and rename it every few years, but it's always been the Arabian territories."

I paused to pull a pen out of Major Thom's shirt pocket to use as a pointer.

"Take a short hop west, across the Red Sea, and you bump into North Africa, which has suffered from its fair share of redistricting. We're mainly interested in the countries directly west of the Arabian peninsula: Egypt; Sudan; and Libya."

Thom grabbed the pen out of my hand. "Sir, you should know the Sahara Desert stretches all the way across the continent, and runs all through these countries."

"In fact," I paused to retrieve my pointer, "much of this area was once called the Arabian Desert. At the time Nostradamus was writing, there wasn't a water body known as the Gulf of Arabia. However, we know how much Nostradamus liked metaphors, and the desert—ocean reference is a common one."

"And, of course, the camel is the ship of the desert," Thom said.

"So," I concluded, "you can see why we believe— firmly believe—that three hundred Foreign Legionnaires on camelback, being swallowed by a sandstorm in the Sahara Desert, is a definite manifestation of a 'The Gulf of Arabia shall bury a great tribe.' "

Major Thom repocketed his pen while we waited for the effusive praise our presentation deserved.

The mole leaned back in his chair and planted his heels in the middle of our map. I took that as a bad sign.

"I'm not going to panic a lot of people and jeopardize our future funding without just cause. The CIA budget goes before Congress next week. This isn't the time to be making waves."

So that was it; Rodent Man had been sent here to make sure we didn't screw up the budgeting process. The world was about to collapse and he was worried about the executive pension plan. I stood up and stalked out. Unfortunately, by the time I'd walked the length of the table to reach the door, the boys had lost interest.

I left the major and the mole to their verbal wrangling and wandered off to write an anonymous, obscene letter to the head of the CIA.

* * *

"Hi, Charlie. It's Richard. Did I wake you?"

At least I think that's what he said. The phone line was crackly, it was four A.M. and I got stuck on the "It's Richard." part.

"I know it's probably late there, but have you got a minute?"

Richard had walked out of my life seven years ago when I went to work for S.T.O.P—N.O.S. He said he couldn't cohabitate with a woman whose paychecks were signed by an imperialistic, bloodthirsty, baby-killing, genocidal, fascist regime. And if I could spend their blood-money, then our whole relationship must have been built on lies.

I couldn't blame him entirely. We met in the first aid tent at a Rolling Stones concert. I had passed out from the heat and he'd smoked some bad grass. After agreeing that Keith Richards *was* the Stones, and watching the man prove it that night, Richard and I bummed around together, cutting classes, attending antiwar protests, and doing volunteer work for Greenpeace. We parted ways when I graduated and went to work.

I tried to convince him that taking a job with the CIA didn't constitute a betrayal of our sociopolitical beliefs since I wouldn't be in the traditional surveillance branch. Richard wouldn't buy it. He joined the Peace Corps and shipped out to Bolivia; said someone had to balance the bad karma I was creating.

"Are you allowed to fraternize with the imperialistic enemy?" I asked him. "Or is that why you called so late?"

"Ah, Daisy-Mae, don't be that way. The Cold War's over."

S.T.O.P.—N.O.S.

The name Daisy-Mae came from a daisy-covered bandanna and halter top that I used to wear everywhere. The straps fastened with velcro, back before velcro was popular, and when there was a lull in the action, Richard used to—well, you figure it out.

"I've mellowed, Daisy."

"Yeah? You still with Greenpeace?" I asked.

"Well, sort of. I finally went back and got my geology degree, from Berkeley."

"I hadn't heard," I said softly.

"That's why I'm calling. I'm head of a Berkeley research team, and I was wondering if you're still into all that occult stuff."

"You could say that."

"Then I got somethin' you want to see."

"Yeah? What's that?"

"Atlantis. It's resurfaced. But it's going to sink again—soon."

"Let me see if I've got this right—Dick. That volcano, or cluster of volcanos, over there is Atlantis," Major Thom said, shielding his eyes from the sun and pointing in the general direction of the island.

We were aboard the Berkeley research yacht, *The Janis J.*

"And when will we be meeting the little men with webbed hands and crested heads?" Thom asked.

To say that Richard and the major hadn't hit it off would be an understatement. Of course, I couldn't blame Thom entirely. I'd made another one of those late-night, do-this phone calls and refused to divulge anything other than our destination. We were anchored just offshore of the Santorini Islands, a small cluster of the greater Kikladhes Islands, all affiliated with Greece.

They were the same Mediterranean islands that had been experiencing all the volcanic activity we'd been reading about. But Thom was having problems coming up to speed with the Atlantis concept.

"Do my back, will ya?" I said to Thom, handing him a bottle of suntan lotion. "And leave my bikini straps alone."

I had already realized the faux pas of my choice in swim wear. It was daisy-covered. The glint in Richard's eye suggested he was getting the wrong message. And Thom was getting unusually friendly. But it was the only suit I had suitable to be worn in mixed company, and there hadn't been time to go shopping. Worst case scenario: I might have to fend off both Thom and Richard. I'd had worse missions.

"Richard, could you run through the whole Atlantis thing again, please?"

"Anything for you, Daisy-Mae," he said with a grin.

"What's this Daisy-Mae shit?" Thom hissed in my ear.

"Shut up and listen," I whispered back.

"That group of volcanos used to be one big island—one big volcanic complex, until about 1400 BC."

"It's not even identified on most maps," Thom interrupted.

"I know," Richard said. "And every map that does identify it has a different name: Kikladhes, Cyclades, Santorini, Thera . . ."

"Don't forget 'Atlantis,' " Thom reminded him.

"Despite that, it's still a pivotal landmass from a geologic, mythical, and Biblical standpoint. Those is-

94

lands were formed by ocean-bed volcanos. Repeated eruptions over hundreds of centuries accumulated enough sediment to break above sea level and ultimately form a mountain. The volcanic activity continued, building the cone higher and higher, but also hollowing it out, as the overlapping volcano cones spewed out the core material. Finally, there wasn't enough of a base to support the mountain formation. In 1400 BC there was an unusually strong eruption, and the whole mountain collapsed."

"Sounds like an exciting event for rock-nerds," Major Thom said.

I jabbed him in the ribs.

"Oof! Tell me why we should care, Chap."

"To start with, the mountain collapsed and sank into the sea, leaving less than what you see now above water. The collapse caused the formation of a huge wave the Tsunami of Antiquity. We're talking waves one hundred twenty feet high. It spewed so much ash in the air that it blacked out the sun for three days. And Crete Island is just seventy-five miles south of here," Richard said, weighing his words heavily.

"So?" Major Thom said.

Thom was being dense. "Crete was home to the Minoans," I told him. I still hadn't grasped the full implications of Richard's words, but I was working on it.

"Minoans?" Thom said. "Early European civilization. Wiped out virtually overnight. No known reason."

"You haven't been keeping up with your history revisions," Richard chided him.

"The explosion?" I asked.

"Uh-huh," Richard said. "Or actually, the effect of the tsunami."

" 'Scuse me, Dick, how do you make the jump from Crete and the Minoans to Atlantis?"

"Plato wrote about an island empire, he called Atlantis, that declared war on Egypt."

"We've all read Plato," Thom interrupted.

I interrupted him. "Supposedly, Atlantis disappeared beneath the water in a single day and night. The mountain collapse! Richard, tell us about the Biblical disaster."

"Remember the battle of miracles Moses and the Pharaoh had over the freedom of the Children of Israel? Remember the signs? The Plague of Darkness, the parting of the Red Sea, the engulfment of the Pharaoh's troops by a great wave? It's all the legendary Thera Island," Richard said.

"You're saying the sinking of Atlantis, the destruction of the Minoan civilization, and a couple of Biblical miracles were all caused by an eruption of that volcano?" Thom asked, skeptically. "Sounds like a bad Indiana Jones movie plot to me."

"Yeah, well, we've got the documentation to prove it, buddy," Richard shot back at him.

"Guys! Chill!" I'd had enough of the macho bullshit. "Great story, Richard. So, why are we here?"

"Because, sweetheart, it's about to happen again. All our signs say those volcanos are about to blow sky high. In a week. Maybe less. And the Tsunami of Antiquity is going to look like a wave in a wading pool by comparison."

"Why? Or more precisely, why now?" I asked him.

"Well, that'd be difficult for a couple of nongeologist types, like yourselves, to understand. Let's just say it's a complicated issue of plate tectonics."

"Cut the condescending crap! Let me guess; this is all being triggered by the increased rate of subduction of the African plate under the Eurasian plate, right?"

I had the extreme pleasure of watching Richard's jaw turn into a fly trap. He stuttered something incoherent. I cut him off.

"We've heard that tune before. It's having world-wide, or continent-wide ramifications, anyway. I want to know why. Why has the subduction rate increased? Answer that, Mr. Geologist."

He shook his head. "I can't. It's not my area. Even the experts are baffled. The continents usually move between one and six centimeters a year. The African plate has more than doubled its speed. And like you said, it's having world-wide ramifications. I can't tell you why, but I can tell you consequences."

He swept his arm toward the islands. "If our predictions are right, the tsunamis alone will wipe out the whole island of Crete. And that doesn't even factor in the damage from the poison gases and ash the volcano will spew out, or the multiple earthquakes the eruption will trigger. We're talking major damage way past Greece."

I was overwhelmed by the possibilities. "A disaster of Biblical proportions!" I whispered.

"Bigger," Richard assured us.

All 200 Kikladhes Islands, along with Crete and the southern coastal areas of Greece, were being evacuated to the northern interior of the country. Against the experts' recommendations, a lot of the Cretans and Athenians decided to batten down the hatches and ride the thing out. In a way, I could sympathize. It's hard to wrap your mind around the idea of evacuating your entire country.

The Red Cross and Greenpeace were coordinating with the country on the evacuation efforts. They had about 100,000 citizens, plus tourists, to relocate.

Two days later Thera blew its top. It took twenty minutes for the first tsunami to hit Athens. In half an hour the sky had turned black. After the first wave of water, the mud slides began. Next came the tornado-force gales.

We were battened down in a huge, underground, atomic-bomb shelter located in northern Athens. It wasn't exactly cozy, and when the mud and water started seeping under the reinforced steel door, I started to wonder if it was safe.

I couldn't pull the rock-nerds away from their monitoring equipment until the water was ankle-deep. A couple of the Red Cross paramedics, who had volunteered to stay on as front-line relief workers, commiserated with me. We scouted around for ways to mop up the floor and tighten the door seals.

Richard was ecstatic. About half the monitors they'd set up continued to function through the waves of disaster. Richard was crowing about all the previously ungathered, raw data they were piling up. Major Thom was right at his side, patting himself on the back, like he'd had something to do with it. Obviously, the boys had found time for a little male-bonding during the crisis.

Personally, I just wanted out of our mud-covered

mausoleum. I occupied my time worrying over the prophecy. Hundreds had died in the sandstorm. The devastation of the storm outside was incalculable. And still, we had a monster, "born of a bear and a sow" looming in the future. A mutant animal? How could that be worse than what we were facing? A return of the dinosaurs? The discovery of King Kong? I was thinking too literally, probably. A product of too many nights spent watching *Creature Feature,* combined with the overwhelming disaster breaking outside.

My thoughts grew progressively more gruesome and black. Finally, one of the paramedics pulled out a bottle of Southern Comfort. We sat down, our backs to the bunker wall, and settled in to do some serious drinking.

"Hey, you guys ever hear the Dylan song, 'Black Diamond Bay'? It's about this weird cast of characters, hanging out in a saloon, on an island that sinks . . ."

We spent the rest of the time passing the bottle and trying to remember all 15 verses.

Seventy-two hours later, we cracked the seal on our tomb. We slipped industrial-strength surgical masks over our faces. The sky was a gritty black, the sun barely visible. The soot in the air stung my eyes. A young rock-nerd came by passing out goggles. I gave thanks to somebody's patron saint for his foresight. Then, carrying high-powered lanterns, we waded up main street Athens, hip-deep in mud. A church bell struck noon.

The *Poseidon,* a one hundred twenty-five-foot ferry, had been deposited on the roof of a governmental building. It sat much closer to the ground now; the whole building had collapsed inward. The tsunami had carried the ferry forty-five miles inland.

Hundreds were dead. The whole country was effectively wiped out. Suddenly, the destruction of the entire Minoan civilization didn't seem so hard to grasp.

There was no water. No electricity. No supplies, except the emergency boxes stashed away in the bunkers. It would take time for aid to reach the city, even longer for the islands. All communication lines were down, except for a couple of ham radios. The Aegean Sea was still unnavigable. Until we could dig out a landing strip, not even a helicopter could land.

As a S.T.O.P.—N.O.S. agent, I was used to reading about disasters, crunching the numbers, analyzing unpleasant situations. But like most governmental workers, I'd never been in the heart of one—never realized the effort and heartache involved in cleaning one up.

Major Thom and I held several heated conversations with Mr. Mole, by ham radio and phone, once the lines were restored. To us, the Thera explosion was the obvious manifestation of "And the mountains of the sea shall raise up rain." He didn't buy it.

Thom and I decided to take a leave of absence from work, stay on, and help with the cleanup.

"What's the bloody point?" Thom tossed his shirt on a rock, bent down, and rolled his jeans up to his knees.

After days of back-breaking work, I thought we deserved a relaxing afternoon at the beach. The whole project was a wash, though. Thom was too pissed at Rodent-Man to enjoy the outing and the beach was buried under a foot of mud and ash. I'd pulled my bikini back out and was catching what few rays could penetrate the ash cloud.

At least Thom was working off some of his frustrations stomping through the muck.

"Why do they bother handing out paychecks, equipping us with state-of-the-art computers, patching us into every information source; broadcast, printed or otherwise, if they aren't going to pay a whit of attention to our findings?

"Why the bloody hell did we spend all those weeks interviewing a bunch of Midwestern loonies who think their dead Uncle Joe is speaking to them through the broccoli patch?"

"Ground control to Major Thom, come in please."

I patted the rock beside me invitingly. With a final huff, he sat down.

"First of all," I told him, "please remember that I am a certified Midwestern loony, so watch the ethnic slurs. Second, some of those broccoli patches *were* uncanny. And third, S.T.O.P.—N.O.S. has been around for centuries. Our expenditures were included in the first budget proposed to the American Continental Congress. Ben Franklin was our bureau leader and struck a deal with Tom Jefferson to get a protective clause written in for us."

I handed my suntan lotion to him. I didn't really need the protection, but I figured it'd give him something to do with his hands.

"It's all written up somewhere in that damned manual you keep reading. You get a lot of seniority after two hundred years. With that much clout, they aren't likely to mess with our budget. 'Course, with a mole in charge, we could be in for some unstable times."

How little I knew how right I was.

* * *

We spent two weeks in the Kikladhes, digging things out, building houses, and unloading supply vehicles. But the last line of the quatrain was still rolling around in the back of my mind. "A monster shall be born in Saxony of a bear and a sow." The mutant creatures in my dreams grew more gruesome and deadly with each passing night. Finally, we packed our bags and returned to D.C. We still had the rest of the world to save.

It was time to bypass Rodent-Man and call somebody with a brain. I dialed Monica, our former bureau chief. After five minutes of verbal wrangling with her three-year-old, I finally convinced little Nathan to put his mom on. Between a series of clicks and occasional bursts of static, I briefed her on the prophecy, manifestations, and apparent lobotomy of the mole, and told her I thought it was time to talk to the President. She was dating the current White House Chief of Staff, so I knew she could pull some strings.

There's no such thing as privacy in an intelligence-gathering office, so I made the call to Monica from home. While I was waiting for her to get back to me, I decided to tap into the Central Database and skim the latest news briefs and data analysis reports. Things had been moving fast. We could have missed a clue, as to who or what the monster might be, in the short time we'd been away. I opened up my laptop, plugged in the modem, and dialed the main frame.

"ACCESS DENIED"

Apparently they'd changed the security codes again. They'd probably put a memo out on it, but I hadn't been into the office yet, and I never read my memos, anyway. Major Thom did. He was so fanatical he filed them.

I grabbed the phone and punched his number. He answered on the second ring, then we waited another thirty seconds for the line to quiet down.

"Sorry about that, Charlie. My phone's been acting up."

I should have been suspicious about that.

"Have you been into the office yet?"

"Dropped by on my way home. Why?" he asked.

"Can you look up the new security number for me? I want to skim a few computer files tonight."

"Don't you have that memorized yet? It's 334—69—"

"Not that one," I said. "The new one."

"The number's not scheduled to change for three more weeks."

I believed him. He made it a point to know these things. But that didn't change the fact that I couldn't log on.

"Maybe you misdialed. Let me try," he said.

Thom had a second phone installed just for his modem, which meant I could stay on the line while he tapped in.

"That's funny," he said. "I'm not getting in either. Hang on, I'm getting interference on this line too. I'm going to run diagnostics."

I knew that'd take a while, so I wandered into the kitchen to make a pot of coffee.

"Bloody hell!"

The phone was barely resting on my shoulder, but I heard Thom explode.

"Those mother-loving bas—"

"What is it?"

"The code hasn't been changed. Our access has been blocked!"

"How?"

"My computer line's been tapped. There's an active program running, trying to infiltrate my hard drive. I'm going to block it and see if I can trace—"

"No!" I shouted. "Disconnect and Discover! Disconnect and *Discover!*" I slammed the phone down and gave in to a bad case of the shakes.

I was glad, now, that I hadn't gotten around to unpacking my suitcase. I grabbed it, my portable computer and my car keys and headed out the door.

I sat at a corner table at the Discover Cafe, slurping my coffee and praying that Thom had understood my message. A few long minutes later, Thom walked in.

"What's going on, Charlie?"

"Get me a refill first," I said, handing him my cup. "The strong stuff."

Thom came back with the coffee and a plate of scones.

"We'll have to contact the Chief, tell him about the breach of security," he said.

"I don't think so."

"Charlie, I know you don't like the man, but this is serious stuff!"

"More serious than you think. I stopped at a pay phone and tried to call the office. I couldn't get through. Just got this rambling message while the line kept clicking. Somebody was trying to trace the call."

Thom buttered a lumpy biscuit and bit into it. Apparently nothing affected his appetite.

"Maybe they've found a double-agent in surveillance," he said through a mouthful. "It's standard procedure to shut down the whole system until they get the mess cleaned up. Probably has nothing to do with S.T.O.P.—N.O.S. at all."

"I'd love to buy into your little fantasy," I said bitterly. "Except, I tried to call Monica back. She hung up on me before I could say more than three words. Somebody got to her. And Monica's not an easy lady to get."

I grabbed a scone and broke it in half. Horrible things. But I needed to keep my strength up.

"What does it mean? What do we do?"

"It means we've been shut down," I said. "What we do is take our database and move to New York."

"We can't get to the database, remember?" As an afterthought, he asked, "Why New York?"

I brushed the crumbs off the table and opened up my computer.

"My dear Thom, you are such a Neo. If you'd taken your head out of that damned C.I.A. manual, I could have told you the inside story on S.T.O.P.—N.O.S. a long time ago."

I booted up my computer. "This isn't the first time the agency's had to do a fast dump of the files and run for the security of the U.N. Every so often we get a renegade C.I.A., MI-5, KGB, or one of those spy-types, storming our offices."

The major looked baffled.

"Why?"

"We're a global organization—you know that. But we do a lot of surveillance work in sensitive areas. Part of our job is to see the big picture. Any prophet or oracle will tell you, it's not always good to know everything about your future."

Thom nodded.

"Sometimes our job includes withholding information," I said. "That creates an uneasy alliance with the individual governments. They think they have exclusive rights to any intelligence we uncover—in the name of National Security, of course."

The computer beeped and the database menu came on the screen.

Thom was astounded. "Even if you maxed out the memory, you couldn't hold half the Central Database."

"True, but with extended memory and hard disk copies, I've got all the prophecies and the critical analysis reports. I can also patch into about half the news wire services. The senior agents all keep a copy of this stuff—updated once a week. We won't have all the comforts and resources we've been used to, but we aren't starting from scratch either."

"Charlie, what are you talking about?"

"The society's been around for five centuries. It's survived thousands of international conflicts and two World Wars. The C.I.A. may have closed our offices, but they haven't shut us down. And we've still got work to do. Or have you forgotten about our active prophecy?"

Thom stuttered, stopped, and tried again. "I'm with you."

"Good!" I was sincerely pleased. I decided not to mention that we wouldn't be getting paychecks anymore. Why dampen his enthusiasm?

"We've got to go underground—now," I told him. "Technically, we haven't done anything wrong, but the

C.I.A. doesn't like people who know so much about them wandering around unsupervised. We'll meet up with other agents in New York."

The U.S. branch of the society was in shambles and would be for years. The American S.T.O.P.—N.O.S. department heads were scrambling for funding from the private sector. Perhaps it hadn't been wise to rely solely on the government, but after two hundred years, you begin to take some things for granted.

I scrounged around New York working part-time for the only operational S.T.O.P.—N.O.S. bureau in the country, and schlepping through a series of odd jobs to pay the rent.

I had dreams of a great, hairy, lumbering beast with a snout rimmed with sharp pointed teeth chasing me through a forest, out into a clearing and into a pond. Only the pond was thick with muck. I kept sinking, but the monster could walk right across it. I woke up before the monster sank his snout fangs into my head.

I sat up sweaty and shaking in my cot.

" 'Nother bad dream, Charlie?"

"I've had worse," I told Thom roughly.

We shared a small studio on the lower east side. It didn't leave much room for privacy.

"Want a cup of coffee?"

"Let's throw caution to the wind and make a full pot," I said, standing up and wrapping the sheet around me. "I'm not exactly anxious to revisit slumberland right now."

"I'll click on the TV. Maybe we can catch a little news."

I nodded my thanks at him, as I filled the coffee pot.

I grinned to myself as I heard James Earl Jones' deep, comforting voice announce, "This is CNN." One of my secret fantasies has that man reading me a bed-time story. I turned around in time to see the late-night anchor shuffling her papers in order.

"The budgeting process has been bloody. It hasn't gotten any easier since the president's mother went on Nightline last Friday and called her son a "tax and spend liberal wimp." And rumblings on Capital Hill say the Attorney General is going to be indicted next week on charges of mail fraud and bribery. He was stung trying to make a political payoff with a few hundred rolls of stamps.

"But first, Disaster hit Germany tonight in the form of two right-wing fringe assassin teams, who struck at the post-election parties of Bruno Schmidt and Hans Kohl. Schmidt had just been announced the winner in the election for Chancellor of united Germany. Kohl had placed second.

"In an astounding move, General Hugo Kurtz—who ran as the head of the radical splinter party, Reicht Now!, pushing a law and economic reform platform—has proclaimed victory, despite having placed a distant third in the elections."

The image of the anchorwoman was replaced by a video of Kurtz, dressed in a general's uniform, sur-rounded by other military types, on an outdoor stage. He was a short, heavyset, balding man. As a matter of necessity, he stood in front of the podium—he was too short to be seen behind it.

"My fellow Germans, today we are faced with a great national tragedy. Our country has been robbed of two brilliant, compassionate, leaders in a time when

Germany is poorly represented on the world stage. But point not your finger at neighbors, or an opposing political party. This was not the work of one of your German brothers or sisters. No! Early evidence proves conclusively that this was the savage act of radical foreign elements, determined that Germany should not shake loose from the chains of poverty and recession. But we will not let foreign extremists dictate the welfare of our great country. We will launch full investigation to capture these international criminals and work toward the return of German stability."

The video tape ended. The anchor's face returned to the screen. "As his first act as Chancellor, Kurtz declared the country under a state of martial law until the criminals can be brought to justice.

"In other news . . ."

"Turn it off, Thom," I croaked at him.

I tried to pour some coffee, but I was shaking so bad I missed the mugs. Thom took the pot from me. His hands weren't exactly steady as they poured, either.

"Charlie? Just where was Saxony?"

"Oh, the term was applied to just about every European country at one time or another."

If I sounded nonchalant, cold, it was because my mind had frozen up.

"Would that include Germany?"

"It would."

"Then the bear and the sow could be the former East and West Germany?"

"Could be."

"And Kurtz could be the monster, the product of reunification?"

"Maybe."

"No!" Thom slammed his hand down on the table. "Not maybe. Kurtz and unified Germany, it's the last line of the prophecy," Major Thom insisted. "I'll lay twenty pounds Kurtz gave the order for those assassinations himself. We should have seen this! He's a madman. It's going to be Hitler and World War II all over again."

His raving shook me out of my cold shock. It was time to do something productive. I started to whimper.

"It can't come to this. There must be another interpretation. Thom, don't let it to come to this!"

I gulped my coffee and tried to get a grip. "I was all for the reunification, closing the bases down, pulling the troops out. I personally, drank half a case of cheap champagne the night they ratified a single currency.

"I used up a week of my vacation time to fly over there when the wall came down. I chipped out my own piece of geologic history!"

"I don't think that counts as geology," Thom said, dubiously.

"The point is," I was hollering at him now but I didn't care. "I was all for the German reunification, and I have the rock to prove it. Hell, I even marched in the independence day parade and drank several gallons of warm German beer to show my support!"

"Several hundred gallons is probably more like it," Thom mumbled.

"F— off!"

"You know, my dad said it would come to this," Thom muttered darkly. "You don't get to be a three-star general for knowing nothing, you know. He predicted this whole imperialistic German dominance thing."

Major Thom was on his feet now, doing an eerily accurate impression of George C. Scott doing Patton.

"My father predicted that if we closed those military bases, if we pulled those missiles out, and stepped down our military presence there, it would leave an economic power vacuum that would ss-uu-cc-kk the whole of Western Europe right down the tub drain. He predicted this, dammit all!"

"Fine!" I yelled back at him. "So plug *him* into our Central Database! But in the meantime, what are we going to do?"

"We'll have to take strong military action," he declared. "A decisive unilateral first strike, to nip this cocky little General Kurtz right in the bud!"

"I thought you were a pacifist," I said aghast.

"Only in interpersonal relationships. On a global scale, there's nothing like a few hundred nuclear warheads to keep an unstable third world country in line."

"I don't want to hear this," I moaned. "Just shut up and interpersonally pacify me."

"German Chancellor Hugo Kurtz signed a nonaggression pact today with several federations of the former Soviet Republic, as German troops swept across the plains of Poland and the Czech Republic, wiping out the last bastions of resistance in the farmlands outside Warsaw.

"Following a nine-hour summit meeting between the U.S. President and the British Prime Minister, the President announced a hands-off policy, saying it was improper for the U.S. to involve itself in a European border dispute. The Prime Minister offered her assistance in negotiating a settlement ..."

I turned the volume down on my headset and looked around for the flight attendant. I had time for one more drink before a nap. Then it would be time to touch down in Mannheim. From there, it was just a short drive to Heidelberg.

We'd wasted a month back in New York, in futile attempts to convince someone that Kurtz must be stopped. We'd sent registered letters and E-Mail files to all our former contacts in Washington. The letters were returned unopened. The E-Mail went unanswered.

We lobbied at the U.N. While we found more sympathetic ears among the delegates there, it was generally agreed that the U.S. was the only super power left. No one had the funds or force to move troops into Germany and fill the vacuum left by the withdrawal of American forces. And no one was quite willing to sponsor an appropriate resolution before the U.N. without stronger, more traditional, evidence.

At S.T.O.P.—N.O.S. we had all the proof we needed. We'd cross-checked with our active seers and through the database. All signs said Kurtz was going to kick off a third world war.

I'd said good-bye to Thom a week earlier. He was shipping out, via the underground, to continue the work in England. I tried not to think about him, just now.

We were still being hunted by the C.I.A. on trumped up, petty ethics charges, designed to embroil us in House and Senate hearings that could take months, even years.

But the C.I.A. were amateurs next to S.T.O.P.—

N.O.S. They couldn't catch us. And they sure as hell weren't going to stop us. We knew what needed to be done.

Things happened fast in Heidelberg. The crowds grew bigger and the security more lax with each speech, each propaganda pitch, Chancellor Kurtz made. My fake I.D. and press pass were enough to get me into the press section. Under the cover of the camera crews and sound technicians, I screwed on the silencer and loaded my gun.

Kurtz still preferred to hold the mike and stand in front of the podium. That, with his rotund build, made aiming easy.

I pulled the trigger three times, tossed the gun into the crowd, and ran for it. Security forces closed in on me before I could clear the press area. But escape hadn't been part of the plan. Even through the pandemonium, I could see paramedics loading a wounded Kurtz into an ambulance. I smiled, satisfied. Because killing Kurtz hadn't been part of the plan, either.

I was thrown to the ground, searched, cuffed, and thrown into a military security vehicle. I knew I was in for the first of many long nights of interrogation. I could have told them then that it wouldn't take much to break me. I'd confess I was a C.I.A. spy. That the president, himself, had ordered the assassination attempt. That even now the U.S. was secretly funneling arms to the Polish resistance. And the German secret service would soon discover the portfolio and documentation of the mission hidden back in my hotel room. The resulting international scandal would draw

America into the war—now, before it got out of hand. In the Society to Oversee and Prevent Negative Oracle Scenarios, we know you can't prevent a prophecy from coming true, but you *can* manage the repercussions.

LAST OF THE RED-LEAD FLEET

by Nancy Holder

Century VI, #94

A King shall be enraged with seditionists
When the armaments of war shall be forbidden
Sweetness in the wild strawberries tainted by poison
They shall die by water, saying "crushed" as they die

Robert Wilkinson, the XO, put his ear against the captain's door. The Old Man was still talking to himself. Of course, that's not what *he* said.

"Sir?" Robert knocked again. The voice on the other side rose, fell, muttered on and on and on. "Sir. Captain Jones, sir." How goddamn ironic to have a skipper named David Jones, that being where the bastard was likely to send them. It would make you laugh, if it didn't make you scream first.

A voice came from behind him. "Uh, sir?" He jumped, turned. It was Andy Morehouse, coming up the ladder; the youngest and possibly the most frightened sailor aboard. Then again, there was no one aboard who wasn't terrified.

"Yes?" Richard asked.

The boy blanched. There was nothing but yellow peach fuzz on his white, unlined cheeks. His eyes were huge and blue, his eyelashes pale, giving him a perpet-

115

ually startled, wide-eyed look that had metamorphosed these last few days into one of complete panic.

He said, "Sir, we're uh, wondering how he is, sir." He was wringing with sweat and he stank, and Robert didn't think it was because he had come to the XO, who by tradition was the least-liked officer, since he policed the men. Saltwater inside the boat, saltwater outside. According to the captain, King Neptune was floating around out there, giving him orders not to return to port. According to their ears, another sub was headed their way, readying for the big showdown, if there had to be one.

"What's the word out there?" Robert's gesture took in the rest of the ship. In his mind's eye he saw the two places he was most worried about—Sherwood Forest, where the missiles stood in shiny rows more like Grecian columns than bandit oaks—and the reactor, down in lower level ops, behind a very thick hatch. And the well-armed Marine guard who stood at alert on the other side. That door opened without authorization, that man shot first, period. Semper Fi, no questions, ever. Those guys were Dobermans.

That was comforting.

Morehouse licked his lips, sweat rolling down his face like a waterfall. The man had sprung a leak, Robert thought giddily, and realized he himself was beginning to lose it. He reined himself in, tight.

"It's okay," he promised. "Tell me."

"Well, sir. Ah . . ." The sailor wiped his forehead and dried his palm on his jeans. His nails were ringed with oil residue. A workin' man. As Robert recalled, Morehouse's parents owned a farm in Illinois. "Frankly, sir, a few of the guys want to go down with the ship. Not a whole lot." He swallowed hard. "The rest of them, they want to know why you don't fuckin' shoot him."

Robert nodded. It was about what he expected. "And where do you stand, sailor?"

Morehouse shook his head. "I don't get it, sir. I just don't understand it. This whole thing is fuckin' *suicide.* How are we ever going to know if everybody disarms? I mean, what's to stop somebody from hiding a couple warheads here and there? And when we've given up all of ours . . ." He moved his shoulders; his entire body was shaking. "But I ain't gonna stand here and get blown up to make a point."

"So you want me to fuckin' shoot him." Morehouse ducked his head. After a moment, he muttered something that Robert couldn't hear. "Andy?" Robert prodded gently.

Morehouse didn't raise his head. "Sir, maybe I do." He stumbled backward and went down the passageway toward the control room. Robert sighed deeply and cupped his mouth and chin, wishing for a cigarette, wishing some other poor asshole was the Executive Officer of the boomer—the nuclear ballistic-missile submarine—the *USS Sharpston.*

At least, in this man's navy.

He leaned against the bulkhead and stared at the wood-grained door with the captain's name painted on it in gold. Total, worldwide, nuclear disarmament. Incredible. Impossible. He had no idea how the kings and presidents and dictators had agreed on it—what they had bargained with, bargained away. It scared him to death. Past death. But somehow they had made it happen. And all the silos were being emptied, all the launchers disabled, and all the hunter-killers and the boomers like the *Sharpston* were coming in. Lay down your weapons, gentlemen, for eternity. But like Morehouse said, all it would take was one welsher, and the rest of the world was screwed. And unglued. For eternity. It was enough to make a man nuts, so he supposed the captain had a right.

He sighed and walked back over to the door, and rapped very, very gently. "Sir . . ."

It flew open. Jones had on his sunglasses and Robert saw his own expression of surprise in the twin glazed reflections. The captain's face was drawn; his cheeks were covered with black and gray stubble. The hair was growing back on his head, but Robert could still see the long ribbons of cuts from the dull straight razor he'd used; something about the new ones being poisoned. According to the captain, everything on the ship was poisoned, and somehow, shaving your head was supposed to help.

"Yes?" Jones demanded. He lifted his chin in the same old way, bulldog arrogant. Beneath his dark blue jacket, his blue poopie suit was clean and pressed, a welcome change from the bathrobe he had worn into the control room when they'd gotten the news. And stayed in for that first day. Maybe it would be all right now; maybe the captain was *back,* in a manner of speaking. Jones had left them about forty-five hours ago when he had received his new orders for this mission from Command Authority. Spent seven hours confirming them six ways to Sunday, even though the four officers had authenticated them together, as was procedure—getting the two codes out of the two safes, reading each syllable, each word to one another, concurring, agreeing that this was the real thing. Then his mind had torpedoed out of his skull—but had yet, it seemed, to detonate.

He gestured for Robert to come into his stateroom as he took off his sunglasses. Robert's hopes were dashed: Jones's eyes still swirled with madness, two big whirlpools sucking his reason in farther and deeper. He did not look good, not one damn bit. Too much pressure per square inch, by half.

Robert's heart did a flip as he went in. The captain probably had a gun. There were also ten M14s, about a dozen twelve-gauge shotguns, and a half-dozen Colt .45s in the shipboard armory.

"Wilkinson, thank God," Jones breathed, gesturing for Robert to sit in the chair in front of the captain's desk set. He pulled the other chair to the foot-end of his narrow bunk. Two chairs, a monk's cot, a desk set, a hang locker. Not much, but by sub standards, the stateroom was a palace.

"Go on," Jones said. Robert complied, his hands on his knees, his spine stiff and straight. Christ, photographs of Jones's wife and kids on the desk. Robert was suddenly aware that he had a terrible headache.

The captain leaned against the door, locked it, and slammed his back against it. "Did anyone follow you?"

Robert closed his eyes and shook his head. "No, sir."

"What? *What?*" Jones leaned toward him. His breath was rank.

Robert's skin prickled; he felt as if he were on fire, nerve endings fried; it was hard enough to handle what was happening without having to deal with the skipper. "No one followed me. No one knows I'm here." Was that a wise thing to say?

"Good." Jones smiled brightly and rubbed his hands together. "Do you want a drink?" Sotto voce, he added, "It's all right. I brought it on board myself."

"Good thinking, sir."

"The room is bugged," he whispered, pointing to the desk, the overhead fluorescent light. Robert nodded knowingly though, of course, that was ridiculous. It would be far more likely that the captain would have forgotten to turn off the intercom beside the desk.

The captain unlatched the hang closet above his head and pulled out a bottle of rum and a small juice glass from the wardroom. He handed the glass to the XO and retrieved another one for himself. "I washed them myself." While the captain unscrewed the bottle, Robert scrutinized his glass. Wished he could smell it, but didn't want to be that obvious.

He held it out to the captain. Jones poured it to the rim. Robert raised a brow; Jones said, "It's the only thing we can eat or drink now, Wilky. He told me so. Everything is tainted. The radiations, you know."

"He . . ."

"Why, His Highness, of course. King Neptune." He made a regal gesture toward his bunk, where the sheets were heaped in the center of the mattress. "I was surprised when you didn't say hello. I have introduced you before." It was not a question. "We'd be dead by now without him. All of us."

"Yes." Robert gulped down half the rum. It burned all the way down with a mellow, blazing heat, but with no sleep and less food, it was a bad idea. He needed all his faculties. The crew needed him. Right now, it was hard to believe any of that mattered. He felt as hopeless as Andy Morehouse: just get a gun and shoot the poor bastard.

"How do, sir," he said to the sheets. The Old Man looked pleased. He said nothing for a long moment; Robert wondered if he was waiting for King Neptune to finish speaking.

Jones poured more rum into Robert's glass and toasted him. "I was glad to see you were a drinking man when we started working together, Wilky," he said. "Can't trust a man who doesn't drink. Either he's an alcoholic, a fag, or a tight-assed religious fanatic."

"Yes, sir."

Jones plopped down heavily in the chair at the end of his bunk with the bottle and the glass in his hands. He didn't offer King Neptune a drink.

They sat in what might pass for companionable silence, though every fiber of Robert's body was tight and ticking like a bomb. He watched the captain covertly, wondering what he should do. Between breaths, his brain flipped back to thoughts of his wife Elise, his mother, his two maiden aunts. Had the civilian populations been informed? Were they celebrating, rioting, assassinating their leaders?

"What are you thinking about?" Jones asked suspiciously.

"Bomb shelters," Robert blurted out, and immediately damned the liquor for loosening his tongue.

"They could be the last hope of the human race." Jones scratched the crown of his head; his fingertips found a scab and he started picking at it. Robert winced inwardly, but said and did nothing. Tick, tick, tick. What if he went crazy, too? What would the crew do then?

"We had one when I was a boy."

"Duck and cover." Jones smiled grimly. "What a load of crap. The Cuban missile crisis was a PR scheme to make Kennedy look like something he wasn't. He was a womanizing pantywaist who couldn't govern. A terrible Commander in Chief. A disgrace." He shook his head; incredibly—or perhaps, not so—he yawned.

"Well, heavy hangs the head who wears the scrambled eggs." He laughed and gestured toward the photographs. "My daughter was so confused when I made Captain. She thought they really were going to put eggs on my hat. When I showed her the braid, she said, 'They don't look like eggs at all!' She was very disappointed. She was, oh, six then." He blinked rapidly and jerked up his head. "I ever tell you she died?"

Robert had started to take another swallow; he stopped with the glass at his lips and said, "No, sir."

"Drowned. Damn fool husband of hers took her sailing. No life jackets. Did you know that in the old navy men didn't learn how to swim? Figured if the sea wanted them, there was no use fighting."

Robert said carefully, "What do you think of that, sir?"

"Wait." The captain turned his head toward the pile of sheets. His face fell, lines and furrows shifting into other lines and furrows. He had lived life hard. He was going crazy hard. "Shoot. He slipped back out."

"Out . . .?"

"Where he belongs." He jabbed a finger toward the head of his bunk, the direction of the hull and the ocean outside. "Where *we* belong, mister."

Robert chewed the inside of his lip. He thought he

might throw up. The booze cut his stomach acid with a rusty razor blade and made his brains as sour as his mouth.

"You know what I'm saying, don't you?" the captain went on. "You do know."

Robert said carefully, "I think we have to return to port." His epitaph, maybe. Without trying to appear too obvious, he scanned the paneled cubicle for any sign of a weapon. For all he knew, it was in the desk. He itched to open the drawers and see. Part of his mind sped ahead, wondering what it was like to be shot; they said you had a grace period of thirty minutes to an hour where you didn't feel it. Then the pain set in, gangbusters, and most people were incapacitated by it. Quick images of a thousand movies clicked by in rapid succession, all of them of men being shot; most of them of men being shot who jumped back up and trounced the bad guy. Men being shot and dying. But not one of them shot inside a sabotaged sub headed permanently for the bottom.

If the captain ordered them to remain submerged, how many of the crew would obey?

"Sir," he said again, while inside a voice begged him, *Don't push it.*

Shifting his weight—*Jump him, now!* shouted the voice in Robert's head—the captain moved to the bunk and flopped on his backside, crabbed to the headboard. He stretched out his legs and settled against the bulkhead. Not a single drop had splashed out of his glass. He slugged it down and poured himself another, motioning to Robert, who shook his head.

"Oh, come on, Wilky," the captain said amiably. "What're you saving yourself for? We're red-lead men." He raised the bottle. "The officers of the red-lead fleet."

"Sir, we're not red-lead. We aren't being decommissioned, we're just—"

"Bullshit!" the captain yelled. "Wilky, please don't tell me you're that stupid. Please don't tell me you don't know what's coming next."

"Just the nuclear weapons, sir. Then we'll go back out." As he spoke, Robert didn't know if he believed that. Why would they let them keep the reactor? He didn't know what to think. He could barely manage a coherent thought. He had to piss like crazy. He had to throw up. He had to make the captain go in. Didn't he? Isn't that what they should be doing?

The captain pulled one leg up to his chest and stretched his head to the left, the right. Hunched his shoulders, straightened them. "Might as well castrate the last bull on earth and then tell him to be fruitful and multiply. There's no sense to it. No logic. That's why I don't believe any of it."

He pointed his finger at Robert, shaking it as he spoke. "It's a hoax. A good one—hell, they know all the codes and the procedures; they can do anything they want. Who puts our codes in the safes in the first place? Gremlins? No way." He folded his arms. "King Neptune's told me no one else is complying, and he's in a position to know, wouldn't you say?"

"Well, sir . . ."

"Look, they wouldn't just send some flash traffic out to the fleets and the troops and the friggin' aircraft. If everyone's doing it, why is it such a secret?"

That bothered Robert, too. But the Joint Chiefs had been holding talks about it for years, and the world's military leaders had been meeting with each other with increasing frequency. Robert's Pentagon friends had held office pools on when the orders to stand down would come. Resumes for civilian jobs were flying thick and fast.

"It's a security check. Or a loyalty check, to see if we'd really do something so fatal to our government." The captain glowered at him. "Whose side are you on, Wilky? Are you a fuckin' Communist?"

Robert said carefully, "Captain, you know the Cold War's over."

"Over, hell. Nothing is over. Unless we hand this boat over to the conspiracy trying to convince us this is standard operating procedure for the whole world! You know those damn ragheads won't hand over everything. No way would our nation agree to this."

Robert heard all his own objections. But he also knew their orders. *Let the politicians sort it out,* he thought. They must have planned for skittish commanders and uncertain crews. They wouldn't have actually been so naive as to assume all they had to do was send you a short, terse request, and you'd pirouette back to port. As Morehouse had said, company was already coming. He could easily imagine the word being given to locate the *Sharpston* and ... urge ... her to comply. And if he didn't do something soon, the crew was going to disintegrate into mutiny or worse.

"Captain," he said, "the men."

"Screw the men. Men live, men die." He pulled his lips back from his mouth, and his face became a huge, ghastly grin that made Robert catch his breath. "Nations are forever."

Robert felt the sweat gathering on his back and

chest. God, one morning you wake up and think, *Thirty-two more days until we surface.* And then a gray-faced kid raps on your door and hands you a piece of paper, turns sideways, and pukes in terror.

It's not just a job . . .

It's a nightmare.

"Captain."

"Dismissed." The captain flicked his hand; it flopped to the mattress like a dead fish. "Go on, Wilky, get the hell outta here."

"Captain, sir, I don't think I should leave without you." Robert rose from his chair and took a step toward the bunk. "I think you should come with me, sir."

The captain raised his head; the whites of his eyes looked yellow, even in the bluish overhead light. He looked very ill. Robert had occasionally wondered what Jones was doing CO'ing a sub. His captain's rank was high for it, and he was too old. A red-lead man, ready for dry dock, a host for the mothballs to hatch inside.

"Sir, come with me, please."

"Why? So you can kill me?" Jones asked in a low, menacing voice. His hand fumbled in the bedclothes—*Oh, shit,* Robert thought—and as Robert had half-suspected all along, brought up a Colt .45, aimed it at Robert, and said, "So you can do the right thing?"

"Sir, no, sir," Robert said automatically. "I do not want to harm you, sir."

"Goddamn mustang." Jones narrowed his eyes at him. "You were an enlisted man, you made good. But do you think that makes you a *real* officer? Have you ever truly grasped the nuances of command?"

Perhaps in another time and place, Robert would have been offended. Now all he heard was that the captain was placing a barrier between them, adding psychic weight to the correctness of his actions, present and perhaps premeditated. They say it didn't hurt, not at first . . .

"Sir, you can't mean to harm me," Robert said as calmly as he could. "I think you're very tired. I'd be happy to—"

"To turn this ship over to our enemies." He laughed harshly. "All I can figure is there's been an alien invasion. 'People of Earth, hand over your weapons!' " His voice rose into a shrill giggle. "It's got to be a test! Or a bad dream. Or I've gone crazy." A single tear welled in the corner of his eye. "Because the America I live to protect would never do this to me, never."

"Sir." There was a knock on the door. Robert jerked, glanced at the door without moving his head, murmured, "Sir, please stow the weapon."

"Captain?" It was Morehouse. "Um, sir?"

Jones bolted off his bunk. "What the hell is he doing here? Has there been a mutiny?" He pointed the gun at the door. His hand was past shaking; it was swaying.

"For God's sake, sir!" Robert moved between the captain and the door. Time slowed down, way down, as he turned his back, hyperaware of the weapon and the bullets inside it; full-metal explosions directly into the center of his dum-dum—oh-so-dumb heart or head or spine. *God.*

"What the hell do you want?" the captain shouted.

"Sir? The Officer of the Deck requested . . ." He took a breath. Robert wondered why him all the time, why a seaman and a boy at that. Why not Chase, the OOD? Where was the chain of command?

"Captain Jones and I are coming out now." Robert took a breath. "The captain hasn't been feeling well, but he's all right now." A chill shuddered up his spine as he gingerly turned his head just a fraction of an inch. "Sir?"

There was a long silence. Robert's sweat chilled to ice. *Don't hurt the boy,* he pleaded. *For God's sake, don't.*

Captain Jones said, "Oh, very well, then, sir." And Robert closed his eyes, partly in relief and partly because he had the sick feeling that Captain Jones wasn't speaking to him, nor to Morehouse. He had the feeling King Neptune was back.

The Old Man got up and smoothed his poopie suit. Robert opened the door and went out first. Morehouse started to say something, coughed into his fist, and walked over to the ladder to give way to the officers as they proceeded forward toward the control room. Robert moved slowly, trying to picture where the gun was, wondering if he should lurch backward and grab it.

"Yes, sir, I hear you sir," Jones muttered, putting his hand over his mouth. "Loose lips."

Sink ships, Robert finished silently. His back tingled, and he kept licking his lips and swallowing, trying very hard not to show that he was afraid.

"What's that, you say?" Jones muttered. "Yes, yes, I see, you're right."

They reached the control room, awash with red lights and men, forty of them, seated at screens, moving about. The screens danced; the periscope gleamed. Robert made way for the captain to enter first, not at all comforted by the fact that he himself was finally out of the direct line of fire. Jones in turn made way, apparently for the phantom King Neptune.

"Captain on the bridge!" The captain was saluted, but all gazes were fixed on Robert. Frightened gazes. Chase, standing with the ship's doctor, slid a glance at Robert. Robert mouthed, *Gun.* The OOD's eyes flickered.

"I assume the con," Jones announced. "Officer of the Deck, you're relieved of conning the ship."

"Aye, sir," Chase said. He drifted backward around the periscope and disappeared down the passageway.

"Diving Officer, make your depth two thousand feet."

There was a rustling as men and officers looked up at him. Two thousand was below crush level. Robert opened his mouth to speak as the captain said angrily, "Diving Officer, I didn't hear you."

"Sir." Robert held up a hand.

"Look, I'm getting my orders from *him,*" Jones said testily, pointing at thin air. "He's going to take us to a safe haven, Wilky. No one will ever find us there. We can wait in readiness, and when this whole damn-fool scheme blows up in their faces, we'll be able to help."

"It's an admirable plan, sir," Robert said, lowering his hand, "but we have orders to return to port. We need to go home, sir."

The captain smiled. "Wilky, that's what I'm trying to tell you. We *are* going home. He's taking us there."

Robert took a breath. Damn it, it was time to do something. Now or never, as they said. God help him.

"Sir, I must ask you to step down. Please relinquish command to me immediately."

For a full minute, Jones stared at him; then, with a short, harsh cry, he balled his fist and lunged wildly at Robert, who ducked easily. "Sir," Robert said. Officers tensed; seamen crouched into fighting postures, poised to intervene; men rose from their chairs. Robert wondered if anyone would try to stop him if he physically restrained the captain.

Jones took a step back as Andy Morehouse bolted toward him. "Stop him!" he shouted. "There are *two* fast-attacks on our butt now! If we dive, they'll probably fire on us! Jesus, XO, save us!"

The captain reached in the pocket of his jacket, pulled out the gun, and aimed it at Robert. He raised his chin and narrowed his eyes, and his hand was steady.

He said, "I am in command."

Reappearing at the mouth of the passageway, Chase signaled to Robert with his fingers: *I am armed.* Dear God. Robert walked toward the captain with his hands up.

"No, sir. No, you are not," Morehouse said, wiping his eyes. The captain's gun arm jerked, tracked the young man's motion. "You're so fucking out of control that it—"

"Stop it! *Stop it!* I am acting on orders from a superior officer!" Jones shook the gun at the boy. "One more word, mister, one more word and—"

"Sir," Robert said calmly, though he was about to wet his pants. "We have just received new orders from that superior. He told me he wants us to return to port." He nodded slowly. "That's what he told me, sir. That's what he wants us to do."

"Don't you lie to the men!" the captain shouted.

"You *traitor!* King Neptune is standing right here, right here, and he is telling me not to listen to you. Not to any of you!" He spun in a circle. Chase moved to the right, around the periscope and the small gate surrounding it. Robert watched them both, his heart pounding.

Jones lunged forward and grabbed Morehouse around the neck, pressed the gun to his temple. "This ship is my responsibility," he hissed. "No one takes my command from me. It was given to me by the highest authority."

"Sir," Robert said, his hands still raised, "let the boy go."

"No. The king says, if you don't obey orders, I'll shoot him. I'll shoot everyone I have to."

Robert's vision telescoped to the boy, the man, and the gun. He was holding his breath, growing dizzy, straining so hard not to panic that he was grinding his teeth. He said, "Chase," and the OOD stood where he was, braced his right hand, and fired at the captain.

With a shout, Jones fell. Morehouse rolled out of his grasp. His shipmates surrounded him, pulled him to his feet, shielding him.

"Jesus Christ!" Morehouse shouted. "Jesus! Jesus!" He collapsed into the arms of his best friend McConnell.

Robert knelt beside the captain. A huge, pulsing wound gaped in the center of his chest; blood was pumping out of it and running onto the deck thick and fast and hot. The doc appeared at Robert's side, took one look, and said, "Damn."

"Sir, sir." Robert leaned over the Old Man. "Sir."

Jones actually smiled. Robert blinked. Then Jones rasped, "It doesn't hurt."

"Sir . . ."

"Your turn. You'll see." He began to gag, his arms moving feebly. He voided himself.

Robert shouted at the doctor, "Can't you do something?"

Then the skipper lay still. His head lolled to one side and blood and chunks of pink tissue spewed out of his mouth. The crew exhaled in one horrified gasp.

Robert shut his eyes. This was his fault. He should have relieved the man immediately, gotten the doc to sedate him, and locked him up.

Jesus, Jesus, forgive me, he prayed, clenching his hands together, bowing his head. He wanted to cry. But the men needed him; he was the captain now. The ship needed him. He drew in a long, steady breath—

—And smelled seawater and seaweed, tangy and ripe.

He opened his eyes.

On the other side of the captain's body, two large feet stood planted on the deck, dripping with water. A stalk of kelp draped the deck beside the left ankle. Robert heard roaring in his ears as he raised his head. He gave a short, harsh shout.

A tall, muscled figure looked down on him. It was a man with sharp features and a flowing white mane of hair entwined with seaweed that hung over his shoulders and across his large chest. He wore a golden crown studded with abalone and black pearls. He was naked except for an iridescent covering like fish scales that rounded his waist and hung down to his thighs. In his right hand he held a golden scepter, an eel coiled around it.

He touched the scepter to Robert's shoulder, and a bone-crushing cold washed through the XO. He gasped.

"Take her down, man." The figure's eyes gleamed, icy arctic maelstroms; his voice a thunder from beneath the sea. "Take her down and keep her down, as you value the land above your head."

"Sir? Sir?" someone called to Richard from far away.

From very far away.

BUCKEYE JIM IN EGYPT

by Mort Castle

Century VII, #24

One who has been enshrouded shall emerge from
 his tomb
The fort of the bridge shall be secured with chains
Poisoned by the eggs of the Barbel fish
Shall be the leader of Lorraine by the Marquis
 Dupont

Prologue

In the beginning, there was darkness.
Then came light.
That is the beginning of everything.

I

The more mundane among us contend Southern Illinois
is called "Egypt" or "Little Egypt" because of its
southernmost town, Cairo, on the Mississippi River.

More probable is that the term came into usage because we are still waiting for a Moses to lead us out of
here right to the Promised Land, although every time
one appears on the scene, we kick him flush in the
backside and tell him to let us tend to our own affairs.

Mort Castle

Brian Robert Moore, weekly columnist,
1920–1973, "I'll Tell You What!" for the
Sesser Sentinel, Eads St. Publications,
Sesser, Illinois

Way up yonder, above the sky,
white bird nests in a green bird's eye.
    "Buckeye Jim"
    An American folk song,
    usually performed on the banjo

Monday, July 12, 1925

Sometimes he forgot who he was.

Sometimes he forgot what he was doing here.

It was just past 7:30 in the morning, and already the thermometer had hit a swampy 80, but it was not the temperature or fatigue that caused the man in the light-weight suit coat to set down his straw valise and banjo case and lean on the rail of the half-mile-long bridge. He needed to think. Gazing down at the rippling, sun-reflecting waters of the Washauconda River helped to bring about a mind calming focus.

He reached into his pocket. He found it: a lucky buckeye. Every time he reached into his pocket, there would be one—and one only. The seed of the horse chestnut was brown and brittle; it felt as though there were something magical and off-center within it. It was exactly like the world.

His smile came slow and easy. Nobody would ever mistake him for handsome, but when he smiled, it made most folks like him.

He knew who he was.

He was Buckeye Jim.

BUCKEYE JIM IN EGYPT

This time.

He knew what he had to do.

Buckeye back in his pocket, he hoisted his grip and banjo. Just then a new, deep green, Oakland All American Six pulled up, the powerful Phaeton model. Of course, in this weather, the windows were down. The driver, in a straw fedora, tie knotted in a half-Windsor, a prominent American flag pin on his collar, leaned toward Buckeye Jim. "How do."

"How do," Buckeye Jim answered, bending down, face framed by the window. "Your automobile is a beaut."

"I do thank you. Might I offer you a ride into Fort Lorraine? I assume that is your intended destination."

"Yes, sir," Buckeye Jim said.

"The Devil is always hiring fiddlers and banjo pickers in hell, but if you're after employment in the mines, Mr. June Legrand's got a one hole privy operation in Fort Lorraine that is likely to oblige. If you don't mind working next to niggers. And if you don't mind being forced to join the union."

Buckeye Jim said nothing as he stowed his gear in the back.

The driver added, "Not saying Legrand's a Bolshevik. Not saying he's a nigger lover. I do wonder if he's a true-blue American."

The auto felt massive. Buckeye Jim wondered if he would ever get used to cars. He did enjoy the smell of new cars. He liked the smell of gently flowing rivers and hot sun on steel bridges. . . .

He suddenly remembered the strong and surprising odor of light, a smell that was itself pure radiance, shattering and banishing the darkness.

137

The driver's name, said the man who wore his nation's flag on his collar, was Mark E. Dupont. ("Thank you for the ride, Mr. Dupont, and people call me Buckeye Jim.") He seemed a friendly fellow, not too jolly or too serious.

Not too much one or the other. He could be a dangerous man, Buckeye Jim reckoned. On several occasions, Buckeye Jim had been killed by this sort of man.

Mark E. Dupont casually mentioned he was assistant superintendent up to the new strip mine owned by Illinois Coal and Power north of Herrin. A new process, strip mining would be the wave of the future, and it was swell. It meant more profit for everyone. Also, Mark E. Dupont mentioned (casually), he'd been elected to Herrin's town council. There had been talk—casual, but who could tell—about his running for mayor.

He started to say something else casual when Buckeye Jim said, "Sure a fine automobile. A real ace."

Dupont chuckled. "Well, I would have been most happy and satisfied with just your standard model, but my boys would not have it."

"You have sons?" Buckeye Jim asked.

Dupont said, "Well, I do have a family, and I do have boys. Two boys, a girl, and a fine, Christian wife who dotes on me.

"But I was not referring to my offspring. I meant the boys in the Klan."

"Clan," Buckeye Jim said quietly.

There were times when his mind became a tedious and troublesome thing.

So many memories . . .

He did *remember* clans. *The MacEldoes? The*

138

BUCKEYE JIM IN EGYPT

McCutcheons? In Scotland. He recalled Scotland as a land of thistles and foggy mornings more gray and ominous than anywhere else on earth. And cutting through the grayness, he could remember the swirling-squeal of the pipes, eerie and mysterious, a summons to war and death ...

He remembered ...

". . . I'm the leader. What you call a Cyclops," Dupont said. " 'Course they have to inflate it some, call me the 'Grand Exalted Cyclops.' " Mark E. Dupont sounded like he didn't mind that "his boys" wanted him to be "grand" and "exalted" and to drive a Phaeton.

"Well, I don't know," Buckeye Jim said.

"A lot of people don't know," Dupont said, "and among 'em is one Mr. C. Cooper Legrand, Jr. I'll be jawing some with him today. Rich man like him, what he can't realize is this was hard-scrabble, bare bone, *poor* country 'fore the mines come. And if all the really big companies from out east choose to leave because Legrand has a head full of foreign thinkin' and a heart that beats pure nigger time like a shufflin' pickaninny ..."

Buckeye Jim said nothing. He was confused. Not infrequently, people thought him dull-witted.

But if you live many lives, and you don't *know what you* should know *and you do know what you* shouldn't *know ...* My, oh, my, and wasn't it a *perplexing* business?

Mr. Dupont was talking about—

". . . the Klan is four-square for the Bible. I'd imagine a right-looking American fellow such as yourself,

139

why, you wouldn't be having any moral or spiritual argumentations with that, would you, Mr. Buckeye Jim?"

With all his poor head had to tote, sometimes Buckeye Jim felt he had no room left over for a sense of humor, but doggone! That *did* make him laugh!

"Mr. Dupont," he said. "I would testify in any court of the land or on Judgment Day that I have *no* dispute with the Bible."

"Well, good, good," Mr. Dupont said. He went on to tell how the Ku Klux Klan defended Americans from foreigners and Communists and Catholics (especially those "Eye-talian Catholics but also Bohunk and Polack" Catholics), and he went on to tell how it brought true Christianity to those as needed the Gospel Truth, and he went on to tell how it put the fear of God in the bootleggers, like those East St. Louis Shelton Brothers, or that Jew Charlie Birger with his roadhouse, the Shady Rest, and he went on and he went on and on and on . . .

Buckeye Jim said, "Looks like we're here."

Like virtually all southern Illinois town squares, Fort Lorraine's was a circle. In the center, an imposing island of civic sanctity, stood the municipal building, new red brick, with broad, white concrete steps. Merchants on the town's center hub included Walker and Sons clothing, the Vick-Cline Pharmacy (where the forty-cent size Fletcher's Castoria was on sale for twenty-nine cents), and Ulricht's Shoe Store.

Buckeye Jim got out and pulled his gear after him.

"Good luck," Dupont said, shaking his hand through the passenger window portal. "You find Fort Lorraine isn't exactly to your liking, that maybe it smells too niggery, you come on up north of Herrin way and perhaps I can do you some good."

"Why, thank you," Buckeye Jim said. You know, Buckeye Jim felt altogether *humorous* today. "Mr. Dupont, you are the very *first* Grand Exalted Cyclops I have met in my entire life and I am likely some older than you take me for."

Mark E. Dupont waved a "Pshaw" hand in pleased self-deprecation.

"And by the way," Buckeye Jim said, "I'm a Jew."

II

With Britain's defeat of France in 1763, the dreams of a French empire in Illinois ended. In the south of the state, such lasting place names as Vincennes, Prairie du Rocher, Bellefontaine are usually so mispronounced in southern Illinois twang as to be unrecognizable to any Frenchman.

But today, in Fort Lorraine, Illinois, in Union Grove Country, "an experiment in planned living" is being conducted that makes many of the local citizenry proclaim their community "a heaven on earth."

The "social scientist" responsible is C. Cooper Legrand, Jr., who owns the Old Legrand and Washauconda River Mining Corporation, one of the smaller operations in the region—"but one of the *safest*," Legrand stresses. A childless widower, C. Cooper Legrand is usually addressed good-naturedly by his employees as "June," or "Juney." With enthusiastic forthrightness, he states, "Yes, we are working *to-*

gether to create a utopia, an earthly paradise if you will. After all, my father created hell."

In addition to owning the mines, the Legrand family built and owns much of the town of Fort Lorraine itself, renting living quarters to its laborers. But these houses are a far cry today from what they were in "the not so good old days." According to the *Illinois Coal Report for 1898,* these dwellings "lacked central heating and running water. One outhouse served six homes. Workers led 'joyless, brutal, dangerous lives,' and had little opportunity to 'even dare to dream of bettering themselves.'"

"My father died in 1910, and I bear him no grudge, and I hope others do not. He was not cruel, merely unenlightened," states Legrand. "I was twenty-two at his passing, and I felt myself ready. I had studied in Europe, in France, England, and Germany. I had visited Russia. I knew that if capitalism did not change, it would be brought down, that there would be a revolution in blood and fire. History would condemn those who reaped inhumane profits from the sufferings of the masses. I envisioned a decent, compassionate capitalism, one that has at its root the understanding that the human experience is one we all share."

Upon assuming the mantle of leadership, Legrand immediately instituted new safety features in the mining operations, and transformed the workers' "squalid huts" into real homes. He opened negotiations with the United Mine Workers of America and his operations today are 100% union.

Not infrequently, C. Cooper Legrand, Jr. is asked if he is a "leftist," or even a Socialist or Communist, and in this part of the country, these are damning labels.

BUCKEYE JIM IN EGYPT

But Legrand laughs at such allegations of "Un-Americanism." "What I am is a *progressive*," he maintains. "I believe in people. I'm working for a better world for all of us, without the invisible walls that have kept people apart for too long."

> From "Utopia in Illinois?", a feature
> article by Roy L. Potts, in The St.
> Louis Tribune-Leader, May 10, 1924.

"Horseshit."

> Mark E. Dupont, Grand Exalted Cyclops
> of the Knights of the Ku Klux Klan; a
> private response to the above article.

The Knights of the Ku Klux Klan stand for the purest ideals of native-born, white, Gentile four-square Americanism:

The tenets of the Christian religion.
The protection and nurturing of white womanhood.
The freedom, under law, of the individual.
The "right to work" of the American working man; his individual liberty to enter into such business negotiations and private and personal contracts as he chooses.

> From a two color handbill entitled "The Fiery
> Cross: America's Guiding Light," written by
> Mark E. Dupont and the Rev. James E.
> Scurlock, January, 1924

"Horseshit."

C. Cooper Legrand, Jr., in a private response to the above quoted handbill, prior to his ripping it to pieces as he laughed.

III

He liked it.

By that afternoon, he'd walked here and he'd walked there, and after a time, he knew Fort Lorraine was the right place.

A little girl on the east side sold him a one penny lemonade, ferociously cold and snapping with lemon.

He saw a blue-jay.

A Negro woman on the front porch of a neat little house in a neighborhood of neat little houses called to him.

"Sir?" She held her little boy by the hand, a child of perhaps five or six.

Buckeye Jim went up the walk. He liked the way she sounded, not the "hiding away" voice black folks often use for white people.

"You lost?"

No.

No one is lost; no one is forsaken, were the words that came to his mind.

There were flowers in the yard. Impatiens. Pink and yellow roses. And tulips. *July, and so hot, and yet the tulips were* still here *and lovely.*

A happy perplexity filled his head, and he felt a small grin growing that he knew to be silly. *Maybe at last, at last, it was coming around! Coming around*

*here, in Fort Lorraine, and maybe this town would be
a light unto the nations ...*

He was, he said, just sort of scouting the territory,
and he told her his name.

She was Mrs. Willoughby. Her little boy was Paulie
Jason. The child drew closer to her. "My Paulie can't
talk. He can hear, but he can't talk. Doctors don't
know as to why it is."

Buckeye Jim put his small straw suitcase down on
the walk. He reached into his pocket. "Yes! I *thought*
I had me one. And it's an extra special lucky one!"

A snap of his thumb launched the buckeye. At the
top of its arc, it hung there ...

... and there it hung.

Then Paulie Jason let loose his momma and slowly,
slowly, his hand swam out as the buckeye dropped
through weighted depths of air to land on his palm and
his fingers closed over it.

Buckeye Jim turned and walked away.

Paulie Jason said, "Good-bye, Mr. Buckeye Jim."

IV

Socialism, communism, and other doctrines
have played no part in the violence and
murder which have brought such ill fame to
the "queen of Egypt."
> William L. Chenery in
> *The Century*

... respect to Mr. Chenery, this self-proclaimed
Sage of Sesser holds that we are just as willing to kill

for doctrines as your most radical, bearded, bomb-toting, Eastern European anarchist. Many of our law enforcement officials and politicians are willing to kill for the doctrine, "Under the Table and in My Palm," while our bootleggers resort to violence to enforce the "Right of Americans to Get Drunk." Our Kluxers, of course, will take up arms in defense of every town's prerogative to conduct festive lynching bees, while I personally know at least two Methodist churches whose congregations load the cannons if you try to take away their covered dish pot luck dinner, which they hold as a sacrament.

Of course, we Egyptians, when we lack doctrines to kill for, will quite happily kill because: A) we've nothing more interesting to do; and B) our nation expects us to act like savages.

> Brian Robert Moore,
> "I'll Tell You What!"

Son of a bitch! Mark E. Dupont, *THE* Grand Exalted Cyclops, did not hold with *unnecessary* violence, but at this particular instant, he could violently put a new Montgomery Ward steel-toe work boot all the way up that man's . . .

Mr. C. Cooper Legrand, Jr., "Call me June," trying to be "plain folks," but oh, the man was just so *full* of himself!

Talk reason *to him.* That's what the Illinois Coal and Power Company wanted its designee (and *rising* member of the *management team!*), Mark E. Dupont to do.

Illinois Coal and Power would like Legrand to sell them his enterprise. Not that Legrand was real competition, not with I C and P's far cheaper strip mining process and nonunion operation ...

—But I like having a coal mine, Mark! It's fun!

Negotiations could begin immediately. Accommodations could be reached with the union. Mr. Legrand could play a role on a board of directors ...

Mr. Legrand, whether you know it or not, there *was* trouble stirring, many of Egypt's citizens did not hold with white and colored living and working together like that—

—Mark, when they came off their shift, all you see is eyes, so you can't tell a colored coal miner from a white one!

—this union thing, well, in the long run, it might *DE*-stroy individual incentive ...

—meant no one was cheated and everyone got what was coming to him. Do unto others and all that, Mark ...

(Like to give you what's coming to you! Like to do unto you until you're done for certain, chucking Bible at me when nobody ever sees *you* at church!

(Hmm, could be some of the fancy learning you got overseas included how to spurn the Lord your God? You an atheist, Juney-Bug? By the way, how long your wife's gone and you still single and no lady around but that giant mammy housekeeper? Could be you more of a *Jane* than a *June*, Mr. Legrand?)

At sunset of a *frustrating* day, Dupont pulled up in front of his home in Herrin. If Dupont had been able to get things moving right, he'd been virtually *promised* the super's position at the Illinois Coal and Power's Fort Lorraine mines!

But . . .

Say, what the hell?

He picked it off the seat of his *new* Oakland All American Six Phaeton.

A buckeye.

That guy this morning, that sort of mush brain . . .

The buckeye felt damn *bad,* he thought.

That's when lightning hit.

Lightning did not blast down from the heavens.

It burst from deep within him, and he felt the searing anguish in his eyes, felt his blood boil, felt his heart blaze and burn and turn to hard, black coal. And he felt a hellish hand wrap around his soul and *squeeze!*

The power of it threw him against the car door with enough force to spring it. He did a back somersault, losing his hat in the process. He pushed himself up to his hands and knees.

"Aaaaah! Aaaaah!" he shrieked, but it was a thin shriek, all breath and tightness. *Jesus! Jesus!*

Save me!

In spiritual and physical agony, his American flag collar pin falling into the disgusting Niagara as he vomited and vomited . . .

. . . in the fetid black and green foaming spew from his guts, he could see incredibly tiny frogs, obscenely clean and shining eyed . . .

The Devil had him! He could not doubt! The Devil . . .

In his anguish, he comprehended it. The Devil could don many guises . . .

Buckeye Jim! "Oh Lord, deliver me," Dupont begged, "for the Devil has laid his fiery hands upon thy servant!"

BUCKEYE JIM IN EGYPT

Somehow, *somehow*, Legrand, atheist *nigger lover DEVIL WORSHIPER!* had arranged it all. He understood that without any evidence but the revelation of his tormented spirit.

Dupont staggered to his feet, slumped against the car. A sudden cramp, and drool and frogs—he could feel them on his tongue and palette!—leaked out of his mouth down his clothes.

Up at his house, he heard the commotion. "What is it? What?!?"

What it was was he was DAMNED!

He lurched into the car.

He needed God's help.

"Please, God, please . . ." he whispered. The automobile jerked away, as he squinted to see through his tears.

He had to get to Granny Gunger!

Give me that old time religion!
It's good enough for me!

Granny Gunger had a regal and hideous demeanor as she presided at the rickety table in her hovel out near the tracks at Whittington Curve, a prime location because, when a train slowed for the turn, coal would tumble from the tender and she'd reap the bounty of Luck and the Illinois Central Railroad.

Granny Gunger came from the hills. She knew dowsing and how to draw fire out of wounds. She could stop bleeding or set bones. She could not regrow an eye, however, and so there was the mucus and muscle rippling empty socket where her drunken father had accidentally thumbed her when all he'd meant to do was punch her.

"You stink, Mister Dupont. You stink like you crawled up a OH-possum's ass," Granny Gunger said. Granny Gunger was known for plain speaking.

Dupont told her why he'd come.

"Frogs," she said. "Frogs is *bad*. You got strong enemies doin' Satan's bidding. Mister Dupont, the Old Deceiver wants you. You're in sorry shape now, and I don't think you'll like eternity in hell much better."

"Help me, Granny!"

"You got faith, Mister Dupont? You got *true* faith and the courage of it?"

"Yes."

"You got a RE-solve for God A'mighty to put you to the test?"

Dupont shivered. "Yes," he whispered.

"You got five dollars?"

He nodded.

Granny Gunger slouched over to the black box, unfastened the chain, opened the padlock, and reached in. Mark E. Dupont prayed as he had never prayed before.

At just under three feet, Sweet Mercy was not the biggest diamondback rattlesnake in the universe, but he was a lovely one, with radiant coloring and perhaps the snakiest eyes ever to grace the mean triangle of a rattler's head.

Granny Gunger kissed Sweet Mercy right at the bony ridge of his nose.

Sweet Mercy rattled happily.

"They shall take up serpents," Granny Gunger quoted scripture. Then she improvised, as she hobbled to Dupont. "For if they be a generation of vipers, what profiteth a man to dwell far from the tabernacle as he goes up to the Land of Goshen?"

Mark E. Dupont thought, prayed, and entreated the Lord.

"Pucker up now," Granny Gunger said. "Let the kiss of salvation come to you."

Dupont closed his eyes. He puckered. He heard Sweet Mercy's rattle. He felt the snake's subtle breath—sugary, like the breath of a baby.

Then Sweet Mercy's forked tongue flicked against the dry, chubby, pursed lips.

Dupont flew to the floor, landing on his heels and the back of his head.

And when he could rise, he did not doubt.

He knew it—because he FELT it! HALLELUJAH!

Free! Saved! Praise God!

Delivered! he thought, as Sweet Mercy got delivered back to his box.

"Now, Mister Dupont," Granny Gunger said, "we got to do us some plannin'! We got to take some precautionary actions. We got to make *sure*. We must confound your enemies."

"Yes."

"I got somethin' special," Granny Gunger said. "It's got night-shade and a bloody thorn and the lips and eggs of a stone blind fish in it."

"What does it do?"

"You'd best believe it does just fine."

After Dupont's departure—preceded by her reminding him of the five dollars he owed her—Granny Gunger sat with Sweet Mercy in her lap, petting the diamondback like a tabby. "Well," she said, "told him

the Old Deceiver wanted him, and now the Old Deceiver's got him."

She laughed.

"Don't you?"

Sweet Mercy rattled in a way that sounded almost
exactly like Granny Gunger's laugh.

V

Prior to beginning another insightful commentary on
our ever-interesting Egypt, I wish to thank those who
have been kind enough to write the *Sentinel* comparing
me with Mr. H. L. Mencken, and offering to tar and
feather us both as soon as we can find the time for this
singular honor. While I greatly admire Mr. Mencken's
writings, I find him far too optimistic about the future
of the allegedly human race.

Now, let's talk about the pride of Egypt: A true
crime lord.

With the passing of the years, it becomes more and
more difficult to distinguish Charlie Birger from the
"legend of Charlie Birger."

I knew and liked Charlie. On occasion, I bought him
an illegal beer at his illegal roadhouse, and he bought
me one. We told one another jokes, few of which could
be printed in this newspaper.

As his acquaintance, then, I will tell you I do not believe that the shady owner of Shady Rest rode the ro-
deo circuit with Tom Mix, but I have seen him on
horseback and cannot doubt his formidable skills.

I do not believe that, following an argument in a St.
Louis speakeasy, Charlie fought to an impromptu

bloody draw with Jack Dempsey, but I believe he would go to the line against anyone of any size because I have seen him do just that.

More folks like Charlie than not, and they had reason. The poor of Harrisburg knew his charity. A good number of men found employment, if not necessarily of the legal variety, because of Birger. He had wit, grace, and courage. He was a man's man, and on occasion displayed a streak of sentimentality that would have been derided in a less masculine fellow.

Above all, Charlie Birger was the steadfast friend. If Charlie liked you, he'd kill anybody for you.

> Brian Robert Moore
> "I'll Tell You What!"

Tuesday, July 13, 1925

A slow afternoon at Shady Rest, so, nothing much else to do, the boys wanted to see him shoot. Charlie felt frisky and in the mood. They went out back, behind the pole barn.

Though a Tommy was his weapon of choice these days—you had to stay modern and keep up with the competition, to say nothing of your enemies!—he took his old Winchester. The boys tossed beer bottles and he snapped off shots from the hip: Eight shots, eight hits.

"That's the way it is done by a shootist, ole hoss," Charlie said. Born in New York City, Charlie Birger spent his youth in the West as a cavalry soldier, a wild horse breaker, a gambler, and a gunfighter, and he still often spoke the palaver of the range. It had been a good life out there; folks played you straight. You were what you were, what you said, and what you did, and that was all that counted.

Here in Egypt, well, let's just say it was considerable different. You couldn't count on all the cards being on the table. But Charlie had done well; they called him the "King of Egypt."

Now the King needed a suitable chariot.

So after a beer, Charlie and some of the boys drove off to West City, where Joe Adams, mayor, gin-mill owner, and proprietor of a Stutz dealership, was working on a new conveyance for His Royal Majesty!

Buckeye Jim got hired by the Old Legrand and Washauconda River Mining Corporation.

In the weeks following this uncelestial event, there were other happenings that might be viewed as more interesting or even "curious."

One of them involved K. J. Pritchard. One afternoon, when, as usual, he was standing on the square, dark glasses and a tin cup, a cardboard sign around his neck saying—

A VETERAN
I WAS BLINDED FOR LIBERTY'S SAKE

—he sensed someone standing in front of him. He said, "The big war. I was in the big one."

"I was in that one, too."

"It was gas. They didn't have to gas us! It was NOT FAIR!!!"

"Nothing ever is, not in war."

"Help me?"

BUCKEYE JIM IN EGYPT

K. J. Pritchard heard something drop into the tin cup. It didn't sound like a coin. Cheap bastard.

With his left hand, he took it out. It felt like . . . It felt like a *buckeye!*

He held it up. Yes, that was just what he was looking at, a . . .

He ripped his dark glasses off, shattered them on the pavement.

The bright sunlight burning his eyes, he wept.

There was a car wreck late one night out past Crenshaw Crossing. A rattletrap Ford full of young boys and younger girls who were full of shine. In the moonlight, you could see the silvery white of bone punching through flesh, and a head squashed the way you'd swear a head couldn't be squashed, and a bloody mess in which you could not tell twisted metal from human meat.

One of the victims, 15-year-old Anna Beulle Diggs, would later say, "I had this strange dream. I heard a voice, kind of like Daddy when he's disappointed and angry both. It said, 'This is foolish, but children ought not to *die* for being foolish. So all of you, you *live*. And sometimes you think about just how *precious* life is.'

"Well, we all *did* live. Maybe it was plain luck, but such a great big lot of luck like that might be a miracle. I think, anyway . . .

"'I don't know why I've kept it, but when they found us, I had this buckeye in my hand, and I have had it as a lucky piece ever since."

It was heavy dark, the frogs and crickets and night sounds, loud, so loud in his throbbing head. Out in front of The Jolly Sports roadhouse, Sam Washington had a gun and no options. With just the one arm, the other blown into sausage in the explosion at the fireworks factory where he had worked, he couldn't find a job, not anymore. He was colored and he couldn't read and he was as tapped out as a man could get.

Once he'd been a pretty good gut-bucket piano player. Not a real professor like Jelly Roll or Willie The Lion, or even the white boy, Art Hodes, but he might have had the makings of a tickler. He used to dream, one arm ago, of going to New York and making records and playing for the swells, just like Mr. Jelly Lord.

Once he had a dream and now he had a gun.

Then there was a white man standing in front of him. He seemed to pop up just like a haunt, but his smile was a man's.

"Mr. Washington, let's make a trade. Let's swap death for life. You give me the pistol. I give you ..."

... the buckeye was in his hand. Suddenly, Sam Washington knew it was all right ...

The man said, "Now what you do is take your dream and go on and live it. Play the piano, Mr. Washington."

"I don't know, sir. You need ten fingers to play piano."

"How many you got?"

"Five."

"So move the five twice as fast."

... strange reports that none other than Jesus, formerly of Nazareth, is paying a visit. Call me a doubting Thomas, but I fear our Egypt an unlikely locale for the Second Coming. Our civic minded Kluxers (and clucks!), enforcing the Volstead Act, will not tolerate His turning water into wine, the unions will move if He attempts to practice His carpentry without getting a card, and few of our churches will listen for five seconds to this "foreigner's" ludicrous doctrines of compassion, charity, and tolerance.

> Brian Robert Moore,
> "I'll Tell You What!"

Tuesday, August 17, 1925
First Shift at Old Coop #3

He had on his British design helmet (the best and safest) and his Davis lamp. Like always, he stepped into the cage first, before the others, all of them: Oren, Dicey, Connie, The Buds (Little Bud and Hey Bud), Hezzie, Luka, a team of 26 men.

No matter how many years they'd been in the mines, the other fellows knew that moment's hesitation, that instant of fear when you understand it is possible for the blackness to engulf you forever.

Buckeye Jim knew darkness. *I was summoned forth from the darkness.*

Don't fear, don't fear. That is what he wanted to tell them, what he wanted to tell everyone. Love one another and do not be afraid.

But they were not ready to hear it yet.

So he smiled the smile that made the others think him a "nice fella," though "no winner in the Mental Olympics, if y'know what I mean." Not that you had to be a chess champion to heft a shovel in a coal mine, and he certainly was one for that!

Buckeye Jim liked the work. He liked the feeling of

using his muscles, his back, arms, and legs. He liked
the idea that darkness, the coal, became heat and
flame.

There was much for Buckeye Jim to like these days.
He lived in Spartacus House, one of two company-
owned residences for single men. It was a lot like an
Army barracks, clean, fresh sheets every week, showers with limitless hot water, and detective and science
magazines, and a Victrola and a player piano, and
pretty pictures on the walls; he paid two dollars a
month room and board. He liked the men he lived and
worked with. Tonight, he'd go on out with them and
have him a beer or two.

And, of course, he liked to play the banjo—

... one *hell* of a picker! Carrying his Thompson
submachine gun, Charlie Birger walked over to the table of Fort Lorraine miners at his roadhouse, The
Shady Rest. After 11, but the joint still had a good
crowd, even though tomorrow was a work day. White
and colored drank at the Shady Rest—and if somebody
purple showed and had a nickel for a beer, he'd be
welcome, too—and there was even a gigantic Ojibway
Indian, Big Tommy Tabeshaw, and so at the place, you
might hear Italian, Polish, Lithuanian, Rumanian, or
Ojibway. (When he was really lost in the firewater,
Tommy talked to himself and to the "Ojibway ghosts"
in his head.)

Charlie told the banjo player that he plainly *admired*
the way he could fram away on that five string.

The banjo player said he appreciated the compliment, but hoped Shady Rest's owner wouldn't get to
framming away on his instrument.

BUCKEYE JIM IN EGYPT

Charlie Birger laughed like hell. No, no, no, his Tommy meant protection for himself and his guests. There were some shit heels, Kluxer bastards mostly, didn't like his catering to a "mixed clientele." And, for that matter, they weren't too delighted with Mr. C. Birger, Esquire's, being a co-religionist of Moses.

"My name is Buckeye Jim." The banjo player offered his hand. He said, *"Shalom Aleichem,"* the traditional Hebrew greeting, "Peace be unto you."

Charlie Birger blanched. *"Aleichem Shalom,"* he said softly. "And unto you, peace." The gleam in his eyes might have been tears. "You're ..."

Buckeye Jim shrugged. *"Vuden?"* Loosely translated, the Yiddish term meant, "What did you expect?"

"I'll be damned," Charlie Birger said. "A hillbilly Yid! A Yid-billy! Well, me, too, I reckon!"

Birger bellowed to the bar, "This gentleman and his friends drink free! Tonight and every night."

He turned back to Buckeye Jim. "You have yourself a friend in Charlie Birger."

"Thank you," Buckeye Jim said. "A man needs all the friends he can get."

VI

Sunday, September 12, 1925

God forgive me, Opal Rae Brown thought. If He did, it would be long before she forgave herself.

Opal Rae puttered about, a huge woman who seemed to fill up all the space in the vast kitchen that had so long been her domain. Oh, Lord, he was a good man and she had to ...

He was a *white* man, she tried to tell herself, and if every white man in the country America decided to swallow a Mason jar full of iodine, lye, and turpentine, now wasn't that just too bad? Besides . . .

Besides, she was scared, she was scared in every one of her 280 pounds. That man, that Mr. Dupont, had never raised his voice as he told her this, and told her that, as he asked her this and then asked her, "You ever smell black skin burning? You are sort of heavy-set, so I imagine it would take a *long* time for the fire to bubble and blister and cook all the meat right off your bones."

He gave her orders and the "secret potion" she was to add to the food (Now don't you worry, just some fish eggs and stuff) and 100 dollars. The money would take her north, she vowed. Nobody burned colored people in New York, not as she had heard, anyway.

She took a deep breath, then another.

Then she took Mr. C. Cooper Legrand, Jr. his evening meal.

The next day, he was in Fort Lorraine's hospital, condition—critical.

Buckeye Jim couldn't sleep. He went for a walk, moonlight his guide. At midnight, that empty moment that is neither one day or another, he was far from Fort Lorraine, deep into the rolling woods. He relished the coolness and earth smells, the myriad night sounds, the eternal celebration and affirmation of life.

Oh, he did not want to die. Not again.

Ahead, on the path that wasn't a path but simply the way he chose, he saw the gleaming eyes. The rattler's precise, gorgeous diamond patterns shone hypnotically. It rose up like a cobra, shifting left and right, the forked tongue a flicker-blur.

Surprised?

"Not hardly," Buckeye Jim said. "Sure you're here. You're everywhere." He took out the lucky buckeye and flipped it, caught it, flipped it. "But you're not going to win, you know. Each time, we get closer."

Fool!

"Fool? Maybe.

"But God needs His fools."

Do you not see? Each time and every time Man is given a chance to damn himself, he says, "Yes, thanks, and might you have a few extra opportunities for my friends?" The victory will be mine!

"No," Buckeye Jim said, "Man is not born to lose." The buckeye flew up high and then higher and came down in his palm. Buckeye Jim grinned.

"Man is born to win."

On Wednesday, condition now "serious/guarded," Legrand had visitors, representatives of the Illinois Coal and Power Company—Mark E. Dupont among them. They did not want to tire him out, to do anything that might slow his recovery.

Inside of 15 minutes, C. Cooper Legrand sold them everything.

VII

Buckeye Jim, weave and spin,
Time to go, Buckeye Jim.
    "Buckeye Jim"
    American folk song

There will always be questions, but I *knew* C. Cooper Legrand, Jr. I drank coffee with him, went to New York with him to hear Emma Goldman, and spent a long, memorable, mentally exhilarating night, arguing with him over the Nihilistic philosophy of Bakunin; both of us agreed that the man had to be an idiot if all he would allow to go undestroyed would be Beethoven's Sixth, the closest the composer ever came to failure.

Juney Legrand was all right.

So to my dying day, I will not accept that he willfully betrayed the people of Fort Lorraine or his dream of a world of brotherhood and harmony.

They did something to him. I know they did. As incredible as this may sound, coming from a man who is reputed to be sane, if surly, I have come to believe there are conspiracies meant to stifle and suppress Mankind as we struggle to attain the next step on the moral and ethical evolutionary ladder.

A conspiracy of ???

The Left will tell you it is a wicked collusion of Capital and Government. Too imaginative pulp magazine fans will offer you theories based on a wicked cabal inside our hollow Earth. Then there are preachers who will tell you it is all the work of the Devil . . .

BUCKEYE JIM IN EGYPT

Brian Robert Moore,
"I'll Tell You What!"

Monday, September 27, 1925

In the basement of Fort Lorraine's Masonic Temple, they argued and argued, called each other names, threw about the words, "scab," "fink," and, a phrase frequently used in the American labor movement: "Dumb son of a bitch!" They would march on the state capital! The nation's capital! A splinter group said there was a case for assassination—if they could figure out who to assassinate.

They waited to hear from the president of the United Mine Workers of America, John L. Lewis. Last time, he said the wrong thing; it provided impetus for the Herrin Massacre of '22.

This time he said nothing.

The Illinois Coal and Power Company meant to take possession of the mines—the town. But damn all and double-damn, it was *not* the property of I C and P; Fort Lorraine was *their* town! The mines were *their* mines. It was their labor that gave them ownership, their muscle and sweat and not a capitalist's dollars!

It was theirs, damn all!

They meant to keep it!

If it took guns to . . .

It went on and on, until, at last—

Now they are ready to listen, Buckeye Jim said to himself. He was sad. He liked these men. He did not want to leave them. He thought about bitter cups. He thought about the Lord's will. He thought about what he had to do.

Then Buckeye Jim said he wanted to talk. He talked easy and slow, flipping a buckeye.

He talked and they heard him.

Funny, how a guy you don't figure all that equipped with smartness can talk to you in a way that makes you say, "Why, yes indeed! That is what we have to do."

That is what they did.

They barricaded the northern approach to Fort Lorraine. They left their guns at home, but they turned over worn-out tin-can cars, piled up bales of hay, and strung barbed wire the way some had learned in the War to End All Wars.

Behind their barricade, they linked arms, the black men and the white men.

They were a living chain across the Washauconda Bridge.

They were ready.

To assist in the I C and P's taking possession of its properties were men in smart-looking uniforms, all duly deputized, bayonets on their rifles.

From Sesser and Marion and Ina and dozens of other towns came nonunion miners, needing work, armed with baseball bats, shotguns, pistols, and pitchforks, determined to get these sorry niggers and Bolsheviks out of their way.

Mark E. Dupont led the largest delegation, the stalwarts of the Klan. The Grand Exalted Cyclops, in his robes of flowing white, a regulation Army Springfield under his arm. Now he'd claim . . . his!

His, damn all! *Mr.* Mark E. Dupont, the new General Superintendent of I C P's Fort Lorraine holdings, had the might and purity and right of the Klan stepping smartly behind him, armed with everything from a Quackenbush boy's model single shot to a log chain!

The forces of the Illinois Coal and Power Company tramped onward.

The men of Fort Lorraine waited.

The army of the Illinois Coal and Power Company came closer, ranks tightening as they trod upon the vast length of the Washauconda Bridge.

Waiting for them, someone called out, "Stand firm! Union men, comrades in the war!"

Men with bayonets, men in miner's hats, men in KKK garb, moved forward.

The men at the barricades sang:

> *"Hold the fort,*
> *Brave union miners!*
> *Show no fear,*
> *Be strong!"*

At the other end of the bridge, taunting voices called, "Let's kill us some niggers!"

"Turkey shoot! They ain't got a gobbler's chance!"

The I C and P troops drew closer. The bridge shook with their out-of-step march. The collage of sounds was sinister and portentous: muttering and shouts, the hiss and whisper and bubblings of the Washauconda below, the click-ready sound of firearms.

You could smell oil and gunpowder.

"You are an unlawful assembly, blocking a public thoroughfare!" Dupont called out. "Give way immediately or perish!" He liked the formality of his proclamation.

He did not like the roared response it drew from a

defender of Fort Lorraine: "You get up on your momma's shoulders and kiss my ass."

When less than a hundred yards separated the men of Fort Lorraine from the I C and P forces, Buckeye Jim suddenly appeared between them.

Quizzical, because nobody *really* saw him walk there, but there he was.

It stopped them all.

Buckeye Jim wasn't flipping a lucky buckeye. Not this time. He had his arms up and out, as though he were Moses helping God, pushing back the walls of water to part the Red Sea. There are some still living who, even to this day, will tell you the man was transfigured.

Buckeye Jim had something to say.

Nothing happened he didn't know about. Not in his kingdom.

Because—you'd better know it and you're mighty well told!—Charlie Birger was the *King* of Egypt!

Fort Lorraine? Good boys, there, and his Yid friend, Buckeye Jim, so . . .

Time for damned sure to hitch the horses to the king's chariot.

Except he didn't need horses.

Everyone stayed quiet. Everyone heard him.

He said, "Some of you don't know me, and some of you know me as Buckeye Jim. But years back, years and years and years ago, I was the one they talk about in the Bible. They call me 'The Widow's Son.' I was dead, just as dead as Mr. Lazarus, but then Jesus called to me and said, 'Come forth from your tomb.'

166

BUCKEYE JIM IN EGYPT

"Well, I was grateful and such, and I politely thanked Him, but I asked him why He had summoned me from the ever-dark of death into the light of life.

"Didn't I like being alive? Didn't I want to do the work of the living God, the God of the living?

"I thought about that and thought about that—

"Until I said, 'Why, yes, I guess I do.'

"Now this is what Jesus told me. This is what He wants me to tell you.

"Jesus came to bring *hope*. He said it was my job to *be* hope, because I'd been dead and now I was alive.

"We are *all* the children of God. The Devil and the darkness will *never* defeat us!

"Jesus told me something more.

"He said He would come again.

"He said He would return—*on the day after He no longer was needed!*

"That means it's up to *us* to set it all right.

"And we *can* start to do that. We can start now."

There was silence.

And almost everyone stood frozen.

But not Mark E. Dupont, who thought, *The Devil can quote scripture for his own purpose.* Dupont slammed the stock of his Springfield into his shoulder and fired.

The bullet caught Buckeye Jim just to the left of the heart. He flew backward, slammed into the bridge railing a slice of an instant after his blood and fragments of bone did, and, loose limbed, flipped over. If his body splashed as it plunged into the river, no one heard it.

The I C and P forces let out a collective yell that

drowned out a sudden roar of thunder in the clear sky above.

They charged.

"Give it all you've got," Charlie Birger commanded. The driver of the brand new armored car obliged. The powerful Stutz engine thrummed. The heavy sheet metal riveted and welded to the auto slowed it and guaranteed nothing could stand in its way. Instead of a windshield or windows, the car had gun slits. Except for treads, it was a tank—and its solid rubber tires weren't about to be knocked out by any varmint hunter's firepower.

It was the lead vehicle of three. Two cars loaded with Birger men followed.

Charlie might have been confused, once they hit the bridge, but the KKK bastards, decked out like Monday wash on the line, why he knew who to shoot! So Charlie popped the heavy hatch, and rose up to let loose with a quick spray from Mr. Tommy. One blast felt so fine, the gun a roaring quiver in his hands, that he fired off another. He heard the guns of his army behind him. He saw the befuddled I C P men turn, trying to figure what the hell. There was sporadic return fire, slugs pinging off the metal around him.

"Welcome to Egypt's O.K. Corral," Charlie yelled. He laughed and fired off another burst.

Then another.

With the next one, he totally hem-stitched Mark E. Dupont.

Inside of three minutes, 43 men lay dead on the Washauconda bridge, most of them Kluxers; another 75 or 81 or 58 (depending on which accounts of the conflict you believe) were wounded and conveyed to area hospitals.

Most historians cite the "Battle of Washauconda Bridge" as the end of the Klan's power in southern Illinois.

Charlie Birger and his warriors retreated to Shady Rest and drank beer. The King could not figure where Buckeye Jim might have disappeared to. He hoped he would turn up. He wished him luck.

Fellow played one *fine* banjo.

Epilogue

Mark E. Dupont received one of the most elaborate Klan funerals in the history of the organization. A vice president of I C and P gave the eulogy, saying Dupont was one of the company's finest *assistant* superintendents; after the funeral, he presented Mrs. Dupont with a check for fifty dollars.

Virtually everyone employed by the Old Legrand and Washauconda River Mining Corporation was fired and had to leave Fort Lorraine. The union did not regain any foothold in the region until FDR.

Charlie Birger had a falling out with Joe Adams, who'd built "The King of Egypt's" armored car, and was convicted of arranging the man's murder.

Charlie was hanged on April 18, 1929, the last man legally executed in this way in the state. Legend had it that the night before his execution, Charlie had a lanky visitor, who talked and joked a while with him, then handed him a buckeye.

Perhaps that is the reason that, on the scaffold, Charlie's last words were, "It *is* a beautiful world.

"Goodbye."

A Final Word or Six

Truth is truth and fiction is fiction—and often the twain do meet. There is more of the former than the latter in this story.

Charlie Birger is still regarded as a Robin Hood by many in Egypt and his final words are those you have read.

Special thanks to Bill Willingham, creator of the *Elementals* comics, and Judy Henske, who sings "Buckeye Jim" beautifully, and to my wife, Jane, a Boneyard Woods Egyptian, who introduced me to the legends, lore, and reality of southern Illinois.

TWENTY YEARS LATER, BY SEPARATION PEAK

by *Kristine Kathryn Rusch*

Century VIII, #41

A fox shall be elected uttering not a word
Playing the saint in public, taking other's property
In order to tyrannize by *coup d'etat*
Placing his foot on the throats of the greatest

I

Seven of us stood in the shadow of Separation Peak. Even though the Peak was twenty miles away, it looked as if we could reach out and touch it. Thunderheads loomed to the west, dark purple laced with lightening. The air was cool despite the higher than normal humidity: what had been seventies in Cheyenne was fifties here. Our rusted cars were parked along the side of I-80, nearly hiding the blue plastic port-a-potty that had somehow survived the decade.

I never expected to stand here. My grandfather once told me that promises made when a man was young were rarely remembered into his middle age.

I didn't know how I would forget.

The wind from the approaching storm whipped our jackets, pressed our thin shirts against our chests. Margarite's breasts showed round and firm despite her

171

forty-five years. She shivered and pulled her jacket tight. I longed to press myself against her and steal a bit of her warmth.

Twenty years. Twenty years and the emotions were as raw as they had been the day we separated.

"I suppose we should start," Sven said. His eyes were dark behind his taped and battered glasses. Scratches on the lenses reflected on his pale skin.

No one looked at me, but I could feel the expectation. *Tell us what to do, Devin. Show us how to be.* But I wasn't going to bow to it. This time they were on their own.

Paolo turned away from me. Chibu kicked a chunk of the interstate. The concrete was shredding under the weight of too many winters. Our cars had broken the weeds in the center, a clear path for any urban tracking guide. Lobo had his back to all of us, the wind teasing his long brown hair. His muscles were still firm, his body still the one I remembered. He and Margarite were almost unchanged. The rest of us had allowed age to sag us, to add lines around our mouths, memory marks beside our eyes.

Quinlin looked at me. His tanned face had taken a leathery quality. "You started it, Devin. You get to end it."

The wind had blown the storm closer. I wasn't going to dodge it any more than I was going to dodge their expectations.

"All right," I said. "Let's see if he's still here."

TWENTY YEARS LATER, BY SEPARATION PEAK
II

Twenty-five years before, in finals week for fall quarter, we held a vote in our American Government Seminar. To this day, I wonder if Professor Wiggins had been a visionary or merely a man trying to grapple with his own fear. We saw nothing, of course. We were children merely pretending to be adults.

Professor Wiggins held his seminars in a lounge on the first floor of Baxter Hall. Twenty students sprawled along couches and slouched in easy chairs. The green decor made everyone's faces sallow, even Paolo and Chibu, whose dark skin would take on a grayish cast.

Two weeks before, we had been appointed electoral college delegates for a mythical presidential election. Then we had studied the system. Our final grade was based on our performance in this afternoon's class.

"I don't understand it," Lobo had whispered to me as we waited for class to begin. "All we do is write our guy's name on a piece of paper and then leave. What's so tough about that?"

I didn't know, but I had a feeling I was going to find out. Even then they looked to me, not just because I was Wiggins' favorite, but because I was heir apparent to the Culhane political dynasty. My father had been a senator, just as his father had before him. Although my parents had been dead for most of my life, and financial necessity (and a jealous aunt and uncle) had shunted me to this tiny backwater college, everyone here knew that I had the power, the charisma, and the political sharpness to reclaim the Culhane family destiny.

Wiggins was up to something—and we weren't going to like it.

He arrived a minute later, carrying a tray of cold sandwiches mounded high and wrapped in plastic carrying a local deli's logo. Two large thermoses of coffee already waited on the table, as did another of hot water. Soda was on ice in a cooler beneath the window. Quinlin had already scouted that out and confirmed what we all suspected: no beer.

Obviously we weren't going to write names on a paper and leave.

Wiggins set the tray down and leaned against his favorite kelly-green overstuffed chair. "You have just flown in from all parts of the country," he said, his gravelly voice taking on a power it didn't usually have. "Because of scheduling conflicts, the meetings begin this morning instead of giving you all a day to recover. While some of you were on the red-eye, and the rest of you were sleeping, the president-elect's plane went down over Indiana, killing all on board. The current president, as we all know, is a lame duck, and his veep has already announced his retirement from public life—"

"Jeez, just like Kastlebaum," Sven whispered to me. President Hurley was a lame duck and his vice president, Mark Kastlebaum had announced that he wasn't going to run in the current election because he had just been diagnosed as HIV-positive.

"—and so, you, my friends, are entrusted with the fate of the country."

"Can't we just hold another election?" Chibu asked. The rest of the class groaned.

"Since we haven't officially started, I will not hold

that remark against you," Wiggins said. "But remember, the popular vote does not choose a president. You do. And as electoral college members, you may place your state's votes behind any candidate—"

"—Or any person," I said.

"Very good, Mr. Culhane." Wiggins smiled. "Any person or any candidate you may like. Are we ready?" The class sighed. He handed me a slip of paper. "Mr. Culhane has my home phone number. You will call me when there is a new president of the United States."

I slipped the phone number in my pocket. That part was for show. I had already memorized Wiggins' home phone. We had spent many a late night talking theory and batting political what-ifs back and forth. We never discussed this one.

Wiggins left with a half-smile on his face, and we fell into it. We argued and screamed and pleaded with each other. We cited case after case, looked up the 12th Amendment to the Constitution which defined the electoral college's role, and decided that we didn't want to throw the vote into the House of Representatives. We examined the hypothetical candidates and their histories. We also toyed with inserting a wild card—a person who had not been on the November ballot—and we even mentioned Milan's name. In the end, we didn't choose an outsider, figuring it would be too much work.

Of course, that was our mistake.

We ate the sandwiches and drank too much coffee. At 10 p.m., pizza and more soda arrived, courtesy of Wiggins, and still we had made no decision. Finally, at 4 a.m., I called a vote. We did as Lobo predicted and each scrawled a name on a piece of paper. Chibu counted the votes. Twenty people divided between two candidates—evenly—and continued to do so with each vote taken thereafter.

Wiggins arrived at 8 a.m. with more coffee and donuts. As he set the donuts on the table, he passed around blue books with the donut boxes. "It's January twentieth, people," he said. "Time to inaugurate a president. Write the name in the blue book of the person who will take the oath of office at noon. You have—" he glanced at his watch, "—one hour."

No sleep and all that wrangling. I wasn't thinking clearly. I ate four chocolate donuts and stared at the empty page in my blue book. Who became president? No one. The vote had to go to the House of Representatives. But the lame duck's term was over. Someone had to head the state.

Finally the chocolate hit and with the sugar high came the answer: The vice president elect. As in all other cases of incapacity of a president, the vice president became president. The vice president would have been voted along the normal course. The electoral college would have had no trouble with that vote. I scrawled down the vice president elect's name, took another donut, and left the room to get a much needed shower and sleep.

When I woke up, I learned that I was the only student to ever pass Wiggins' final.

III

We trudged along the rocky surface of the Divide toward Separation Peak. Losing sight of the Interstate filled me with a dread that seemed irrational now. No one wanted to get lost in the Rocky Mountains, but we weren't going very far. The Interstate itself was no protection: few people had the resources it took to buy a tank of gas. That we all made it to the reunion spoke of our determination instead of our wealth.

It also spoke of our fear of Milan.

By unspoken agreement, Lobo led. His athlete's muscles could respond to any danger quickly and he seemed to remember the trail that time and weather had dispersed. The wind had died down to an unnatural calm, and in the distance thunder boomed. The air smelled of rain.

I dug my hands into my pockets, fingers toying with the frayed edges of the holes that had long ago torn through the seams. The jacket wouldn't provide much protection when the storm broke. Perhaps it would wait until we were done, and I could return to the relative safety of my car. At least my windows were intact. Sven's weren't.

"Here," Lobo said.

We fanned out around him. The rocks still formed a cairn—an obvious grave to anyone who was looking. But no one had looked. Not once in twenty years. Even the animals had left the site untouched.

Nights alone in my small apartment I had envisioned that cairn, top busted open, the body gone. The night before we came, I dreamed that Milan was standing next to the open grave, laughing at us.

I walked over to the cairn and ran my hand along the sharp pointed rocks. I had set the last rock on top, my fingers dirt- and blood-covered. Even then, we hadn't believed Milan was dead. We had joined hands over the grave and vowed to return twenty years later, to make sure Milan's body remained at rest.

I don't know what the others feared. I told them I was afraid someone would find his body and make him a martyr. But really, I thought Milan more than human. I never expected him to remain in a prison of my own making.

I clenched my fists and pulled my arms against my sides.

"I'll be a son of a bitch," Chibu said. He glanced at me, his black bangs nearly covering his eyes. "So what do we do now?"

IV

I loved Milan. Not in a carnal way, but in that deep, abiding, worshipful love only a young idealist could have.

He had been the hero of my college days, the savior the country was waiting for. Each generation had a man like him—a hope for the future, untapped as yet by the electoral process. Teddy Kennedy in late '68 before Chappaquidick, Mario Cuomo after his speech in '84; Constance Brownwin in '96—politicians who didn't run, who never really spoke, and yet the country waited for them to ride into the government, turn it around, and save us from ourselves.

When Brownwin died four years later, a tainted President-elect, her vice presidential choice already considered more incompetent than Dan Quayle, the electoral college turned not to the candidates who had lost to the Brownwin team but to Milan. And when he, with grace and reluctance, stepped in—the first white knight ever allowed to play the role—very few people in the country complained. Only a handful of commentators pointed out that Milan had never held an elected office, and even fewer noted that Brownwin's plane had flown out of Milan's home airport or that Milan's newspapers had first initiated the charges of the vice president elect's incompetence.

I first saw Milan on a CNN Special Report. They called him The Man Behind the Throne, and The Greatest Hope for America's Future. They had film clips of him walking out of buildings, his lean graceful body belonging to a movie star instead of a corporate executive. He never gave speeches and rarely made public comments. He never acknowledged the crowds as he walked by; and he never smiled for the cameras.

I read everything I could find about him. I studied his impoverished roots, the fortune he had made in the computer industry, the way he turned that fortune into billions.

Even then, though, his enemies had a way of disappearing, and his detractors often changed their minds. I had one of the few copies of *Milan the Fox* written by a renowned political commentator who turned up dead weeks after his book trashing Milan was pulled from the shelves.

But Wiggins hated him and after the election, Wiggins withdrew. His lectures were rote, his eyes often gazed as if they were staring at far-away places. Our late-night phone calls stopped, and I never even thought to invite him to my graduation party two years later.

But he thought of me. He tried to call me in the

179

week before he died. His name had become so much a part of my past by then that it took me a day or so to place it. It took another day for me to return the call.

His phone had been disconnected.

He had resigned from the department.

His family had no idea where he was.

And I forgot about it until Paolo handed me the file, almost two years later.

V

The wind had a chill to it. Strands of Margarite's hair whipped around her face and stuck to her lips. She brushed it away absently. "I don't know," she said. "This looks too new, too fresh. Shouldn't the rocks be weather worn?"

"It takes years for rocks to wear away," Sven said.

"I don't like it," Quinlin said. "I think we should check."

"Oh, for God's sake, it was a stupid agreement to make in the first place." Lobo crossed his arms and leaned back on his heels. "We've been acting as if Milan had supernatural powers. He didn't. No one can rise from the dead."

"If anyone could, he could." Chibu said.

The first drops of icy rain splashed on my face. I glanced up. The black clouds in the distance had that melted look brought by hard rain. "We had better decide soon."

"If Milan were still alive, we wouldn't be in this mess," Paolo said.

"Are you saying what we did was wrong?" Margarite was standing alone, arms wrapped around her waist as if to keep herself warm.

"He's saying that Mussolini made the trains run on time," Quinlin said.

"No, I'm not," Paolo said. He walked over to the cairn and ran a hand along the rocks' sharp surface. His brown skin stood out in sharp relief to the pale gray of the stone. "Don't you guys wonder how it might have been? Don't you think about whether or not things would have been better? Sometimes I dream about it and I wake up wishing for that righteousness of youth."

"Wiggins hated Milan." Chibu had knitted his fingers together. His knuckles were white.

"Wiggins was a political science professor at a small private school that eventually lost its endowment. If he was one of the world's great thinkers, he would have been at Harvard or Yale. If he were one of the world's great politicians, he would have been in office somewhere instead of planning odd final exams." Paolo picked up a rock and ran his finger along the sharp edge. "By the age of twenty-four, I had done more government service than he had. That should tell you something."

I remembered the file Paolo had given me, the stern look on his face all those years ago. What had happened to him to change his mind? Had he been victim of the riots that shook D.C.? Did he live, like I did, in an area so remote, so cold, that just survival was difficult? Did he sleep on a bed or on the hard, dead ground?

He had to have some wealth. He had a car, after all. Margarite took the rock out of his hand and set it back on top of the cairn. "We didn't do anything wrong."

"We killed a man," Paolo said.

"We killed a monster," she said, "and saved thousands of lives."

"Did we?" Paolo asked. "Or did we condemn them to die more slowly in this wasteland?" He brushed his hand on his faded jeans. The rain fell harder, its steady patter a counterpoint to the words. I shivered.

"Let's dig him up," I said. "We need to remember."

VI

Milan greeted me himself on my first day of work. He called me into the Oval Office, and I went in promptly at nine, my throat dry, my heart hammering against my chest. I had spoken to other political interns from previous administrations. The only time they had met the President had been on the day they left, the day they had their pictures taken with the Chief Executive. And here I was, sitting in a room filled with history, on the day I arrived.

The office had the damp dusty smell of an ancient building. Most of the furniture was for show except the brown leather chair on the other side of the desk. Milan had brought back the Kennedy furnishings, including the huge brown desk that John-John had played under while heads of state visited. John-John. I had never been able to reconcile that little boy with the skirt-chasing celebrity lawyer who was twenty years my senior.

The only thing that brought the room into the 21st

century was the small terminal on a wooden computer desk to the side of the chair.

The desk was empty except for a file, and the room was empty except for me. I stood on the expensive rug embossed with the Presidential seal and tried not to look nervous, although each muscle was held rigidly in place.

Then the door opened, and Milan made the entrance he was famous for. His black hair was swept away from his face and his dark eyes snapped with energy. He was taller than I expected and whipcord thin, moving with the grace of a natural athlete.

"Mr. Culhane," he said, with that deep warm voice. "I hope I haven't kept you waiting too long."

"N–no. I just got here." I felt twelve years old again, being humored by an adult for a small accomplishment.

His glance seemed to catch my discomfort. "Sit. Let's talk."

I took the wingbacked chair to the right of the desk. The cushions were hard as wood.

"Mr. Culhane," he said. "I plan to treat my young interns differently than my predecessors did. Young minds are a national treasure, and I think yours is more valuable than most. I chose you myself."

I swallowed. "Thank you, sir."

He leaned back and templed his fingers. "I read your files. I understand that you are an expert in Constitutional history. You must find me quite interesting."

"Your election was unusual," I said, voice trembling, "but not illegal."

He smiled, revealing teeth whiter than any I'd ever seen. "Yes, unlike John Kennedy's electoral college victory or that of Rutherford B. Hayes. The dead did not vote for me nor did I bribe any state officials." He put his hands down on the desk. His actions seemed less like nervous fidgeting and more like they were calculated for effect. "Still, I find my every move questioned. Even Gerald Ford had been elected to an office, although it wasn't the office of President. I have never responded to a mandate of the people—and that terrifies the underlings here in the White House and all of Congress. You know about the amendment?"

"To ban the electoral college? Yes, sir." I hadn't moved at all. My body felt rooted to that hard chair.

"And what do you think of it?"

"I think it was only a matter of time before someone proposed it. The average American has never understood the electoral college, and now it's placed someone in office without a popular vote. People are scared because they don't understand." My voice had gained strength as I spoke.

"But you understand. I want to know what you think of the amendment."

I swallowed, uncertain of the test. "The founding fathers believed that the people were not educated enough and not interested enough to directly choose their own government."

"Not all of the founding fathers believed that."

"Enough of them."

"And you agree?"

My hands were moist. I kept them resting on my knees. "Except for a handful of people, everyone I knew voted based on press coverage and campaign ads. They read nothing and often didn't know the background and voting records of the candidates they chose."

Milan laughed. The sound startled me. "Mr. Culhane, you are truly the son of a politician. Three different answer to the same question and none of them reveal how *you* feel about the process. We will go no farther until you are frank with me."

Frank. I had to stand up. I rarely let people know what I thought about anything. But I was standing before the President of the United States, a man who claimed he had hand-picked me to be a student intern in the White House. A man with a plan. And unless I told him the truth, I would not know what that plan was.

"All right." My voice had an airy quality to it. It felt as if I were speaking through someone else's throat. "To be honest with you, sir. The fact that you have been chosen to lead the country in this manner frightens me. You have a wonderful business track record. You have treated your minority employees well. You seem to have a head for global affairs, and yet you have run a corporation not a government. I worry about your ability to compromise. I worry about the nation's ability to accept you."

"I will face a referendum in a few short years," he said quietly. "I can be voted out of office."

"Or you can resign. Or you can be impeached. Honestly, sir, when they said that the electoral college had chosen you, I expected you to offer to serve a shortened term while we held emergency elections."

"The Constitution does not provide for that."

"No," I said. "It doesn't."

"Nor does it provide for many things," Milan said.

He stood, too. He was a few inches taller than me, but it seemed like more because he was so thin. "It doesn't provide for most of the jobs in the federal government, and it doesn't provide for the position I am going to offer you."

I looked up at him. The feeling of being a child in an adult's presence returned. "Sir?"

"I would like you to be one of my personal advisors. I need youth, energy, an understanding of the system, and a willingness to look for loopholes." His voice took on the rhythm of a campaign speech. "You were right, Mr. Culhane. I have run corporations. I want to run this government like a business. I want to show the people that decisiveness—not politics—can improve their lives. And perhaps, after that, they'll be able to make changes in the two-hundred-year-old document that rules our lives. Informed changes instead of fear-based ones. Are you willing to work with me on that, Mr. Culhane?"

I didn't understand it, entirely. Even now, as I run through that speech in my mind, I do not know exactly what Milan wanted. Although I know what he achieved.

"I'll work with you," I said, and thereby sealed his doom.

VII

The rain came down in hard pelting sheets. My hair was plastered to my skin, and my clothing hung like heavy armor on my frame. The wind had died down, but the frigid drops more than made up for the chill.

TWENTY YEARS LATER, BY SEPARATION PEAK

My hands were red and raw as I pulled on the rocks before me.

The others worked in silence around me. The clatter of falling rocks was half-hidden under the rain's steady drumbeat. An occasional peal of thunder boomed overhead. I did not watch for the lightning. I did not want to know how close the storm was to us.

Margarite's lips had turned blue. Chibu's left hand was bleeding. Lobo had cleared twice as much as the rest of us, the pile of brown stones resting at his feet. Only Paolo refused to help. He sat on the grass like a scrawny Buddha, his arms crossed over his chest, impervious to the rain.

"What happens if you don't find him?" he asked.

"We'll find him." Quinlin sprayed water as he replied. His curly hair had gone straight with the weight of the rain.

But I wasn't so sure. I didn't remember putting this many rocks on the cairn. I didn't remember the rocks being so heavy. My muscles strained, and my back hurt, but still I didn't stop.

Paolo leaned back and put his hands on the wet grass behind him. I could feel his gaze on me. "What are you looking for, Devin? Your conscience?"

A shiver ran down my spine. "I have a conscience," I said.

Paolo unfolded himself like a deer sleeping in the grass. He stood, towering over me. "I suppose you do, after a fashion. And that's why you expect the ghost of Milan to smite you, and why you made this silly pact in the first place."

I stopped working for a moment and caught my

breath. "If you had no plans to keep our agreement, why did you come?"

"To take a good hard look at my past and my choices."

His voice was soft, but his tone had a self-righteous edge I didn't like. I wiped my hands on my already stained jeans and felt the damp cloth press against the cold skin of my thighs. "Milan had too much power," I said.

"Only because you helped him achieve it," Paolo said. "Then you discarded him when you discovered that your idol had feet of clay."

"Milan was an evil man," I said.

Paolo shrugged. "Perhaps. But I often wonder if we're any different."

VIII

Milan laughed a lot in the late night meetings. We came to his apartments—four other interns and myself—and huddled around the president as if he were a popular professor. He acted the role, handing out assignment after assignment, and we completed them all, like good little devoted servants.

He would order pizza and beer and place them on the Duncan Fife table near the fireplace. We would pull armchairs over, and eat the pizza with our fingers—no napkins or plates—and let the grease run down our hands.

"Alexander Hamilton believed that a president should be elected for life," he said one evening.

"That's why the compromise happened," I said. "A

four-year elected term with no limitations on the amount of time served."

"The Twenty-second Amendment changed the limitation to two terms," Milan said, reaching for the pepperoni pizza with anchovies that sat in the middle of the desk.

"Because FDR's four terms were too much for the Republicans," I said. "And he died in office, just like a king."

"So the secret, then, is pleasing the opposing party should the Twenty-second Amendment be repealed."

I shook my head. "You have to be more global than that," I said. "You make the new amendment throw out term limitations—which every politician suffers under now—and you make the amendment retroactive to include politicians in power when the amendment is proposed."

Milan laughed—the warm, throaty sound that he always made when one of us did well. "You are devious, Culhane," he said, biting into his pizza. "I'm sure that's why I like you."

IX

Paolo and I were staring at each other. Margarite stepped between us. She looked thinner, less beautiful with her hair glued to her face and her cheeks red with cold. "We can't change it," she said to Paolo.

Rocks clattered to the ground beside us. Lobo, Chibu, and Quinlin were still working. Sven was watching us. He crossed his arms, a Norwegian god ravished by age and bad times.

"You have no right to be holier than the rest of us, Paolo," Sven said. "You're the one who blew the whistle. None of this would have happened without you."

"I know that," Paolo said. "But it wouldn't have happened without the rest of us either."

He was right. I had thought over the scenario night after night as I huddled in front of my woodstove in my tiny, worthless apartment in Cheyenne: Our friendships engineered by Wiggins, our relationships forged by his class. Whether it was vision or merely luck, we would never know. But we had been the perfect team to take down Milan.

Margarite: the only daughter of a skilled diplomat. Doors opened for her where the rest of us saw only walls.

Chibu: raised as a migrant farm worker, in college only by the grace of the system and a Texas teacher who had believed in him. Saved by brains and a circle of friends. The *vox populi,* arbiter of the simple way, speaking an underclass' logic.

Lobo: his father's reentry into the states had been denied the year Lobo entered college for trading illegally with countries not recognized by the United States. Trading arms.

Sven: whose father owned the largest exercise equipment firm in the Midwest. If anyone needed money, Sven knew how to find it.

Paolo: a lawyer's son with a passion for the truth. His clerking position with a judge who was later appointed to the Supreme Court opened another door.

Quinlin: whose father was serving a life term in New York State for a crime billed as the most gruesome murder of the century. Computer digitized photographs of the "hobos" who had been found near the grassy knoll in Dallas in 1963 revealed one with Quinlin's father's face.

Friends of friends of friends.

It all boiled down to who I knew.

X

Paolo met me in Tony's Deli, a rundown establishment on a backwater street in the slums just inside Maryland. I was surprised at how much the neighborhood had improved. When Milan had taken office, a business would not have been able to survive here, no matter how marginally.

Inside, the place smelled of onions and beer. It had a warmth that I never would have guessed from its unpainted exterior.

It was two weeks into Milan's new term—the one he had achieved through a slim popular vote and a large electoral college victory—and I hadn't seen Paolo in nearly a year.

Paolo remained in his clerking position, the traditional job held by a traditional man. He was still thin, his tailored suit hugging his frame. He carried a laptop and hugged a file to his chest. Clerking for Justice Levin in the Supreme Court building had benefited Paolo as much as interning for Milan had benefited me.

I had already taken a scarred table far from the window. Behind the steamy glass counter, a large man in a butcher's apron piled beef on rye for me. Paolo ordered, grabbed a pint of lager, and sat down.

191

"Still working to repeal the Twenty-second Amendment?" he asked with no preamble.

"It's not work," I said. "We've got more than enough support in both houses to ratify the change on the first vote."

Paolo sipped his lager. The deli man brought me my sandwich, which stood higher than my palm. "Yours be coming in a minute," he said to Paolo. Paolo nodded.

I pressed the pieces of the sandwich between my fingers and tried to take a graceful bite. A bit of mustard-covered lettuce slapped against my chin. I brushed it away.

"I hear that this version of the new amendment lacks a clause."

"Which one is that?" I asked around my food.

"This Article shall not apply to anyone holding office when the Congress proposed this Article. . . .' " Paolo's smile did not reach his eyes. "No wonder you're getting it through."

I shrugged. "You have to know how to manipulate the system."

"Milan is good at that."

The deli man set down an oversized turkey and cream cheese in front of Paolo. Paolo nodded and handed him the empty bottle of lager.

His comment had made me defensive. But, then, a lot made me defensive in those days. "What do you mean?"

"You know that the Rider Bill which just passed gives Milan the equivalent of permanent emergency powers."

The rye was tart, the beef fresh, and the mustard hot.

192

TWENTY YEARS LATER, BY SEPARATION PEAK

I hadn't had a sandwich that good in days. "I trust that your branch will overturn it."

"I thought this smacked of you," Paolo pushed his untouched sandwich aside. "Look, Devin. The justices hate that new law, but it won't get overturned for a year, maybe more. You and Milan knew that when it got proposed. That gives him time to consolidate and make even bigger changes. Once the Twenty-second Amendment is repealed, he'll be able to do whatever he wants."

"He's already done a lot of good," I said. I set my sandwich down and wiped my mouth. Crumbs littered the table in front of me.

"He's already done a lot of bad. Did you know there was a link tying him to Brownwin's plane crash?"

"So give the information to the media. They're supposed to start that kind of shitstorm."

Paolo laughed. "As if that would do any good. Milan clipped their feathers last term. And besides, three days after the link contacted us, she died."

The food twisted in my stomach. "Milan is not tied to any murders. He's done everything above ground."

"Everything you see maybe," Paolo said. "But it's time you see more."

He slid the file across the table to me, then picked up his sandwich. "Got a bag for me, Petey? I'm late for the office."

The deli man pulled a crumpled white bag from behind the counter. "This okay?" he asked.

"Sure." Paolo stuffed the sandwich and a few napkins inside. Then he looked at me. "Happy reading, Devin. When you're through, leave a message with Levin's secretary and I'll find you."

Then he grabbed the bag and his laptop, and left.

I opened the file and nearly jumped when I saw Wiggins' face staring back at me. The first four pages were in his handwriting, documenting Milan's history of corruption from his college years (when he had been a student with Wiggins) to the first ten years of his business. There was more: a history of dead associates, and embezzled funds. Plus a complete analysis of the changes in the states of Montana and Wyoming since Milan took office. From Wiggins' point of view, the pattern of corruption by the president was the same as the pattern of corruption by the young man building his business.

But it wasn't that which stopped me. It was the pictures of Wiggins toward the back of the file: naked, too skinny, covered with bruises and lacerations, eyes open in death. He had been found on a dry reservoir bottom a week before delayed spring run-off would have covered him forever.

I closed the file and pinched the bridge of my nose. Wiggins. I owed so much to that old man. And I hadn't contacted him since coming to D.C. because I had been hurt that Wiggins hadn't acknowledged my appointment. I returned his one phone call but never tried to track him down when he mysteriously disappeared. Now we would never reconcile. Now we would never talk.

I took a deep breath and closed the file. Just because Wiggins was dead didn't mean that Milan had anything to do with it.

And I would prove it.

TWENTY YEARS LATER, BY SEPARATION PEAK

XI

The rain stopped. Small pools of water had formed in the holes left by the rocks. The trail had become mud. The wind was gone, but I shivered anyway. Paolo had shut up after Sven's challenge, and we had all gone back to work.

No one spoke. The clink of rocks against each other provided the only noise. Paolo had moved a few feet away from us, staring at Separation Peak.

The others had the same feverish look that I knew was on my face. We would find Milan. We would cover him. We would make sure he was dead. We needed that. We needed to know that Milan would never haunt us again.

"This is ridiculous." Margarite wiped her face with the back of her dirt-covered hand. Her gaze met mine. I knew nothing about her any more. The last time I had seen her had been on this bit of land, in front of his cairn. Since then, a government had fallen apart, the world suffered the largest economic crisis ever, and the United States had gone from a major power to a third world country.

Yet all of the living we had done, all of the years we had spent apart, seemed less important than finding Milan one last time.

Lobo stopped pulling rocks off the cairn too. He peered inside. "I think you people need to see this," he said.

XII

Friends of friends of friends.

A friend in Justice put me on the trail of a man who had seen Wiggins last. Another friend in the FBI tied Milan to the death. And a third friend, a former journalist, showed me the pattern. All of Milan's old colleagues were dead. Most of his detractors had been silenced.

All of the electoral college had been bribed.

Friends of friends of friends. I followed the path Paolo had sent me on like a police dog sniffing a cocaine trail. Then I flew back to Wyoming, gathered the group together, and we had our first conversation.

We had our second after the *New York Times* massacre. Our third when the order went through to shut down the computer nets. Hundreds of people died at the hands of government troops called in to quell local emergencies. Even more disappeared. Milan was consolidating his power.

When the Thirty-fifth Amendment passed, repealing the Twenty-second and placing no limit on Milan's stay in office, our group met for the fourth and final time.

I never knew the details. I don't even think Quinlin knew. His father escaped from prison about the same time as Milan's murder, and I overheard Quinlin explain to Chibu that the real coffin had been switched with one that had a different body inside—easy to do, since no one opened the coffin after Milan had been placed in it. No one wanted to see a man with his face blown away. Margarite found the burial site—a lonely place at the top of the continental divide where she had been brutalized by a trucker and no one had come to her aid. No one had driven by—even though it was the days of long haul traveling and easy gas. She believed it appropriate that Milan would be placed to rest there.

We arrived on the morning of May 29th to find the body had already arrived. The coffin was gone. Someone had left a body bag behind a rock. Paolo had opened it and then turned and got sick in the grass. The smell was rich and fetid, the smell of decaying flesh, something I had only encountered roadside before—as I drove past a dead and abandoned deer.

No one else looked at the corpse.

We left him inside the body bag and built the cairn around it. Then we swore to return in twenty years, thinking the world would be a better place.

Politicians should never predict the future.

Milan's vice president—the man Brownwin had chosen and Milan had kept—turned out to be truly inept. Milan's changes had weakened Congress and pulled power from the states, leaving most of the strength in a now-incompetent executive. When the global economic crisis hit—the one Milan had foreseen and been planning for, according to papers that turned up later—America shattered.

And we all shattered with it.

XIII

The body bag was open. The zipper's teeth were rusted and spread out the width of a man. Someone had disturbed the grave. We pulled rocks off the cairn with renewed intensity. Even Paolo helped. Our breathing was

197

ragged, our fingers flayed and bleeding. We finally yanked the last of the rocks off the top of the body and stared down.

The sun had come out and illuminated the darkness inside.

The rocks had crushed most of the bones. Milan's big hands had become skeletal fingers, identifiable only by the heavy gold watch and matching ring he wore on his right. His skull had no eye sockets, no cheek bones and no teeth, only the cranium with a bit of gray matter still lodged in the back. His silver presidential belt buckle had fallen into his pelvis, and his fake leather shoes still covered his feet.

The smell of rot was long gone, replaced by a dusty, dry scent—the smell of rocks, the smell of opportunities long gone.

My legs would no longer support me. I sat down beside the cairn. One by one the others viewed his remains and turned away, like polite mourners at a funeral. I reached inside and touched his index finger. The three bones rolled apart.

A shudder welled up inside me. I hadn't looked the first time. I hadn't seen that long, graceful body motionless, a bloody mess where the face should have been.

But Paolo had.

"He's really dead," I whispered.

Paolo turned from his position near the edge of the trail. "Yes, Devin. He's really dead."

The soft voice, gone forever. That laugh—silenced. The probing mind that knew how to find the answers to questions other people had only dreamed of—shattered.

TWENTY YEARS LATER, BY SEPARATION PEAK

By my hand.

As clearly as if I had wielded the gun myself.

Paolo's expression softened. He walked toward me, then sat down beside me. The ground's wetness had seeped into my jeans, making me even colder.

"You didn't know, did you?" he asked.

I could barely breathe. My whole body was shaking. All these years I had lied to myself. All these years, I had hoped—hoped—that Milan would come back and ask the right question which would save us from ourselves.

I had loved him once—thinking him to be a minor deity.

Then I had hated him for loving power and games more than people. I had hated him—not for the deaths, but for the corruption.

I had hated him, but I had never stopped believing in him.

No wonder he had liked me. I had been just like him.

I put my face in my hands. Paolo grabbed my shoulder and squeezed. Then the grass squished as he walked away.

Paolo had been wrong. What Milan would have done didn't matter. The only thing that had mattered was what we had done.

We had had the power to change things at our fingertips, and we had taken the coward's way out.

I had taken the coward's way.

I gripped the side of the cairn and stood up, staring at those bones for one last moment. They looked so frail, all that remained of a man who had once held an entire country in his grip. A man with a vision, a man with a plan.

A man who killed to get what he wanted.

Chibu, Lobo, and Margarite were staring at me. Quinlin, Sven, and Paolo watched me, too. Waiting, as always, for me to tell them what to do. Waiting for some kind of guidance, some kind of leadership.

I had none to give them.

WAGING PEACE

by *Nina Kiriki Hoffman*

Century IX, #95

The New One shall lead the army
Near Apame, just until the riverbank
Bearing help from the Milanese elite
The Duke without eyes, in Milan, in an iron cage

The peace marchers gathered in De La Guerra Plaza.

I was fifteen and driver licenseless in November of 1969, and normally I would have had to depend on my mom for transportation to the start of the march; our family marched for peace or vigiled with the Quakers in front of the Art Museum on State Street about once a week. But this was a big march, scheduled to coincide with major events in Washington, D.C., and San Francisco, and I was in Free School, which was treating the whole thing as a field trip. The entire student body and all the teachers had driven from our school building in the foothills to downtown in rusting VW buses and Ford vans with bumper stickers that said things like "Save Lives, Not Face" and "U.S. Out of Vietnam."

Signs were stacked up near the curb of the service road through the plaza, and people were choosing. I picked up the standard "War Is Not Healthy for Chil-

201

dren and Other Living Things," but ditched it when I found a sign that read, "America Cooks Children." It reminded me of W. C. Fields. I had been acquiring an education in old movies that summer from our next-door neighbor, a woman who put up with the three youngest boys in our family visiting her when things got too weird for us at home. She had gotten me and my two brothers hooked on thirties movies, poker, and murder mysteries. She told us about movie stars' backgrounds, so I knew about W. C.'s feud with Baby LeRoy. I knew W. C. Fields had said something like, "Sure, I like kids . . . if they're cooked right."

Some of the other kids from Free School got mad when they saw what a good sign I had. "Come on, Rob, that's not fair," said Sheila. She wore a beaded anklet with Indian brass bells on it. Every other step, you could hear her coming. She also wore a dress made from a thin Indian print cotton bedspread. I could almost see her breasts through it. She said, "You got to sit in the front seat, and you got out of the bus first."

Since we were supposed to be learning cooperation instead of competition, and since one of our teachers was nearby (not that we respected anybody's authority, but he was teaching us Mandarin Chinese, and I liked that class, especially the calligraphy), and since I had kind of a thing about Sheila, I said I'd switch signs with her after a few blocks.

We had come early. More and more people crowded onto the lawn in the plaza and eventually into the service road. The air smelled like sun-baked adobe, mowed grass, and exhaust. At the far end of the plaza stood the old Governor's Palace from the town's Spanish days, now housing the Santa Teresa *Times* offices. If any reporters had come out to watch the gathering of peace forces, I couldn't tell.

Another beautiful sunny day in Southern California. God, I wished I had a car.

I spotted someone Dad had invited to dinner once, a research scientist from the University. Dad worked at a think tank and sometimes invited people over. The scientist's name was Mike Something-that-starts-with-P, and he was young and intense and had granny glasses, long hair, and a jaw that stuck forward even when he was smiling. The six children in my family usually demolished visitors with clever rudeness disguised as friendliness, but Mike Something had held his own, I remembered, and had even told some jokes we laughed at. In fact, he had talked about biology in a way that made it almost as interesting as science fiction.

Mike was talking to a mean-looking older man with a crewcut and a suit, which put him in the "suspicious" category as far as I was concerned. Rumors abounded about the FBI infiltrating the peace movement. Some said they sent guys around to try to get people to say they had Communist leanings. But usually you could spot the FBI guys by their bad wigs, fake thrift-store clothes, and clean shaves—kind of the way hippies dressed on *Dragnet*. This guy looked too much like an FBI guy to actually be one. So just who was he?

I was a big James Bond and *Man from U.N.C.L.E.* fan, even though Bond, Solo, and Kuryakin worked for the Establishment. I wondered why Mike was talking to a crewcut. I decided to spy on them.

"Hold this," I said, handing my sign to Sheila.

"Chauvinist pig," she said.

"Oink," I said, and slithered through the crowd.

Mike and Crewcut were having words, but very quietly. I stood with my back to them five feet away, among other people, and I couldn't make out what they were saying at all. I turned and pretended to be looking toward a palm tree.

"She's not ready to be out in public," Mike said, a little louder.

"She's the prototype," said Crewcut. "We have to test her sometime."

"Now is not the time," Mike said. He glanced around, his eyes narrowed. I faced away before his gaze reached me. I thought camouflage, projecting: just another skinny kid in tire-soled huaraches, wear-whitened jeans and a satin-backed thrift-store vest.

God, I wished I had muscles.

Yeah, and some spy technology. Glasses with a hearing-enhancer built into the earpieces, and a mirror coating on the inside so I could see behind me. A tape recorder the size of a cigarette pack. I also liked the thought of plastic explosives disguised as chewing gum.

"You're making a big mistake," Mike said at last.

"I can cut off your funding," said Crewcut. Then he said, "Come on. You're as curious as I am. Besides, with all those age accelerators in her, she won't last. We have to use her now. And we've got three more ripening. Come on."

I heard them moving off behind me. When I turned around, I saw them heading toward a van covered with giant painted flowers and pastel peace signs. Its back windows were blacked out.

Messages came through the crowd about forming up

and heading out. People milled more purposefully, but there were so many present it would take us a while to get set up. I paused, torn. I wanted to see what the scientist and the crewcut were up to, and I wanted to go back and find Sheila again and fight with her.

Then the woman appeared.

She stood on the back bumper of a van so we could all see her. She had black hair in a Prince Valiant haircut. She was wearing an outfit like the kind I saw at the KPFK Renaissance Fair, a belted gray tunic sort of thing, tight black pants or maybe just tights, and riding boots. Her intense dark eyes scanned the crowd. When she looked at me, I felt prickly and warm and peculiar, as if someone had shocked me.

"My friends," she cried. Her voice was deep and strong. "My friends."

Everybody turned to look at her.

God, I wished I had a car, muscles, and some fake I.D. I'd never been in an actual bar, but I suspected that was where to take someone you wanted to impress.

"I lead you now to battle, for God and for the Right," she said, raising her arm in a clenched fist. Not exactly what we were used to hearing at these events; but I felt this surge of energy run through me. I straightened.

"Give me my standard," she cried, and somebody handed her a really big white sign that said, "We Shall Overcome."

"Onward, my children. To me!" she cried, turning away from us, jumping down from the bumper, the sign held high. As she turned I saw something in her ear, a hearing aid not quite as pink and perfect as her cheek.

In silence everyone massed together, almost in formation, and we started marching—not the usual amble and chat, amble and chant, but left-right-left. Though I could see her sign, I couldn't see past taller people in front of me to the woman herself, and I wanted to. I also couldn't seem to shove forward the way I usually did. I had my place, between a large older woman in a muumuu carrying a sign that said, "There is No Way to Peace; Peace Is the Way" and a muscular guy wearing a twisted red bandanna as a headband. I stared at the back of the T-shirt in front of me. It bore the legend "Frodo Lives" in psychedelic print. I marched.

When we reached State Street, the march was supposed to turn left, toward the ocean. The plan was to cross Highway 101, stopping traffic for however long we could, and then walk along the shore past City College and up to Ledbetter Beach, where somebody was waiting with a big supply of candles in cups, and we would sit in vigil as darkness fell and think about all the people marching all across the country that day, the way they had in October for Vietnam Moratorium Day.

I had been in Europe that summer. My two brothers and I went on a package tour with a lot of old people and a few young ones, seven countries in thirty days, while my mom checked herself into a mental hospital and had a breakdown. On July 20th, we'd been riding a bus through Rome. We stopped at the Colosseum and the Catacombs. The Catacombs had creeped me out, but I liked them almost best of everything we saw. After wandering underground among the bones of people who had died fifteen hundred years earlier, we came up into evening, and my older brother bought a newspaper. We couldn't read the text, but we didn't need to. The whole front page was just one picture: a footprint.

A footprint on the moon.

"Just imagine," said my brother. "Everywhere on Earth, this is probably front page news."

We got back on our tour bus to head for our hotel and I was still imagining it, the whole world resonating to a single event. And I, who had routinely gone to see the principal because I refused to say the Pledge of Allegiance in school ("Liberty and justice for all? Ha!" Sometimes at night Mom read aloud to us. She read *Nigger!* by Dick Gregory to us, along with Tolkien), on the night of the moon landing, I was proud to be an American.

With the right lever, we could move the world.

The march was supposed to head down toward the beach, but the big white sign gestured, the compelling voice cried, "Onward!" and we followed, north on State Street's sidewalk toward the mountains and the Mission.

I stared at the word "Frodo" and thought about walking on the moon and wondered why I was marching like a soldier when I planned to burn my draft card as soon as I got it. Something clicked in my head and I edged out of formation and over toward the street. I had to see that woman again.

By the time I had dodged cars and worked my way up the column to the front we had gone about three more blocks. A lot had happened in three blocks.

The woman was still carrying her sign high and marching with determination, but her hair had grown half a foot, and the top part of it was silver and white.

"Onward, children!" she cried, half turning to look back. The face that had been smooth as a peach was now wrinkled. Her eyes still burned, though. Her back was straight. She made me think I was watching a comet walking along the ground.

I stood in the street as the march moved past me, trying to understand what I had seen.

She had been standing on a bumper when I first saw her. I closed my eyes, ignoring the horns honking at me, the cars edging around me. She had been standing on the bumper of a van painted with big flowers and peace signs.

She had been young—not much older than I—and now she was . . . ancient.

Prototype. Age accelerators.

I rushed ahead again.

Crewcut was marching two rows behind her. He wasn't carrying a sign, but he had something in his hand. He held it up to his mouth and whispered, and the woman at the head of the march turned and called, "We are near, children!" She flourished her sign.

Mike Something was marching on the street side of the column, about three rows back. I jumped up on the sidewalk and edged in beside him, staring at his face. He didn't even notice. His eyes didn't blink. He was watching the woman.

She stopped in the wide space in front of the Bank of America. "We will lay siege to them," she cried, "these enemy occupiers of our country. We will drive them into the ocean! Our country will be ours once more!"

She was wasting away. Her hair was falling out, her cheeks were sinking in, even her back bent, but her voice was still strong. I felt very strange. There was a prickling under my skin and my cheeks felt hot. I glanced at Mike. A tear ran down his cheek. I thought, muscles and cars and fake I.D., none of it can save her. None of it matters.

The peace marchers kept coming and coming, surrounding the small clear space where she stood in front of the big double doors into the bank. A security guard inside was peering through the glass, his hand resting on his truncheon. Distant sirens sounded. Cars were honking, gulls were crying.

"We shall prevail," the woman cried, holding both arms high. She burst into flame.

It was the longest night I ever spent.

I couldn't move away because nobody else did. I grabbed Mike's shirt and held on. I closed my eyes and wished I could close my nose. America cooks children.

Mike was gulping and sobbing. Some of the others were too. Nobody said anything. The police came and used bullhorns to yell, "Break it up. Break it up." Somewhere way out on the edge of the crowd people started to move. Eventually there was room for us to move. I kept my grip on Mike's shirt. He was too stunned to brush me off.

We wandered away. He seemed to be in a trance and I didn't care where we went. Eventually we found a park bench somewhere and sat down.

"Who was she?" I asked. I had to repeat it several times.

"Joan," he said. "Joan of Arc." His voice was flat.

"What?"

"Her heart didn't burn."

I thought back to the scene in front of the bank. I had not looked to see what was left. I hadn't watched the burning. I'd looked at the inside of my eyelids, pressed my face into the crook of my elbow. I didn't want to think about what might have burned and what might not have.

"Five hundred years ago, she was burned at the stake, but her heart didn't burn." He was still talking like a robot, each syllable coming out without intonation. "The executioner took it to the convent of the Friars' Preacher and said he feared he was damned, for he had burned a holy woman. And the monks kept her heart."

"Her heart," I said.

Mike stared at some nearby eucalyptus trees and didn't say anything else. We both sat there until after midnight. I don't know how I got home.

I heard later that President Nixon sat in the White House watching college football, with sharpshooters hidden all around to protect him in case of violence, while the largest political mass march and demonstration in U.S. history went on outside on Pennsylvania Avenue.

I never heard of another Joan; I never saw Mike or the crewcut after that night.

In 1972, as a conscientious objector, I started alternative service in a hospital. I emptied a lot of bedpans as an orderly, and I ended up working in the burn ward.

THE FIRE OF THE DARK

by Lawrence Greenberg

Century X, #10

Corrupted by murder and vast adulteries
Is the great enemy of the human race
One who will be worse than his grandfathers, uncles,
  or father
In iron, fire, bloody and inhuman

Extract from a letter written by the novelist Johann Schemm to Gregor Strasse, January 1936:

I cannot, my dear Gregor, remember a time when I was more inspired to be what I am—a creative artist living and working in the greatest nation on earth. I am full of energy; I am fired with enthusiasm, and we, all of us, are truly blessed now to be graced with a man who has no fear—who is not afraid to stand up and proclaim to the entire world that, yes, there are such things as loyalty and courageous dedication to the progress of an entire race—not merely a few select members. Yet we the German people, in fact, are those select members of the entire human race, presented with a unique opportunity to seize the moment, to capture the imagination of the entire planet with the boldness of our actions. I know beyond any doubt that we will not fail in this undertaking.

211

Lawrence Greenberg

Diary extract of Albert Rosenberg, statesman, January 1936:

It is difficult to understand how Herr Goebbels believes he can help effect the dramatic metamorphosis he continues to proclaim is in the process of overtaking this country. What he espouses is nothing short of what I would term psychotic mediocrity—by which I mean that his fanatical methods will do no more than bring about a state of mass confusion within which no one will shine. At least, no creative worker. For how can the individual artist express his prowess when his will must be completely subservient to that of the state?

Now, I have no serious argument with the turn this nation has taken—indeed, I believe it is the best development that could occur for us. But part of the greatness of our land is the sacred domain of the creative spirit who rises to meet the challenge of the culture's growing need for advancement by pushing himself ever on to achieve the apex of his career. Perhaps these are portentous words. I do not know. Perhaps history may judge them so. And then again, it may not.

Notes found in the desk of Frau Wilhelmina Krause, amanuensis to Josef Goebbels, May 1936:

We now know that film is one of the most modern and far reaching ways of influencing the masses today. This is as my master Herr Goebbels has stated. He will use film to transform our society. He is so fiercely loyal to the cause of liberty that there is absolutely no question that Germany will triumph over all others. Herr Goebbels has attained the status of one whom others must obey. This is surely not to detract from the glory of our mighty leader who must not only be obeyed, but unquestioningly followed, exalted, yes, even deified. I revere him, as I do my mother and father. As I do my husband and children. And yet, Herr Goebbels—oh, what a man is he! When he takes me in his arms and fondles me—when he caresses my body, when he places his lips to the nipples of my bare breasts, and, yes, when he penetrates me as he has so often, here, right here on the floor of my little office with the door closed—it is all I can do to stop from fainting, from idolizing him, from shouting his name aloud. Because Herr Goebbels is so great a man, I have even shared the details of these intimate meetings with my dear Friedrich. At first, he was aghast. But I convinced him of the need Herr Goebbels has for what he calls my buxom, voluptuous body to better fan the flame of inspiration in his important work. And, although reluctantly, Friedrich has consented to allow me to serve my master willingly, with great devotion and dedication to the cause of our state.

During his conferences with Der Fuhrer, which I have been privileged to attend for the purpose of note taking, my beloved master has demonstrated again and again that the medium of film will conquer the will of the little people such as myself. And all the virile, mighty men who have come to attend the conferences—they, too, agree with this statement. On rare occasions I wonder why it is that there are seemingly no women who have assumed powerful roles in our beloved Reich.

But of course those are the times when I forget, much to my shame, the place of women here. It is to serve, to nurture, to provide a warm and loving hearth for their men who struggle valiantly to overcome the forces that will always be set against them. And it is then that I begin to weep quietly and yearn for, dare I say it, both my Friedrich and my master at the same time. And even, would that it could ever take place, the strong, courageous leader of our people. How I long for him to anoint me with his manhood. Gladly would I open my legs for him. Oh, come to me, my mighty warlord! Do with me what you will! I am eternally your willing slave.

Extract from a letter written by the filmmaker Karl Ritzler to Hans Jonst, playwright, May 1936:

There have now been a number of discussions between myself and Herr Goebbels. It is quite apparent that we have much in common, and thus were able to agree on so many matters. The Gleichschaltung will insure that all of our activities are culturally consistent. It is most encouraging to realize that there have been many such meetings—most of them with quite a number of writers, artists, sculptors, composers, and filmmakers such as myself—during which Herr Goebbels has outlined his rules for this great coordination which will make us all so very proud of who and when and where we are. I, for one, am looking forward with great eagerness to set forth my ideas aligned with the magnificent assimilation which der Fuhrer and Herr Goebbels have designed.

Extract from a letter written by Franz Lehrmann of the Technical Department, Film and Cinemas, to Karl Ritzler, filmmaker, May 1936:
My dear Karl:

This is a most amazing development! Stefan of our

department—you remember him; you met him at the last Bundesreich party where I introduced you—along with Georg Leiser, Eva Hinz, and myself have come up with a new film camera which is no larger than two fists together, and which operates with a minimum of noise. We have tested it with our simultaneously developed film stock of miniature proportions which actually took much longer to perfect than did the camera itself. And it works! It all works! A true miracle! The advantages for espionage work are incalculable. We have designed the camera to hold enough film for one hour of shooting—a truly remarkable accomplishment considering the size of the device and the capacity of a normal film camera. I have no doubt whatsoever that we will be able to secure knowledge of enemy activities far more effectively than any other nation—especially those who dare to defy us. I am eager to put our child through its paces, to test its limits, its sureness of vision, its scope. And I am sure that opportunities for its use will come quickly and dramatically.

Diary extract of Rudolf Pohl, Commandant, Ahnenerbe, May 1936:

We have now found what appears to be one of the objects being sought by Der Fuhrer. It is truly inspiring to be part of this select organization, the Occult Research Bureau, dedicated to the task of retrieving the sacred objects that will serve to further increase our leader's power, and therefore the might of our entire nation.

Dr. H. had mentioned to General Rolm that the item would in all likelihood be embedded deep in the earth; I received this information from the General. Follow-

ing the instructions of Herr Doctor—who seems to
have the second sight uncannily stronger than anyone
else in recent memory—we traveled to Aurigen, a tiny
village in the Alps of Switzerland. This was the settlement closest to the mountainous area which he described. It is certainly comforting to us all that we
could confine our journey to German Switzerland.
From this village, we six set out on foot to retrieve the
object. The six are myself, Sergeant Josef Gruen, and
four of our finest Schutzstaffel, especially recruited for
the Ahnenerbe—Kurtz, Hahnemann, Steinmetz, and
Gruber. Now truth be told, I am not by any means a
psychic—not even remotely close to having those
qualities—but Herr Doctor was assured that such faculties were not necessary. And that was because, as he
indicated to General Rolm, we would know the item
when we came upon it. Apparently, he did not provide
any real description of exactly what it was we were
looking for. Thus, we had very little to go on. However, Der Fuhrer and Dr. H. have been working together very closely for the last year and a half or so;
therefore, I did not press for any details.

About an hour and a half after starting out, we arrived at a charming little recess where we stopped for
our hearty lunch. I mention this not to detail our eating
habits, but because it was during this brief respite that
Kurtz brought something most curious to my attention.
From where he was positioned, leaning against an outcropping, he observed a small area of rock distinctly
lighter in color than that surrounding it. He pointed in
its direction and I immediately saw what he was referring to. Perhaps, I thought, this is what the doctor
meant in saying we would know the object when we

saw it. This area of rock was situated not more than a hundred meters or so from where we were. I cut short our midday meal and indicated that we should descend immediately to the site. We did so, and discovered that the lighter rock was also a bit softer than normal rock and grainier in texture as well.

My men commenced picking and digging; within a relatively short time, we came upon a stratum even lighter and grainier than the top layer. And in due course, surprisingly enough, we hit sand—pure white sand. Rather than stopping to gawk at such an unusual phenomenon, we applied ourselves diligently to what confronted us and were eventually rewarded for our efforts. However, when Steinmetz hit something solid, no sooner had his shovel made contact with whatever it was than he began shaking violently all over. The others immediately dropped their tools and went to assist him. The poor fellow had to lie down; even fifteen minutes or so afterward, he was still trembling noticeably. Gruen therefore instructed the others to exercise extreme caution in uncovering the item. Unfortunately, because no one remembered where Steinmetz had struck the thing, Hahnemann suffered a similar fate. This time, however, Gruber and Kurtz saw exactly where Hahnemann's shovel had made contact and they avoided doing so, digging around the thing until they had at least exposed the shape of what we assumed was the object we were searching for. Considering that two of our men had had such a noticeable reaction to contact with it, this seemed like a safe assumption. I could only marvel at Herr Doctor's uncanny accuracy in predicting the location of this item.

The object was rectangular in form—indeed it was

for all intents and purposes nothing more than a box. We now had the problem of securing it without causing harm to ourselves. This seemed a matter for some concern until Kurtz—quite a perceptive fellow—observed that in both cases of personal injury, it was metal that had touched the object; that perhaps there was some sort of electromagnetic force which the object gave off that had thus been transmitted through the medium of our picks and shovels. I concurred; we were, after all, dealing with an object that might very well have decidedly unusual properties. This would mean that theoretically at least it should be perfectly safe to grasp it with our hands or even touch it with our clothing (i.e., gloves, coats, and so on).

I asked Gruen to test my theory. He looked at me blankly for a few seconds and followed his momentary lapse with a rather abrupt "Yes, sir," immediately after which he grasped the thing with both hands and pulled it out of the sand. He was completely unaffected. We all gave out a cheer—even Steinmetz and Hahnemann who by this time had seemingly recovered from their prior state and were now both sitting up.

This box was oddly shaped—long and narrow, like a miniature coffin but with strangely rounded edges. Once we had brushed off the sand still clinging to it, we observed that it was covered with all manner of symbols the like of which none of us had ever seen. These symbols were of the same material as the box itself—not inlaid, yet not carved into it either. Rather, and this does admittedly sound peculiar, they were integrally part of the box; they formed the shape of the box. After examining the object thoroughly, we discovered neither lid nor latch. At that point, there was little else to do but wrap it up in cloth and bring it back with us.

By this time, Steinmetz and Hahnemann seemed to have recovered fully and we were all in excellent spirits, confident that we had found what we had been instructed to, and that this find would surely lead to the greater glory of our beloved Third Reich.

Diary extract of General Friedrich Rolm, Schutzstaffel, May 1936:

Commandant Pohl has retrieved the object and turned it over to me with a full report which I have now read. It is unfortunate that the Commandant retained possession of this item in his own quarters for a full day prior to giving it up, and also unfortunate that in his report he noted his examination of the "box" in his attempt to find a mechanism to open it.

Herr Doctor has conveyed to me that it was the orders of Der Fuhrer that this item be delivered directly to Dr. H. without delay. This was made clear to the Commandant at the outset of his little expedition. For failure to comply with this direct order, he will be imprisoned with minimal nourishment for not less than 40 days.

As an aside, I am still curious as to the nature of my communication with Dr. H. All of our "talks" have been held in a construct similar to a Catholic church confessional booth, the difference being the panel separating the two parties in this device has only the narrowest of slits, three of them running vertically top to bottom, to transmit the sound of a man's voice. It is virtually impossible to see the other person. Since Herr Doctor is already seated within the construct on all occasions when I have conversed with him in the room I call the "speaking chamber," I have never actually seen the man. Still, he is very close to our leader, so I listen carefully to his statements. His voice is thin and high, akin to the sound of some reed instrument. I gave Dr. H. the box at our most recent session by leaving it on my seat immediately before I left. This talk proved to be the most unusual of the entire series I have had with him.

Upon entering the construct, I sensed a greater than normal level of agitation or excitement. There seemed to be more movement than what normally occurred on the other side of the panel—fidgeting, I suppose one would call it. No sooner had I sat down than the doctor whined, "You have the item?" I have not heard him speak with so grating a voice before.

"Yes," I said. "It is here with me."

"Excellent, excellent!" he whined. And he jumped in his seat. Or so it seemed. "It looks like a box, does it not?"

"Yes," I repeated.

"Ah, that is most excellent indeed. It is not really a box, you know, my dear General. Ah, yes, but you would not know that, would you? No, of course not. Ah, well. Never mind, never mind. At the end of our little talk, just leave the item on your seat and I will collect it. Now tell me, did your man have any difficulty finding it?"

I then related to him the details as presented in Pohl's report. During this description he made a series of snuffling noises, as though he were afflicted with a cold of some sort. Yet they appeared to be sounds of pleasure, strange as that may seem. I do not know exactly why I say this, only that I sensed it. It was most peculiar. The doctor seemed particularly interested in the two Schutzstaffel men who had hit the object with their shovels, and with the Commandant who had kept the item in his quarters prior to turning it over to me. He specifically inquired as to their state of health and when I responded that there was no perceivable problem, he let out some sort of odd clucking sound.

At the conclusion of this description, Dr. H. said, "Oh, thank you so much for your little story, General. I'm afraid our little talks have come to an end. Leave the item on your seat and hasten back to your duties, which I'm certain are quite pressing."

I had no hesitation in leaving on this occasion. Just before exiting the speaking chamber, I looked quickly over my shoulder in an attempt to catch a glimpse of the doctor. I was not successful. However, at the very moment prior to the closing of the door, I was certain I observed something I had never seen before. There was some sort of dark fluid seeping out of the construct from his side. It was not blood. This I am sure of.

Directive from the office of Josef Goebbels, Minister of Popular Enlightenment and Propaganda, June 1936:

For treason against the state in the form of consistent and direct opposition to the Gleichschaltung, Albert Rosenberg of 54 Kinderstrasse, Berlin, is to be apprehended and summarily executed by hanging. In particular, the execution will be public and should be made known to all recognized creative artists in our society as a symbol of the consequences of rebellion against the power and nobility of the Third Reich.

Lawrence Greenberg

Report of Dr. Manfred Schirmer, Reichstag Hospital, Medical Corps, mid June 1936:

The soldiers W. Steinmetz and O. Hahnemann were admitted to our facility here in Berlin on this day. They are both young men, 24 and 28 respectively. Both men were suffering from a series of unusual ailments, the like of which defies description. In both cases, there were open festering sores over the back, the shoulders, the chest, and limbs. The sores all oozed some sort of thick, sluggish fluid, the nature of which I could not determine. It is certainly not blood. Nor is it pus; it is too dark and thick for that. It is very dark brown, almost black in color, and continues to seep from all of the sores regardless of what type of compress is applied. The exudate is also quite warm, enough to nearly burn the skin.

In addition, both men complained of severe bouts of vomiting during which clumps of heavy dark matter are ejected. And there is something perhaps even more peculiar. Both men also described episodes of night terrors in which large shadowy forms predominate. What is most strange about this phenomenon is the remarkable similarity of their reports. These forms seem to be constantly hovering in the air and there are small whiplike appendages that lash out periodically. I did not know what to make of this at all.

I asked the men first, if they knew where they had contracted this disease, and second if they had been in physical contact with anyone. It is clear to me that these symptoms—at least the physical ones—approach those of some sort of pandemic. Regarding the first question, the men did not know. Hahnemann mentioned that they had both suffered fits of shaking in

222

connection with the unearthing of some sort of box. I asked him to explain what happened, but when he related the incident, I dismissed it outright. One does not contract symptoms like these from contact with a box. As to the second question, both answered in the affirmative. They had both engaged in sexual intercourse with their wives. Steinmetz, the better proportioned of the two, mentioned that he had also enjoyed the favors of a young woman encountered at a local alehouse, as well as an older woman, an artist. Unfortunately, he knew only the first name of the younger woman, although he did know the name of the drinking establishment. The liaison with the artist was even more perfunctory, and so he had no information about her at all.

I left them with some medication for their emesis, which, frankly, I think will not help them. Perhaps it may give them a bit of hope. I did not know what else to do in this case. As for the sores, the most that could be done was instructing them to apply a penicillin compound every few hours. This as well seemed to me quite futile. I could do nothing for their unusual nocturnal visions. I asked that they return to me every week for the next month to check their condition.

While they were in the office, I telephoned their superior officer to insure that the men would both be placed under quarantine immediately upon their departure from the hospital. Additionally, I requested that there be strict observation of both mens' wives, and that effort be made to locate the girl from the tavern and that she be observed as well for similar indications. I have never seen these symptoms before. And I hope not to again.

Lawrence Greenberg

Recording on magnetic tape made of Commandant Rudolf Pohl in his cell in Kreslau Prison, late June 1936:

It comes up, it all comes up, here it is the 21st day here and all of it comes up, it's coming back up, I can just spit it out, can't I, I can just get rid of all of it, like these boiling ruptures small volcanoes, all over me, are getting rid of whatever is inside me now. I can just let it all out, these pieces of myself, like I am, I can bring it all up, so like me, these dark lumps, all of it, everything I have. Yes, yes, General, I took the box back with me to my room, yes, that's right, that's right, I did and then I tried to open it—oh, excuse me, here I come again (sounds of vomiting). Oh, yes, excuse me, are you listening to me, I know you are, yes, that's what we're known for, isn't it? Yes, I used my hunting knife, I cut it, I tried to cut it open, I hit it with my skillet, that's right my cast iron pan, and oh, yes, I remember—oh, damn these burning sores, again more of this coming out of me. What is this, what is this rotten shit? What is this that I have become now? (pause; sounds of weeping).

And it is all because of this, this ridiculous, this box? No, no, not the box. It is because of what we are, because of what we do, because we do not know what is, what is good, do we? We do not know, we do not—oh, God, have mercy upon us, in your wisdom, creator of, of all things, of these things, the ones I see at night, I don't know if they are dreams or what they are or not, every night, they come to me every night, these big dark things—oh, God, why, these shadows, these big black shadow things, am I raving, why can't they just go, just not be there, make them go

224

away, stop it, stop it, STOP IT! (there is a long scream and the recording ends).

Diary extract of Johann Schemm, novelist, July 1936:

On this auspicious day in early July, I and many others were witness to the public hanging of Albert Rosenberg who has vehemently opposed the Gleichschaltung from its inception. There was a total of perhaps 200 or 250 of us—writers, painters, filmmakers, sculptors, composers, and others. The scaffold was surrounded by a cadre of the SS, as well it should have been. When Rosenberg was brought into view, a barrage of jeers and insults was let loose. The condemned man was asked by the presiding officer if he had any last words. Of course, had Rosenberg been a Jew, which he is not, that favor would not have been granted. He replied that he did and turned to face us.

And then, like a bolt of black lightning, a woman—positioned not far from where I was standing and obviously insane—ran out from our group towards the scaffold screaming, "The mind of the artist is sacred! Rosenberg is right! The Gleichschaltung is a travesty of society!" and so on. The woman was hideously disfigured—full of dark festering pustules covering her face and arms. No wonder none of the SS bothered to apprehend her. Instead, one of them shot her through the head. Immediately upon falling to the ground, her body gave forth a copious stream of some thick dark fluid, certainly not blood by my reckoning. It appeared as though this substance was quite foul-smelling; all those in her vicinity turned away with expressions of disgust on their faces.

Rosenberg then regarded us with bowed head and

said, "I cannot put it more forcefully than did this woman." He then turned and nodded that he was ready for his death. He was strung up without hesitation. The body jerked for a few seconds and then we all saw the corpse turn slowly. The presiding officer made a short speech concerning the significance of the Gleichschaltung for all of us which we applauded. We then returned to our respective homes.

Diary extract of Karl Ritzler, filmmaker, July 1936:

Franz and his colleagues have done a remarkable job of designing and building this little film camera. By now, I have had the opportunity to use the device myself surreptitiously. I took the liberty of filming the tryst of two lovers in a secluded part of the Schwarzwald (yet suffused with enough sunlight for my work) and captured the entire course of their involvement from the first moments of gentle kissing to its culmination in vigorous copulation. I am quite grateful to the Technical Department for their discretion in developing and processing the film. The quality of the resulting film was excellent—better, it seems to me, than that produced by a standard film camera.

In the meantime, Herr Goebbels has announced to the "members" of the Gleichschaltung that we may all be on the brink of a monumental advance in the evolution of the Reich. He was not any more specific than that but stated that in short order, Der Fuhrer would himself make an announcement concerning his intensive work with Dr. H. I am led to believe that the two have discovered some phenomenon from which we may all benefit.

THE FIRE OF THE DARK

Further notes found in the desk of Frau Wilhelmina Krause, amanuensis to Josef Goebbels, July 1936:

I do not know how to describe what has happened to me, it is so wonderful. Surely there are enormous changes in store for our dear nation, more awesome than words can ever say. If I can relate my own experience, maybe that will put this miraculous development into perspective.

Four days ago, Herr Goebbels approached me and asked that I step into his office. I thought that we would have another of our inspirational sessions, but this was not to be. Instead, my master asked me to sit in one of his fine chairs. Then he walked around and sat at his desk and gazed at me for a few seconds. Finally he said, "Do you know, Wilhelmina, how important our Fuhrer is?"

I was surprised by his question, but answered Herr Goebbels straight away.

"Yes, sir. Certainly. He is the most important man in history."

My master smiled at me.

"Yes, he is. And he has just asked me for a favor." He stopped for a moment. "And do you know what that is?"

I was a little bit confused by his question. "No, sir."

"He wants to borrow you."

"I'm sorry, sir?"

"He wants to see you in his chambers. You are to go to him at once."

I was shocked and could only sit in place, staring at my master in complete disbelief. Finally I realized what he had said and made to leave at once.

"Oh, and Wilhelmina," Herr Goebbels continued.

"You may write down what transpires during your visit, but be sure to keep your notes in a more secure place than where we found your earlier writings."

I blushed and bowed my head quickly.

"Yes, sir."

"Very well. Now go." And he pointed the way down to the end of the corridor.

I hastened toward my rendezvous with destiny. And it was certainly to be that, as I discovered. I knocked on the unmarked door, guarded on either side. Neither of the men said anything to stop me. The door was opened by one of Der Fuhrer's personal aides, a man I had seen in the building from time to time. He nodded curtly to me and gestured that I should come in. I entered the vestibule, and he closed the door after me. Still without saying a word, he escorted me inside to our great leader's office. He knocked twice on the door quickly. I heard a rather distinctive voice say, "Come," and the aide opened the door to a large, high-ceilinged room decorated with banners and pictures of the mighty men of our glorious past.

Der Fuhrer arose from his desk with a flower in his hand and looked directly at me.

"Come in, my dear," he said, offering me the flower. It was a rose. I heard the door close behind me. I did not know what to say or do. He extended the flower further to me. That was the sign for me, finally, to come towards him. I walked those steps so nervously that I thought my legs would give out under me. At last I reached his desk and took the rose. Then he indicated that I should sit, which I did. I felt a little more relaxed, but was still awestruck at being in the presence of such a great man.

228

THE FIRE OF THE DARK

Our mighty leader sat back in his chair, keeping his gaze upon me.

"I am sure you don't know why you are here, Frau Krause." He spoke in his distinctive voice.

"'N–no, sir, I don't," I stammered.

"You have no need to worry, my dear. You have done nothing wrong. In fact, the reason I called you here was to help me."

I could not believe what he was saying. "To help you?"

"Yes, that is correct. I want to demonstrate conclusively that we are about to enter the next stage of man's evolution. That we will soon attain the status, all of us good, healthy German people like you and me, of the superman that Nietzsche mentions in his writing. Wouldn't you like to assist me in that undertaking?"

"Oh, yes, sir. Oh, yes, yes, of course."

He smiled at me. It was a wonderful sight.

"Excellent, my dear. Then if you would please just come with me." He arose from his desk and beckoned me to follow him. I had no idea where Der Fuhrer was taking me. Surely it was not out the door I had come in. No, it was not. He walked to the back corner of his office where a large bookcase stood, full of important looking volumes. And then our great leader pulled one of the books toward him and the entire bookcase swung in. Der Fuhrer had a secret room!

He signaled that I should follow him and, of course, I did. My amazement was growing at the mind and character of this powerful ruler. And when I stepped into the hidden chamber, I was astounded. This room had an even higher ceiling than his office and was larger also. And it was decorated much differently. Instead of images of our past leaders and the symbols of our mighty nation, the walls were covered with the work of an artist I had never seen before. The paintings were of many women, all of them naked, and every one of them was singly impaled on a metal spearlike stake. All of them were facing upward toward the sky which was dark gray. There were black women and yellow women and red women and brown women. The only white women in the paintings had the Jewish symbol, the six sided star, marked on their foreheads. Sometimes the mark was on their arms or legs or their sides. And there was something else in the paintings which I could not understand. Floating in the gray sky above these thousands of dying women were a number of very large black shapes. Most of these shapes had many tentacles dangling from them. Several also had blazing red eyes that looked down upon the women in an impersonal way. Here and there, the creatures had gotten hold of the women with their tentacles and were bringing them upward. These dark shadow things were many times larger than the women.

I was awed and baffled and I suppose my feelings clearly showed on my face, because Der Fuhrer said, "I see you are wondering what all this is about. Yes, Frau Krause?"

"Oh, sir, I—." I paused and really did not know what to say.

"Please do not worry. A fine German woman like yourself has nothing to fear. And now you will assist me in demonstrating the evolution of the superman, yes?"

"Oh, yes, sir. Yes, of course, sir."

"Excellent. Now wait here. Do not move." And our

mighty leader turned and walked toward the rear of this large chamber where I noticed there was a folding screen that looked like it was made of black wood. He went behind the screen and after a minute or two, I heard Der Fuhrer speaking in a tongue I did not understand. Since he spoke in a low voice, I suppose it is possible that I could not tell what he was saying. But I was not sure of my conclusion.

After a few minutes, Der Fuhrer returned to where I waited for him. It is difficult to relate this, but he looked very different. His eyes were blazing and his mouth seemed harder, somehow. His whole face looked tighter. I guess that is the best way to describe it. Yet he seemed full of a strange kind of energy. When he smiled at me, his teeth looked hungry.

"Ah, r'lyeh, fhtagn, my dear Frau, ah, indeed. Now I am the man wolf I have always longed to be."

I did not understand his words. But it did not matter. For I could see in his eyes what he meant. And then our great leader came over until he was standing directly in front of me and took hold of my dress and ripped it away from me. And then he ripped away my underthings and I stood naked before him with only my shoes on my feet. I was paralyzed with fear, afraid that he would do to me what had been done to the women in the paintings. But Der Fuhrer did no such thing. Instead, he encircled me with his arms and lifted me above him. I did not know he was so strong. And then when he began to play with me, swinging me up and down, and around and around, I longed for him more than I had ever longed for any man. I became delirious with desire, yearning for him.

At last he set me down. I was swooning with love

for him and knelt before him and looked up at him, pleading to let me do what I was sure he wanted me to. He looked down upon me and patted my head. And then Der Fuhrer nodded. Eagerly I reached for the buttons of his pants and undid them as quickly as I could. And then I grasped hold of his manhood and brought it out. And that was when I gasped and felt the blood rush from my head. It was very large and it was black, blacker than night, glistening, shining, pure shadow black, the black of the creatures in the paintings, and full of thick hair. As I held it in my hand, it grew even larger and soon it was I think ten inches long or more. I knew that he was unlike other men, and so I knew that I should not be shocked by what I was seeing and feeling. Der Fuhrer began to laugh and at the same time, he pushed my face into his enormous member. I opened my mouth and encircled his thing with it and he put it even farther into me, grasping my head and pushing forward. My tongue licked and circled it again and again. It was an iron bar, it was very warm, it was hot and more rigid than any man's. I sucked as hard as I could as he pumped it inside my mouth and it felt like he was going to fill my mouth with his seed, but then he pulled me up to my feet.

That was when he said, "I know what you wrote in your notes, woman. I know what you do with Josef and how he doesn't tell his wife. And now you will have your chance with me. And I will have the true test of our new species." Then Der Fuhrer encircled me again with his arms and this time he lifted me high enough to thrust his gigantic glistening upright manhood into me. It was so warm that I thought I would pass out. But it also felt so strong and so wonderful, so different, so pure and so unbelievably sexual, that I could only hold onto him, my mighty warlord, wrapping my bare legs around him and clutching his shoulders with both my hands as he had his way with me. It felt like he did not want to stop. He made strange howling sounds as he filled me with his love, so loud and piercing that I thought someone might enter the room. But I did not care. I gasped and screamed with pleasure. I knew I wanted him more than anyone I had ever met. "Oh, my great lord," I sobbed to him, again and again. He thrust into me over and over, howling the entire time, and then after I think it must have been almost forty minutes, he shouted, "Yes, and now it happens," and that was when he let loose the hottest and most powerful stream of seed I have ever felt in my entire life. He shot it into me like a supernatural force, and that is what I think it really must have been. I would have been thrown back had he not been holding me in his arms so tightly. Yet strangely, even with its power and its heat, it did not hurt me. I felt myself absorb it as quickly as it plunged into me. He was the greatest of men and my most ferocious warlord lover and I wanted him to do whatever he wanted with me. I bucked with him as he took me, my most virile warrior, the king of the world, knowing that I was his queen, at least just for that moment, knowing that I would bear his magnificent child.

And when he had finally finished with me, he set me down and said, "Now you will give rise to my offspring, the first of the new race of men. You are blessed among women. You are and shall always be an honored citizen of the glorious Third Reich." Saying that, he kissed me tenderly on the forehead and then said, "Now, Frau Krause, we must get you some clothes. Kindly wait behind the folding screen in the back and be good enough not to touch anything you see."

Trembling with both ecstasy and shock, I hastened back to the black screen and hid myself behind it while he summoned one of his staff to find a replacement for my torn apart dress. And what I saw there was certainly nothing that I would call unusual. There was a small table covered with a black cloth. Resting on the table was a small, narrow, smooth-edged box. There was nothing else that I could see. But I felt something. It was that same tense, wild energy that Der Fuhrer had possessed, or maybe been possessed with right before he ripped off my dress. I felt it and it made me tremble even more and long for him. I wanted to run back to him and throw myself at his mercy and feel him inside me again. But I could not. I waited with enormous agitation and longing. Only a few minutes later, a stout woman approached me with a clean set of handsome clothes which she handed to me in silence. I thanked her and she left as quietly as she had come.

After I dressed and returned to Der Fuhrer, he said to me, "And now my dear woman, I want you to come back to your good husband and relate to him, if you wish, what has happened here. You have my blessing. And you may also write of this in the notes you have been keeping, if you are so inclined. I trust you will keep certain aspects of our meeting completely private."

I bowed to him and said, "Oh, yes, sir. Yes, of course." And then because I could not help myself, I cried out, "Oh, my Fuhrer, my great leader, will I ever see you again? Please, sir, please, let me! I long for you so." And then I broke down in tears like a little girl.

Our great warlord, our mighty leader, regarded me with the eyes of one who has seen much in his life and said, "No, my dear Frau, no. I have too much to do. However, if you need anything, please be sure to mention what it is to Herr Goebbels, and I will insure that it is taken care of. I should also tell you that I will be checking the progress of the developing life inside you through Dr. Schirmer, one of our finest physicians at the Reichstag Hospital. He will visit you from time to time and tell me what I need to know. And of course, when you are ready to bring this child into the world, I will be there in the hospital, waiting with great anticipation the coming of our destiny. Now, dear Frau, return to your duties and allow me, if you please, to return to mine."

Der Fuhrer bowed to me and gestured at the same time toward the entrance to the chamber. I bowed to him as well, but when I arose, he was walking toward the folding screen. I left the great chamber still trembling and returned to Herr Goebbels' office and then to mine. My master said not a word, but nodded to me as I came in the door.

Everything that I have written down here happened to me as I described it. And now, as our great leader said, I will await the coming of our destiny. I have not yet told Friedrich of these things. I am sure he will be amazed and absolutely delighted with the news.

Report of Dr. Manfred Schirmer, Reichstag Hospital, Medical Corps, July 1936:

The condition of the soldiers W. Steinmetz and O. Hahnemann has worsened considerably. They are now swathed in bandages from head to foot. A disclosure of the flesh beneath any bandaged area reveals a dark, foul-smelling mass of necrotic tissue. The decay has spread from the previous state to the point now where there is hardly any skin that has not been affected in both men. In addition, the vomiting has increased in frequency, as have the night terrors. These latter two facts I learned from the men's poorly written statements, not verbally, owing to the extensive decay in the facial area precluding the use of the tongue and lips for coherent communication. Indeed, eating has become quite difficult and the two men in the last week or so have had to rely on liquid nourishment to sustain themselves. Even so, the emesis continues to be composed of the same dark chunky matter observed earlier.

And at this time, it is my duty to make an additional observation. Completely apart from the advanced nature of this condition, it appears that both of these men appear to be changing. That is, metamorphosing into something altogether different from anything resembling a member of the human species. This is indicated not only by massive necrosis of dermic tissue, but also by gross distension of the limbs and something perhaps even more frightening. Along the spinal column, extending from the lumbar all the way to the cervical areas, there appear to be a series of excresences. These resemble nothing so much as clusters of tiny appendages which have the same dark appearance as the exudate from the necrotic tissue. They are more substantial in consistency and rather smooth in texture. This phenomenon is unlike any I have ever seen and without question surpasses what I have come across in all my medical experience as the most bizarre manifestation of any disease or illness. I have excised a small piece of this tissue for further study.

In the meantime, there is little else that can be done for these men other than continuous observation and feeding. The metamorphosis that they are undergoing, if I may make a more personal observation, seems to be taking them into a realm heretofore unknown to man. It is impossible to say with any certainty at this time if they are regressing or instead moving into a biological state that perhaps in some way exceeds that of man himself.

The young woman with whom Steinmetz had engaged in sexual activity was located. She and the two wives have also been quarantined. All three show signs of the same condition as the two men, although not as advanced at this time. Several of the staff assigned to the enclosure reserved for these five people have complained vehemently about their appearance and odor and have asked either that they be reassigned to a different unit or that the patients be removed to a different area. Two of the more aggressive staff suggested that the five be exterminated. I have rejected this option because of the remarkable transformation they are experiencing which necessitates close and continuous examination. Although previously I found this entire set of phenomena loathsome, at this time I find it far too unusual to dismiss.

If only it were possible to know what these individuals were thinking and feeling. Or do they continue to have thoughts and feelings? Have those quintessentially human functions been replaced by some other class of experience which cannot even be imagined? Perhaps one day I shall discover the answer to these questions.

Diary extract of Karl Ritzler, filmmaker, July 1936:

I have just participated in a private meeting with our Minister of Popular Enlightenment and Propaganda to whom I was summoned quite discreetly. Herr Goebbels informed me that there is to be an announcement and a demonstration of great import within the week by Der Fuhrer and Dr. H. Herr Goebbels will use his influence to see to it that I attend the meeting as one of the two representatives of the artistic community. The other is to be the novelist Johann Schemm.

There is a specific reason for my presence at this event. Herr Goebbels requested that I make use of the newly developed miniature film camera to film the proceedings. This would be done without the knowledge of Der Fuhrer or Herr Doctor, and so I would be required to exercise extreme caution and ingenuity to accomplish the task. I am sworn to the utmost secrecy concerning this activity. The Minister mentioned that I would be closely watched from just after our meeting to the occasion of Der Fuhrer's announcement and were I to disclose my intentions to any person I would be shot on sight. I swore to Herr Goebbels that I would never reveal the substance of our discussion to a living soul. He seemed satisfied with my rejoinder and requested that I leave his office immediately upon the conclusion of our meeting. On my way out, he mentioned that I would be notified of the time and place of the great announcement.

THE FIRE OF THE DARK

Recording on magnetic tape made of Commandant Rudolf Pohl in his cell in Kreslau Prison, July 1936:

Agh, I am, cthulu, mlwaghn, no (sounds of vomiting). Plwthawn, help, nlwyn gnulwp, please, fhtagn rlyeh, shoot, (some sort of snuffling sound). Ylgnwa nthapl, kill me, agh, kill, wnthlyga, die now, die, kill me (vomiting). (Snuffling again, followed by a long, rumbling wail, then four or five gunshots).

Final notes from the desk of Frau Wilhelmina Krause, amanuensis to Josef Goebbels, August 1936:

It is very difficult to write this for so many reasons. Friedrich has left me with our children, claiming that there is no way I can be a good and decent mother after I told him what happened with Der Fuhrer. I thought he would be proud of me, but instead he called me a tramp and a harlot.

"But Friedrich," I cried, "I'm going to have Der Fuhrer's child! Doesn't that mean anything to you?"

He spat in my face. "How do you know it won't be Herr Goebbels' child? Or perhaps the child of Herr Goering? Or Herr von Ribbentrop? I cannot take this, woman. You are a trollop and I will not be married to you any more." He slapped me and then covered his face with his hands and wept. I moved to him, but he pushed me away.

"Don't even come close to me," he said. "I will be gone by this evening. Yes, with Heinrich and Mitzi. Don't try to stop me."

And so he left. And now there is an empty space in my heart. I am trying to fill it with the presence of Der Fuhrer's child, but it does not happen. And that is another reason why this is so difficult to write. There is something very odd going on inside me and I am sure it is because of this child I am carrying. I do not mean to sound disrespectful, but I believe this is not a normal experience. The baby is making strange sounds that I hear in the middle of the night more than any other time. They are very deep rumbling sounds, like a train, but it is a train that is moving much too slowly. I am sure it is much too early for any sounds at all, even if they are strange ones like these. It is also much too early for what else is going on. There are movements. But how can this be, less than one month after Der Fuhrer gave me this child? The movements are very strong, like the child wants to rip through me. I pray to heaven this will not happen. Oh I know we do not believe in heaven now, it is such an old-fashioned idea, but I cannot help it. I am very frightened.

And I am also frightened by what is happening to me. There are a number of strange sores that have shown up on my legs and arms. Two of them have burst open and a horrible smelling dark liquid comes out of them. I have asked to see Dr. Schirmer and I have been told that he will be here soon. I cannot wait. I am very frightened. I do not know what to do. I wish Der Fuhrer could help me now. I wish anybody at all could help me. Please—oh, God—please help me.

Diary extract of Karl Ritzler, filmmaker, August 1936:
The great announcement by Der Fuhrer and Dr. H. has been postponed indefinitely owing to what appears to be Herr Doctor's disappearance. This is what Herr Goebbels communicated to me. Therefore, the Minister

has given me new instructions. What I must now do could be infinitely more dangerous than the previous plan of action.

The Minister is to meet in private with Der Fuhrer and only six others, all of whom are high level officials. I assume that refers to Goering, Hess, Himmler, von Ribbentrop, and Bormann, among others. This private meeting replaces what I understand was to be another of Der Fuhrer's grand public spectacles, which would have been held in the evening, complete with a torchlight parade. The private meeting will be held in Der Fuhrer's office.

I will attempt to gain entry to the office by posing as a member of the Totenkopf SS accompanying Herr Goebbels as a bodyguard, under the pretext of the Minister having received a letter from an unknown person threatening to kill him. I will be able to conceal the film camera within my clothing. Herr Goebbels will request that I be stationed in the vicinity of the meeting to insure the Minister's safety. He is certain that Der Fuhrer will have no objection. I will then attempt to film the proceedings of the meeting right where I am standing. The camera will be lodged just beneath my voluminous topcoat and the lens will be pointed directly at the conferees through a hole especially cut out for that purpose. I will attempt to position my arm so as to hide this hole when I am in close proximity to the attendees. Then, when I have been stationed at my post, I will drop my arm and reach inside my topcoat to activate the film camera.

I can only hope that everything will go according to plan. If it does not, it is not Herr Goebbels who will suffer.

Lawrence Greenberg

Report of Dr. Manfred Schirmer, Reichstag Hospital, Medical Corps, August 1936:

The patient Wilhelmina Krause was admitted today with multiple complications including an abnormally advanced pregnancy and symptoms similar to the two soldiers, their wives, and the young girl from the tavern. While the latter symptoms by this time were familiar to me, the advanced pregnancy was certainly the most unusual of its type in my experience and, likely enough, in that of the remainder of the staff here.

The patient's abdomen was grossly distended. According to her, the child was the offspring of Der Fuhrer which, given her state, seemed hardly credible. She was shrieking and wailing for the entire period she remained in the hospital. Once we had firmly tied her to an operating table, she repeatedly asked in a choking voice whatever nurse was within earshot and myself as well if Der Fuhrer was here in the hospital with her. When given a negative reply, she moaned and screamed all the more.

In addition to the gross distension of the abdomen, there were sounds of a highly unusual nature emanating from that same area. The sounds were low and rumbling, sometimes even like growling. The patient also complained of severe shooting pains which, she said, would last for only a few seconds but which were so intense as to occasionally induce fainting. When she was describing this symptom, she must have experienced one such episode, for she gasped audibly and nearly passed out. At the same time, I noticed a bizarre movement in the abdominal area—a sudden convexity in the lower right. This episode was one of several which began coming increasingly frequently until the patient was, for all intents and purposes, close to co-matose. And then—

And then there was a brief instant when Frau Krause opened her eyes and would have bolted upright had she not been tied down. This was when she screamed, "Let me die! I want to die!" and then passed out completely. What happened next gave just cause to her outburst. For whatever it was inside her ripped its way out of her. It was not a human child—anyone in the room at the time can attest to that. It was black as ebony, blacker than the blackest night, and it was the most grotesque thing I have ever seen in my life—far more than the two mutating soldiers. What little humanity it possessed was distorted almost beyond recognition. It blinked its bright red insectlike eyes at me once and then using its unearthly appendages—mere vestiges of human limbs—it made its way over the corpse of its poor mother, down the operating table and across the floor before all of us, who were too shocked to respond to the presence of this monstrosity. It seemed momen-tarily stymied by the room's closed door, but with little hesitation, it crawled up until it reached the doorknob, twisted it until it opened, crawled back down, and pushing the door open further, it left the room. We none of us reacted with anything but paralyzed shock.

Scarcely had we recovered from this horror when another incident occurred which left us further horri-fied, if such were possible. A mental patient who must have temporarily broken free of his quarters came rushing into the room screaming, "It's here, it's here!" and then before we could do anything to stop him, be-gan licking the trail of black ichor the "child" had left over the corpse of its mother. Within seconds, an attendant raced in and pulled the insane man from his ghastly endeavors. The two struggled fiercely and in their fight, the mental patient licked the attendant's face, smearing it with the same exudate. Then the attendant punched the insane man who fell to the ground, unconscious for the moment. The attendant apologized profusely to us all and left the room, dragging the patient behind him.

By the time any of us had thought to look out the door for a sign of the "child", it was too late. The thing was nowhere in sight.

Diary extract of Josef Goebbels, Minister of Popular Enlightenment and Propaganda, August 1936:

Last night, two days before the private meeting called by Der Fuhrer, I had occasion to speak with him at his residence concerning the future of our society. At the same time that I was so strongly moved, even hypnotized by his words, I could not help but wonder about the man. Is he really human? I would not swear to it. There are times when he gives me the chills. And soon after these thoughts came to me, Der Fuhrer's behavior suddenly changed, as if to verify their presence in my mind. He yelled for help. Sitting on the edge of his bed, he was as though paralyzed. He was seized with a panic which made him tremble violently. He uttered confused, unintelligible vociferations. Then he muttered, "It's him! It's him! He's here!" His lips had turned blue. He was dripping with sweat. He screamed, "There! Over there! In the corner! Who is it?" He began jumping up and down and howling.

I left as quickly as I could while he was in that state and hastened back to my home, to the comfort and warmth of my family. I am now convinced, more than ever, that while Der Fuhrer is the right man to lead this nation, it is imperative that, as much as possible, his actions in private be monitored. For this reason I am justified in secretly filming the forthcoming meeting.

Diary extract of Karl Ritzler, filmmaker, August 1936:

Surely I am the most fortunate man on earth. And the most astounded by what I have witnessed this night. And, as well, the most grateful to Herr Goebbels and whatever powers protected us both from the fire of the dark.

I arrived at Herr Goebbels' office at the appointed time in the garb of the Totenkopf SS with the film camera hidden safely beneath my topcoat. The Minister nodded briefly to me after I told him the camera was secure. Without further ado, we walked down the corridor to Der Fuhrer's office. We encountered no resistance on our way inside. However, once in the vestibule, Der Fuhrer's aide inquired of Herr Goebbels the reason for my presence. The Minister took him aside and in a low voice explained why I was accompanying him. The aide nodded vigorously and indicated that we should proceed.

When we entered Der Fuhrer's office, I, at least, was somewhat surprised. For those attending this private meeting were not whom I expected. Instead of Himmler, Hess, and the others whose presence I assumed, there was a group of five men and one woman, none of whom I had ever seen. They were standing in front of Der Fuhrer's large desk facing its occupant. When we walked in, they all turned to greet us and at the same time stood aside, allowing Der Fuhrer to greet us as well. The aide, who had followed us, made his way up to his master and whispered in his ear. Der Fuhrer nodded once, and the aide left in short order.

I had never seen our leader at such a small distance before. He was shorter than I judged him at the public rallies, but the intensity of his demeanor certainly offset whatever he might have lost by his diminutive stature. His eyes blazed with a fierce darkness that was difficult to regard for any length of time. His mouth seemed locked in place; his lips were thin and tight. His brows looked permanently furrowed. When he spoke, his voice was harsh yet somehow completely captivating. This, I think, was owing to the ferocious sincerity of his words.

As for the others in attendance, they were a strange looking lot indeed. The woman was quite stout with close cropped black hair that looked pasted on. She had a rather blank expression on her face which never changed during the entire course of the meeting. Her name was Petra Blavatsky. She was the niece of the well known Madame Helena Blavatsky.

The five men were all introduced to Herr Goebbels by Der Fuhrer as some of the leading thinkers of the Third Reich. One was tall and gaunt, almost cadaverous looking. This was Helmut Reichert, a theoretical physicist. Another, Rolf Kramen, was even stouter than Fraulein Blavatsky. His bald head glistened with ever present sweat. His specialty was biological chemistry. Dernsford Chamberlain was an Englishman, son of the great Houston Stewart Chamberlain whose work, *Foundations of the Twentieth Century,* I had read excerpts from, as had many of the Nazi intelligentsia. The son resembled his father in the set of his jaw and his receding hairline. And there was Hans Horbiger, who looked more than anything else like a Biblical prophet with his long white hair and equally long beard. His Doctrine of Eternal Ice had been embraced by Der Fuhrer as the cosmological gospel of the Third Reich. Finally, there was Rudolf Glauer, also known as Heinrich von Sebbotendorf, the founder of the secret and powerful Thule Society which our leader had proudly claimed to have joined in his earlier days. Herr Glauer was, I thought, a timid looking man with almost nondescript features.

"Well, gentlemen," Der Fuhrer said, "and madame," nodding toward Fraulein Blavatsky, "I am delighted that you could all find your way here this evening. I wish us to meet further inside. If you would all follow me, please." So saying, he walked to the rear of his office and stopped in front of one of the large bookcases there. He then pulled out a large volume whereupon the bookcase moved inward, opening into a large hidden room. Der Fuhrer led the way inside.

This room was noticeably larger than the office we had come from. And its ceiling was painted with a mural so bizarre I could not help but gasp. Unfortunately, I had little time to take note of the details; as soon as all of us were inside, Der Fuhrer immediately motioned the group to sit at a round conference table which stood in the middle of the room. I took my position not far from the table and in short order, activated the camera. Thanks to two rather large candelabras suspended from the strangely decorated ceiling, I had ample light for my film work.

The leader of our people began by walking around the group, peering closely at every person as if studying the details of each face. This included Herr Goebbels. No one said a word. Once he had completed this task, he returned to his seat and, standing, began the meeting as follows:

"I had told you all that Herr Doctor could not be with us this evening because he had disappeared. This is not quite correct. This you may discover in due time. But, for now, we will discuss the purpose of our meeting."

And here Der Fuhrer spoke of the necessity for all Germans to strive for greatness, to attain the highest possible level of accomplishment in their chosen fields, and, more important than anything else, to understand the necessity for change. Change, he said, was synonymous with growth and development. Change was the nature of life. And the most essential change was that of man becoming what he was meant to be—a superman.

"We shall bring out a religion peculiar to our race," he said, "one which embraces not only the concept of the superman, but the knowledge, the means to attain such a status. Make no mistake about it. The superman is living amongst us now! He is here! I have seen this New Man. He is intrepid and cruel. I was afraid of him. Do any of you dare to meet him, to know him as he really is? Do any of you wish to meet the destiny of the human race—that which each of you yourselves have the opportunity to become?"

Der Fuhrer regarded the group with a look of such fierceness that none of them answered him. That, at least, seemed one of the reasons for their lack of response.

THE FIRE OF THE DARK

"I will take your silence as consent," he said forcefully. "So now you shall see."

And with that, he retreated to the rear of the large room where stood a black folding screen. He walked behind the screen and emerged quickly, carrying a small box. Der Fuhrer then placed the box on the conference table.

"Thanks to the profound knowledge of our colleague Dr. H., we were able to unearth this artifact. It has been of immense help to our cause. Let me demonstrate to you its workings so that you may see for yourselves the power with which we can effect the great change from man to superman."

He closed his eyes and after only a minute or so, began chanting in a language completely unknown to me.

"Cthulu f'htagn. Nyarlahotep f'htagn. Ahriman f'htagn. Hastur f'htagn. Shuggoth f'htagn. Glaaki f'htagn. Zoth-Ommog f'htagn. Yidhra f'htagn. Yog-Sothoth f'htagn. Azathoth f'htagn. Tsathoggua f'htagn. Lloigor f'htagn. Dagon f'htagn. Atlach-Nacha f'htagn. Zhar f'htagn. Ghroth f'htagn. Ymnar f'htagn. Ngyr-Khorath f'htagn. Ubbo-Sathla f'htagn. Shug-Niggorath f'htagn. R'lyeh f'taglhnya ph'glyapyn nl'wga bnhya! Gah'lm l'phnggu pwao! Djlya ggnlnu cyylgna!"

The silence that the conferees had answered Der Fuhrer's questions and statements with before was now infinitely more profound. What then took place staggered the imagination. The box began to glow from within. The light that emanated was dark blue and in only a few seconds it permeated the entire chamber. And that was when, to my regret, the quality of the film began to diminish considerably, as I discovered later while running the footage. This light was like a blue fire; the room began to grow warmer. Soon most of the attendees were showing signs of discomfort with the rapidly building heat. As this heat increased, so too did the intensity of the light. Yet by intensity here I mean not the brightness, but the darkness, if that can be imagined. And in the heat of this blue darkness, Der Fuhrer shrieked, "R'lyeh mlw'gfah nglyu f'htagn!" followed by "The superman is amongst us! He is here! He is—Herr Doctor!"

He pointed toward the ceiling and everyone, myself included, looked upward. The ceiling, covered with the weird designs so reminiscent in theme of Vlad the Impaler, began to shimmer. This phenomenon was not the effect of the light upon the ceiling; it was the actual fabric of matter itself that was moving in an infinite number of infinitely small wavelike distortions. That is perhaps the most accurate way to describe it. This shimmering itself increased in intensity until the ceiling was actually vibrating—that is, the wavelike distortions increased in size. The vibratory activity was both visually and mentally painful, yet impossible to ignore. At the same time that everyone present was staring blankly at this bizarre spectacle, they were holding their heads with expressions of agony on their faces. That is, everyone but Der Fuhrer. His harsh laughter seemed a fitting aural counterpart to what we were all experiencing. The vibrating became, finally, large waves of matter, as though a giant had found the ceiling to be a dirty carpet and grabbed hold of it with both hands to shake it out.

Then occurred the climax of these wavelike distortions. The rolling increased in intensity until the entire ceiling was like an enormous flag flapping in a brisk wind. And this enormous flapping wave parted close to if not directly at the midpoint of the ceiling. It was like that old Biblical story of Moses and the Red Sea. Only instead of water parting to reveal dry land, this was matter parting to reveal black empty space. And instead of a prophet walking on the dry land with his followers behind him, there was something so ghastly that it cannot be believed. It was a monster—huge, black, glistening—whose hundreds of appendages whipped around in all directions, as though searching randomly for what would appease its hunger as quickly as possible. With its appearance, the painful thrumming of the vibrations was replaced by an abysmally low rumbling sound. And while the room prior to the appearance of this gargantuan horror was intensely warm, now it became unbearably hot. Fraulein Blavatsky and Herr Glauer could do nothing but scream, yet remained seated in place. All the others, including Herr Goebbels and myself, were completely transfixed, paralyzed in complete terror and silent awe.

"Behold the creation of the superman!" Der Fuhrer shrieked. "This is Herr Doctor! This is the New Man in his ultimate form!"

The continuous screaming of the fraulein and Herr Glauer must have ultimately attracted the abomination to them. Two impossibly long tentacles lashed out; each found one of the two hapless victims who was encircled and, still screaming, engulfed in what could perhaps be termed the thing's maw, though certainly there was no shape or outline to delineate such a structure.

With that occurrence, we all bolted out of our seats

and ran for the door. (Of course, that did not include Der Fuhrer.) I heard Herr Professor Horbiger exclaim, "Ach du leiber!" Everyone remaining was able to escape the fire of the dark—except, unfortunately, Herr Professor Kramen. His portly waddle did not take him far enough as quickly as he would have liked. A brief glance over my shoulder confirmed that another tentacle had found him. The last thing everyone heard before we were all out of earshot was Kramen's high-pitched scream and Der Fuhrer's laughter. Once outside the office building, each person rapidly went his own way without saying a word to anyone else. As to what transpired within that room after our departure, I have no knowledge.

There is scant likelihood that anyone of rational mind will believe this story and, as previously mentioned, because of the unusual light, the film footage from the latter part of the meeting is faulty. The only segment that remains demonstrating the absolutely surrealistic character of what happened is that of Der Fuhrer chanting in that strange language.

I tried to make an appointment with Herr Goebbels, but his secretary told me, again and again, that he was not available. I will, then, retain this film in a secure place and disclose to no one my involvement in this incident.

Report of Dr. Manfred Schirmer, Reichstag Hospital, Medical Corps, August 1936:

No, this is not an actual report. It is—I do not know exactly what it is. It is a relating of what has happened and of what may happen. It is, perhaps, a warning to those who may find my papers after I am gone. It is a testament to the madness of this era. It is, more than anything else, a futile cry for mercy from whoever or whatever can grant it. I have no doubt now that mercy will not come for us.

It did not take long to discover that Frau Krause's "child" was destroyed by an officer whose wounds had healed sufficiently to allow him movement. One look at the detestable thing and he drew his Luger and fired into it as many shots as were in the gun's chamber. This took place directly in the hospital room where the other patients present reacted with justifiable shock. I did not know the whereabouts of the event. Otherwise I would have cautioned those who came to dispose of the remains to refrain completely from touching the thing. I do not know if any physical contact occurred.

The two mutated soldiers eventually began babbling in a tongue I have never heard, interspersed with wails of total anguish. They had mutated to such an extent that even I could not sanction their survival. For that reason, they, too, were destroyed. I had no choice but to authorize as well the special treatment of their wives and the young girl.

But I am certain this is not ended. How exactly did Frau Krause become pregnant? What being could have sired such a monstrosity? Could the "father" of her child be the source of all this grotesque destruction of our people? And what of the young girl? Had she engaged in sexual contact with anyone other than the unfortunate soldier? And what of the mental patient who licked up the "child's" ichor? And the hospital attendant whom the insane man licked? And the woman artist? And those who disposed of the remains of the "child"? I myself must have made contact with one or more of the patients suffering these strange symptoms. For now I find that several of those sores have burst forth on my body, oozing the same dark, thick fluid. It does not help matters to have found out only yesterday that my wife is now with child.

It seems more than likely that what I had previously wondered concerning the thoughts and feelings of those mutated soldiers will now come to pass for me. That is, unless I end my life now and spare myself the inevitable anguish that must occur. Of course, I would have to do the same for Hilda. No rational man would want his wife to suffer as I would, or to bring anything even remotely resembling Frau Krause's "child" into this world. Would he?

Extract from a letter written by the novelist Johann Schemm to Gregor Strasse, September 1936:

Ah, my dear Gregor, we are truly living in glorious times. Our society continues to grow and prosper and I have found great success with my writing. Only yesterday, Reinhold Semmler, the well known publisher, agreed to a large print release of my latest novel *The Joyful Leader.* I am overjoyed and honored to be one of the select writers whom Herr Semmler has favored with his firm. I know now that there is no doubt not only of my continued good fortune, but that of our great nation. Let us give thanks to Der Fuhrer for his excellent leadership as he ably guides our ship of state through the perils of this world. I am sure that you, too, Gregor, are prospering. Please let me know through what course your own life takes you. I wish you all the best.

THE FIRE OF THE DARK

Directive from the office of Josef Goebbels, Minister of Popular Enlightenment and Propaganda, September 1936:

The filmmaker Karl Ritzler is to be picked up for questioning in the matter of suspected misappropriation and unauthorized use of an experimental piece of equipment from the Technical Department, Film and Cinemas.

NOTES

Most of the characters in this story are fictitious. But aside from the obvious real historical figures (Hitler, Goebbels, Madame Blavatsky), several others did exist. There actually was a Hans Horbiger who did espouse the Doctrine of Eternal Ice which, in fact, was embraced by Hitler as the Third Reich's cosmological gospel. (And he actually did look like a Biblical prophet, as described in the story.) And Houston Stewart Chamberlain was also real—an Englishman who did write the work cited, *Foundations of the Twentieth Century,* in which he lauded the emergence of a new fascist German state. However, he had no son that I know of. Similarly, Madame Blavatsky had no niece named Petra as far as I know. And there was a Rudolf Glauer (who did use the pseudonym Heinrich von Sebbotendorf) who was the founder of the Thule Society, a group of occultists to which Hitler did belong in his earlier days. Dr. H. is based somewhat on the real personage of Karl Haushofer, a professor, who was a major influence on Hitler. Haushofer's son, who later defected to the Allies, stated that his father was responsible for letting loose on the world the "Beast of the Apocalypse."

Other aspects of the story are based on fact as well. The Gleichschaltung was established by Goebbels to insure that all creative works—film, fiction, art, and so on—conformed to the philosophy of the Third Reich. And there was a Film and Cinemas Bureau which approved all films made by German directors. This bureau was one of several for which Goebbels was responsible. (And the bureau did have a Technical Department.) In addition, the Ahnenerbe actually did exist. This Occult Bureau had the mission of discovering and/or retrieving relics of value to the German state and insuring that they made their way back to the confines of the Third Reich. This is documented in, among other works, *The Spear of Destiny* by Trevor Ravenscroft.

I have taken some obvious liberties with the details of Hitler's and Goebbels' personal history. Yet the description that Goebbels gives of Hitler's paranoia in his bedroom is documented—i.e., when Hitler begins to rant, sweat, and see things that are not there. And Goebbels' doubts about Hitler's humanity, and that "he gives me the chills" are statements Goebbels actually made. Also, part of Hitler's speech to the private meeting group near the end of the story are words he actually spoke—those referring to the superman.

PLAYING IN THE STREET

by Dean Wesley Smith

Century X, #72

In the year of 1999 and seven months
Shall come a great and horrible King
To revive the great King of the Barbarians
Before and after, Mars rules by whim

Moscow, Idaho. July, 2013

A fine layer of gray dust covered everything. Old
cars, rusted, tires flat, lined the street like a huge metal
fence. Every car coated with the dust. No animal footprints, not even that of a cat crawling on the hood and
sleeping in the sun. Nothing since the gray dust fell.

Litter had spilled out of a garbage can in front of
one house and was now glued in place by the dust. The
trees were dead black skeletons, making the street appear to be in the grip of winter all year long. A stop
light at the street's end, three dark round eyes in the
sky, watched the complete lack of movement on the
quiet suburban scene. It watched the mailboxes and
the child's bike. It watched the basketball hoop above
the garage door of the split-level and the bare areas
that had once been green yards.

Before. The evidence of before was all along the
street. It lined the street. It was the street. There had

been a time of life here before the dust had settled over it. The dust had fallen at night, then it had rained and the dust had become hard, like a child's clay exposed to the air too long. It still looked mostly like a layer of gray dust, but it never altered. Not even the winter snows and spring melts could move or change it. And there was nothing anyone could do to clean it up. The dust was there to stay for centuries to come, of that there was no doubt.

The unblinking glass eyes of the old, rusted cars watched silently as the dust held its strangle hold on the neighborhood.

Now there was only silence.

Now there was only now.

And dust.

I am always careful to walk in my own footsteps. The boots of my protective suit leave large, patterned prints in the top thin layer of dust and I am careful on this street to match those prints step for step. Not doing so would feel as if I was tearing up a piece of my own history.

I always park my government van near the old grocery store and start down the street under the stoplight, keeping to the inside of the sidewalk. Seven houses down from the light is a light blue, two-story house, with a two car garage. An average house for this neighborhood and this part of the little city.

But this house is special.

Through the door is an open wood foyer. Beyond that a plush living room and then beyond that a dining room with oak tables, dishes in glass cabinets, and an empty fruit bowl in the middle of the table. Everything looks so dated, yet so familiar, as if I have just stepped into a time machine and gone back twenty years.

The rugs are rotted, the drapes hang partially ripped from the hooks by age and their own weight, and the normal dust of the years gives everything a washed out look. But the living room is still a beautiful sight to me; comfortable and yet elegant.

There is a brick fireplace against the wall opposite the front door. On the mantel of that fireplace is a picture, faded slightly, but still clear under the glass of its frame.

It is a picture of three children playing in the street in front of the house. Playing a game of catch with a football between the rows of parked cars and in the small green front yards. In the background beyond the stoplight a car is caught in the frozen motion of the *now* of the picture. There is no dust, so the colors of the picture are bright, vibrant in their life.

The three children are smiling and the cars are mostly clean. It is a picture of a street that feels like home. The children feel comfortable playing there. I remember, since I am in that picture. I am the one with the football. I was twelve. I was comfortable and happy and alive, even though at the time I never thought of it in those terms.

The picture was taken ten summers before Grandpa died and everything changed.

But I remember the time when the picture was taken, everything about life seemed enjoyable along that street. I give the street far more good times than bad. But that, too, may be nothing more than my memory coloring and adding to the scene in the picture. Sometimes I wonder.

Beside that picture on the fireplace mantel is another picture. This picture is an older one, more faded, of a young couple standing on the steps in front of the same house. She is dressed as a bride. He a groom.

Both are smiling and his arm is around her waist, holding her while she holds a large bouquet of flowers. In the reflection of the picture window behind and to the right of them is a clear picture of the street. People are standing in the driveway and on the sidewalk beside the unplanted yard. There are two empty fields across the street where houses are not yet built. The street and the neighborhood are both very young, almost as young as the smiling couple.

They are my parents. They used to live in this home.

They are still here, in bed upstairs, two skeletons covered with the dust of years. The real dust outside caught them while they slept, as it did most of this city. They died not knowing that death was floating down on them.

I consider them lucky. But it is still hard standing at the foot of that bed, looking at their skeletons. I have done so a hundred times and will probably do so another hundred.

My mother, Mrs. Richard Gilet, Dot to her friends, was still a slim woman at fifty when she died. Her arm was draped across my father's chest. I find that to be a sign that they were happy the night they died. Richard Gilet, Rich to his friends, was sleeping on his back, one arm raised over his head above the pillow. The bone of that arm holds what is left of his hair in place. What is left of Mother's dark brown hair had dropped in a bunch around the top of her pillow. The sheets and quilt were pulled up to mid chest level and their remains make very little dent under the quilt.

I am glad I did not come in here until many years after the dust. I do not think I could have stood in this room, imagining that I could smell them rotting in the summer heat through my protective suit. I am glad that the air has already taken their eyes and their skin and left the bones and hair. It is better that way.

With them as only skeletons I can still sometimes retrieve the memories of bouncing on the bed to wake them on Christmas morning. I can still remember them that morning; sleepy, smiling, the smell of them filling the room. Sometimes the memory is so strong I want to jump on the bed again to wake them.

But I do not. I need the reality of them sleeping here after death much more than I need the quick release of jumping on the bed and messing up their last scene.

At least so far. But at times that urge to jump into bed with them is very strong. Someday I may fail to resist it.

I am now older than my father was. I find life interesting that with the dust and everything since the dust, I am still here. I really don't understand what brings me to this room time after time. I have yet to visit my own room, just down the hall. I loved my own room. It was always a safe place for me.

Yet I always just visit here, in my parent's bedroom, always careful to remain in my own footprints and not move fast enough to mess anything up.

It seems odd that I have access to this small city, this frozen museum of a life twenty years past. This is a city of death. In my lifetime, and for many lifetimes to follow, no human or animal will be able to live here or walk here unprotected. But since I am the one who told the world, who gave the history of it all, who knows the most about what happened, the government sees fit to let me in.

I suppose they understand that someday I will open the protective suit and stay with my parents. But that is never talked about and for the moment they are happy to let me in and have me report back on what little I see. I am one of the very few crazy enough to even want to be here.

Yet because of my father and his father, I know what happened to this small city. And I know I feel responsible. Somehow I should have tried to stop them. I knew we didn't know enough. I knew we should have reported our findings to the government and gotten help. But I was still fairly young and just out of graduate school and my voice and my worries were not enough to stop them. My father and the others had been so sure of themselves. So sure they understood. So sure that the understanding would take them places they never imagined.

I looked at the skeletons of my sleeping parents. Maybe this trip down the street was the right time to open up my protective suit and join them.

I stood there in the same exact spot where I always stood, staring at their last embrace.

Not yet. Maybe next time.

Boise, Idaho. March 14, 1913
Idaho Governor Frank Stunenburg dropped down out of the passenger seat of the Model T. He stood thin and tall, almost too tall for a Westerner. He had sharp, dark eyes and a smile that disarmed even his most

staunch detractors. He brushed the dust off his well-worn suit and turned back to retrieve a package from beside the seat that contained material his wife had asked him to pick up. "Thanks, John," he yelled to the attorney general over the loud sputtering of the engine. "Going to have to get me one of these since they built the Governor's mansion way out here."

"That you are, Frank." John waved and swung the Model T around and started it bumping down the dirt road back toward the center of town. The governor watched, thinking that sometimes he wished things weren't moving so fast. He enjoyed horses and always had. Riding in those automobiles was hard on the kidneys. But technology was moving fast. Too fast. And when the world heard about the discovery under that mountain outside of Moscow, it would move even faster.

He shook his head. He still wasn't going to believe what they had told him until he got up there and took a look for himself.

He sighed. It had been a hard day all the way around. Actually a hard month, with the union mining problems up North. He wished like hell they could have just included that part of the state in the Montana territory. But they hadn't. Back East it had all been political compromise with no attention to how difficult it was to move from the southern part of Idaho to the northern.

So, as governor, he was stuck with the unions and the problems and all the killing going on in a place that took five days during the summer to get to and was impossible to travel to in the winter. Somehow the killing and the union had to be stopped. But no one seemed to know just how to do it. He had come down hard anti-union and that stance had divided the legislature in Boise. A fistfight had even broken out yesterday on the House floor.

He could hardly wait to see what the legislators would do with the Moscow discovery.

Frank looked up at the not completely finished mansion and the young trees that surrounded it. It felt good to be home, even though they had only lived here a short time. Someday he knew the new mansion would be a place Idaho governors would be proud to live. But it, too, had caused a huge amount of resentment between the people in the north and the government in Boise in the south. Northerners were still fuming over the theft of the state seal from the northern city of Lewiston and the government's move to Boise. It had been a midnight raid and a three-day nonstop ride more than twenty years ago. But it wasn't anywhere near forgotten.

Between the Moscow discovery, the seat of government and the union problems in the northern mines, he would be lucky to keep the young state in one piece over the next few years.

A new white fence ran across the front of the mansion and down the left side. A stream and a grove of maple trees bordered the right side. It was a beautiful setting above the growing main city. The government planners had been right to build it here. He was proud to be its first resident.

Frank hefted the package and started for the front gate. For the last month the gate had stood wide open, held that way by a large rock. But now it was closed. Frank thought nothing of it.

PLAYING IN THE STREET

He switched his wife's package to his left hand, flipped the latch up on the gate, and pulled.

The explosion sent most of the Governor of Idaho flying back into the middle of the road and left a crater the size of a house in front of the new governor's mansion.

North of Moscow, Idaho. October 6, 1979

"Your grandfather's notes say it is about here," my dad said as he pushed aside the underbrush and climbed over a small ridge of rock. I looked up at the red back of dad's hunting jacket as he picked his way up through the pine trees and underbrush. I couldn't believe I was with him on this crazy treasure hunt. We were a good half mile up the mountain above Grandpa's house and I was beginning to think we were going to be lost. Or worse, shot by a stupid deer hunter who thought our crashing through the brush was a reason to shoot.

It was bad enough that my crazy grandfather had died, especially right in the middle of my senior football season and the roughest semester I had signed up for in four years. But now dad was acting like a strange kid since he found Grandpa's journal.

Three hours ago Dad had been up in the attic cleaning out and sorting Grandpa's things. When he came down, he looked as if he had seen a ghost. Mom asked him if he was all right and he handed her a yellow paper and then a journal that had *Gold Mine* written on the outside in gold pen. He said it was Grandpa's handwriting.

"Take a look at this," Dad said, and sat down at the kitchen table where Grandpa used to sit and smoke.

The house still held the thick, rich smell of his pipe smoke, but with the windows open and the cool fall air from the surrounding forest coming in, the place was almost bearable.

I crowded in behind Mom and we both read. The first entry in the journal said that Grandpa and Grandma had moved to Moscow from Boise back in 1914 to find a lost gold mine.

Dad flipped quickly ahead in the journal. Grandpa and Grandma had lived in Moscow and a large number of the entries for the next year tell about Grandpa's search for the mine. In May of 1915 his journal says he found the abandoned mine on the back side of Moscow Mountain. But the mouth of the mine had caved in and he would need money and time to dig it out. He was going to very quietly check around town to see if anyone had a claim filed. For some reason that entry seemed almost paranoid.

The next entry in the journal a week later was about how much trouble he would have getting a claim to the land because the previous owner had disappeared years before under very strange circumstances.

Next entry was very short. "May have mentioned the mine to the wrong person."

There was another short entry a month later about meeting a man named Carl and the other members of the Wheelbarrow Association. The entry said they were the ones who had collapsed the entrance to the old mine, called the Lost Wheelbarrow Mine. Grandpa said in the entry that he had dinner with the men of the association and there was no way they were going to allow him to open the mine back up.

He feared for his and Grandma's life, since it was

obvious these men would do anything to keep the mine closed. And had numbers of times before.

The last entry was a month later. All it said was, "They took me inside the mine. Now I understand. Joined the Association. Youngest member. Let us hope I will be the last."

Then in a different color ink Grandpa had scratched, "I was right about the governor."

There was nothing else in the journal except a deed showing that Grandpa owned a huge chunk of the back side of Moscow Mountain and a map drawn years later after Grandmother had died in 1955. Grandpa had built a house on the back side of Moscow Mountain the next year. The map gave exact directions to the mine from the house. The location on the map of the mine was inside the land that Grandpa owned and the deed gave clear ownership of the Lost Wheelbarrow Mine to Grandpa. And now Dad. Grandpa had scratched on the side of the deed, "No gold left."

By the time Mom and I finished reading, Dad could hardly contain himself. He had never heard Grandpa talk at all about the mine or why Grandpa and Grandma had moved to Moscow or why Grandpa had moved to the back of Moscow Mountain. It just hadn't occurred to Dad to ask. In fact Dad had no idea that Grandpa had owned so much forest land.

Dad wanted to go see if we could find the mine and Mom wanted nothing to do with it. So Mom decided to keep cleaning while Dad and I went up to the mountain looking for the old mine site. It was a wild goose chase, as far as I was concerned, but Mom wouldn't let Dad go alone because he had had heart pains last year. I was elected.

Dad scrambled over the top of a slight ridge and disappeared through some underbrush. A moment later I heard him say, "Got it." Then, as if I hadn't been right behind him the entire time he yelled "Gary, it's over here."

I ducked under brush and around a large pine and came out into a slight clearing about fifty yards wide. It looked as if someone had kept the trees and brush cut back. Across the clearing in front of me the mountain side went up sharply and there was a rock outcropping to the right. Even with the growth of brush under the outcropping I could see where a long time before there had been a cut into the side of the hill. Dad was standing in front of the cut, looking through the brush.

I moved up beside him. "Any opening?" I asked.

Dad shook his head. "Doesn't look like it." He broke back some limbs and climbed around where the opening should have been. After a minute he said, "No luck."

He backed out into the clearing and stood looking around. "Your grandfather must have kept this area cut back for some reason. It looks as if there is the remains of a road coming in here." I looked to the right where he had pointed. It still took me a moment to see the faint possibility of a road cut into the hillside, now overgrown with sixty-year-old trees.

Granted, it was fascinating thinking that way back in the past someone had dug a mine here. It was sort of thrilling to think there was some mystery about it that Grandpa had kept to himself. But mostly right then I was worried about passing a City Planning test tomorrow morning and then making it through football practice at three. I had already missed three practices because of Grandpa's death.

"Dad. Mind if we head back now?"

He stood for a moment, hands on hips, staring at the cut in the mountain, nodding. "No problem," he said. "But guess where I'm going to spend next summer?"

"Water-skiing behind our new boat?"

He laughed. "Well, just maybe. We might buy one. Right after I open up this old mine."

He started off down the hill before I even had a chance to groan. I knew for a fact I was going to get stuck helping him.

Moscow, Idaho. October 17, 1979

Actually it was while I was standing under a hot shower trying to clear some of the aches from grueling football practice that I figured out how to get into Grandpa's old mine. Grandpa himself had told us in his journal, but we just hadn't seen it.

Since we had found the journal, Dad had become a different man. He was pricing equipment for digging and making all sorts of plans to get inside that mountain. He and I had been back up there twice and his excitement was starting to be catching. I found myself daydreaming about it in class and now standing in the shower after practice I figured out that there had to be another way in.

I got dressed as quickly as I could and headed for the University library. After a full hour I had discovered a huge number of books on gold mines and mining. But nothing I could use right off. So I did the next most logical thing. I headed over to the College of Mines. It was supposed to be the best in the country, so it seemed realistic that someone there would be able to answer my question.

And I was right. A mining grad student named Carol occupied the giant wooden front desk in the college office. She stood, on a good day, five foot even, and had big brown eyes and a smile that made me stammer. The desk dwarfed her, yet somehow she held her own against it.

She listened patiently to my request and then took me to a huge book of diagrams about how most gold mines were dug in the northwest, depending on location and ground formation.

I told her what the area around Grandpa's mine looked like, approximately when it was dug, and told her it was in this area. She showed me how those mines would have been dug, made me copies of diagrams, and then asked if there was anything else she could help me with.

"Actually, there is," I said. "I was wondering if it was normal, and how, and maybe why, someone would open a second entrance to a mine."

"Sure. They did it like this," she said and flipped to a section farther back in the same volume. It took her a moment to find what she was looking for, then pointed it out to me. "Almost always they went sideways along the same line and started a new shaft. Usually the second shaft would angle in to help cut down distance to the surface after a main shaft had followed a vein too far underground."

I stared at the illustration. It seemed so simple in drawings, but I knew what that hillside looked like, covered in thick trees and brush. This was not going to be as easy as it sounded.

"Of course," Carol said, "if the original shaft went down or up following the vein, then they would start the second shaft to attempt to match the rise or fall."

I sighed. "What you are telling me is if there is a second shaft it could be anywhere in a radius of 500 feet around the first shaft."

Again she laughed. I was starting to enjoy that sound even though she was mostly laughing at my problem. "Actually, it could be a lot farther than five hundred feet. Some of the old gold mines in this area went on for thousands of feet underground."

"Great. Just great. You want to spend some time with me Saturday hiking in the mountains looking for a mine?" I actually meant the question almost jokingly.

"I'd love to," she said, "on one condition."

"What's that?"

"You tell me your name."

I did and we also agreed to have dinner Friday evening. I left thanking Grandpa and his stupid mine. The week was looking up.

Moscow, Idaho. October 21, 2025.

This would be my last trip into the dead city. It seemed sort of obvious that I should make this trip on the anniversary of the date Carol and I found the second entrance to the mine.

I plan on leaving the government van just inside the edge of the what is not so laughingly called the *Dead Zone* and walk the rest of the way. I should be able to cover my tracks enough that it will never occur to anyone to trace me to my parent's old home. Besides, as long as they get the van back, no one is going to waste much time on an old man like me. Not after all these years.

Carol would have laughed at this as being stupid. But Carol died of cancer years ago. I always blamed the mountain for her death. I supposed now it is responsible for mine. But I am old and don't have much time left anyway. If she were still alive, she would have known where I would have gone. She would have tried to stop me. But she is no longer with me. Has not been for years. Now I would rather just be left alone.

I think she would have understood that.

I park the van near the road beside what had been an old gas station. The bright yellow of the van stands out against the dull gray of the dust. They will have no problem finding it.

I leave tracks into the gas station and then out the other side, letting my prints blend into others I have made over the years. Then I move out onto the road and start walking toward town, staying within the tracks the van has left during my hundreds of visits. My footprints will never show.

I walked slowly, taking my time. I am old and the hills around this little city are steep. Besides, I am in no hurry.

Boise, Idaho. August 16, 1913

Harold Gilet stood against the back wall of the hot courtroom and watched Clarence Darrow stride back and forth in front of the jury of twelve men, all dressed in suits, all looking very uncomfortable in the heat. Hundreds of reporters and spectators jammed the room, their notepads held at ready, some scratching down what Darrow was saying, others using the pads as fans.

The huge open windows of the courthouse let in the street noise and once in a while a breath of breeze, but not near enough to suit Harold. He used today's newspaper to fan himself, but even that didn't seem to help. The heat and the smell of packed human flesh was overwhelming.

But he couldn't leave. He had to stay to get his suspicions confirmed one way or another. The governor had been killed because of a gold mine outside of Moscow, not because of the union problems in the silver mines farther north.

But as yet, in all the days of the trial, not one word of the old gold mine had been spoken. It was as if no one knew about it.

Senator Borah, the Boy Orator as they called him in Washington, D.C., sat peacefully at a table in front of the judge with Idaho State's Attorney General. Harold could tell that the senator was listening intently to every word Darrow said. Darrow was considered the hottest young attorney in the nation. When he had offered to defend John Stevens for free in the bombing death of the governor, the attorney general had called Washington and asked if Senator Borah would come home and help in the prosecution for the state.

Of course, the case had brought the press. Besides having a governor assassinated, the future of the unions in the silver mines of Northern Idaho rode on this trial. And the future of a lot of mining unions all over the country.

If Stevens could be proven to have union connections and the governor was killed on the orders of the unions as everyone suspected, the mine's owners would win. The unions would be dead. But if Stevens was just a lone wolf, taking his hatred of the mines, and what they had done to him and his family, out on the governor, then that would not hurt the unions. And the fighting would continue.

But Harold Gilet was sure the governor's death was because of another mine completely. A lost gold mine outside of the northern town of Moscow. He had overheard the wildest conversation possible two days before the governor was killed.

He had been up in Idaho City, courting Mary, his soon to be wife. Her dad had a small placer claim there and had built Mary and her mother a cabin just above the creek. Harold had camped down and across the creek in a small grove of pine trees. Somewhere in the early morning hours he woke to the sound of a horse just beyond the grove. His fire had died down to nothing more than embers and through the trees he could see the faint flickering of a light.

With gun in one hand, he crept from his bedroll and moved silently toward the light. Beside the creek trail a man stood, holding the reins of a horse with one hand and a small lantern with the other. He seemed to be staring off down the trail in the direction of Idaho City.

So Harold settled in and waited. In this part of the country, unless you wanted to be shot, you never sneaked up on another man. Too many claim jumpers still worked the mountains.

In a very short time another rider approached and dismounted. He was wearing the clothes of a gentleman even at this time of the night. Harold could even see the chain of the man's pocket watch hanging from his vest. He was obviously from Idaho City or Boise.

"You got the caps?" the gentleman asked the other, who was dressed like a dirt miner and wore a rain slicker, even though it wasn't raining. Harold now wished he had gotten closer because he couldn't see either of their faces in the flickering lantern light.

The miner patted the horse's saddle bags. "All set. I'll pick up the dynamite down on the river."

"Good," the gentleman said. "Make sure you make it look right. Then get back north to Moscow."

"Don't you worry. The union will take the fall. You sure about this?"

Harold could see the gentleman nod. "Absolutely. We can't let word of the gold mine get out. Outside of Moscow, he's the only one who knows about it. It was a mistake to tell him about it. With him gone and the mine on the back side of that mountain, no one is going to find it. Better that it stays lost."

Without a handshake or another word both men mounted up and rode off in different directions. Harold went back to bed, wondering what that had been all about. The next day Mary agreed to be his wife and two days later he heard about the governor being killed by a bomb.

He and Mary were married in Idaho City and then moved down to Boise. When the trial started, Harold crowded into the courtroom every day with the reporters. He had thought about going to the attorney general with what he had heard, but he couldn't identify the men and the more he thought about it the more none of what he had heard made sense. He decided to wait and see if anything about a lost gold mine came up in the trial. If it did, he would then tell what he had heard.

But not one word was ever said about a lost gold mine outside of Moscow. Stevens was convicted, without a connection made between him and the unions. Over the next year Harold couldn't seem to shake the idea of there being a lost gold mine outside of Moscow. A mine that had gotten the governor of the state killed.

So with the help of Mary's father, the following summer they moved to Moscow with the idea that Harold would get an engineering degree. That summer Harold helped with the wheat harvest around Moscow and that fall he started school at the new land grant university there.

On weekends, without telling anyone, he explored the back side of Moscow Mountain.

Moscow, Idaho. October 21, 1979

Carol ended up knowing a great deal more about mountain hiking than I did. She discovered that fact over dinner Friday and later at her apartment. I didn't much care. By Saturday morning I was in love with the short, brown-haired grad student. She could lead me into any wilderness area she wanted, any time she wanted.

But where she did lead me first thing Saturday morning was to the local outdoor supply store. She had me buy a good pair of boots and a thick pair of gloves. We picked up a pack, a small ax, and a folding shovel. Also three flashlights and a good lantern, just in case. By the time we added food, matches, and toilet paper, I was out two hundred bucks.

PLAYING IN THE STREET

We left my car at my grandfather's place where Dad joined us. After I introduced him to Carol, he whistled at my new boots and gloves and nodded thoughtfully at the sight of the shovel, ax, and flashlights. I had told Dad the day before what we were planning on looking for and when. He had gotten really excited and decided to join us. At first I had been annoyed at that. I had hoped to spend the time alone with Carol. But after spending the night with her, it now didn't matter. I just knew we were going to be spending a lot of time together for years to come.

Dad had packed us a large knapsack of lunch and when we reached the mine site, he dropped the sack on a stump and sat down beside it. I could tell he was breathing hard, but I couldn't tell if it was from the climb or the excitement. Carol was fine, not even winded. I thought I was in good shape from football, but that climb had still made me suck a little air. Carol just kept on impressing me.

Carol dropped her small pack and moved over in front of the old mine entrance. She climbed in around the bushes, studying the old entrance to the mine and then the rocks around it. "Looks to me," she said, pointing at the angle of the rock outcropping, "that they followed the vein in here and went down at a slight angle and to the right."

"So we look to down there?" I asked, pointing in the direction of the old road.

She shrugged. "Seems as logical as any place to start. Remember, chances are it won't look like a mine entrance. And it might go straight down to start and then turn inward."

"So what exactly should we look for?" Dad said.

Again Carol shrugged. "Anything that looks odd. Maybe nothing more than a slight depression in the side of the hill."

"Simple enough," I said.

Carol only laughed.

Of course, she was right. It turned out anything but simple. We spread out and slowly angled our way down the hill to the right of the mine, climbing over logs, slipping on loose sticks, scratching our faces and arms on sharp brush.

Two hours and two breaks later it was Dad who finally spotted the entrance.

"Gary. Carol. Over here," he called out and I scrambled up through some thick brush to reach his side just as Carol came down through the trees above him.

At first I couldn't see what he was looking at. But then slowly it became clear. Behind some branches and slightly to the side of a huge pine there were some old wooden planks covered with dirt and rock. Actually the only reason he had even found it was that a deer had used the area to bed down and had knocked off some of the layers of rock, dirt, and pine needles, uncovering one of the boards.

"Wow," Carol said, studying the old board and the area around it. "Someone really didn't want this found, did they?"

"Sure seems that way," Dad said. "Actually, the more I read the old journal, the more I think this place was something much more than a gold mine."

"Well," I said. "Let's open it up and find out, shall we? Carol, any suggestions as to how we might go about this?"

"Carefully, would be my suggestion. Very carefully.

PLAYING IN THE STREET

These old mines can be very dangerous. Wood exposed to the elements for seventy or eighty years will be completely rotten."

We spent the next hour slowly opening up the hole. The one thing we hadn't remembered to bring was a hammer, so the shovel and ax served for most of the duty.

The second entrance turned out to be a hole about five feet square that went straight down into the ground about ten feet. An old wooden ladder was secured against one wall. The shaft of the mine turned directly into the hillside. Obviously this entrance had been built to be covered easily and hidden. Carol said she was impressed that there were no signs at all of tailings. She said they must have hauled all the dirt out by bucket and then by wheelbarrow.

It was two in the afternoon before we finally had the entrance cleared enough to go in. Carol was getting as excited as Dad and I were. It was fun watching her and her radiant smile as she worked at cleaning back the brush and old wood.

Dad had brought a short rope with him, so we tied it to the closest pine and tossed it down into the hole. "Chances are the old ladder is rotted. But we might as will try to use it. Just keep hold of the rope."

"Let me try first," Carol said, "since I'm the smallest."

Dad nodded and Carol dropped on her stomach and then slowly inched her way over the lip of the hole and down. The ladder held her and the floor of the hole was solid dirt. I didn't bother with the ladder. I just lowered myself over the edge and dropped to the bottom. Then with Carol on one side and me on the other we helped Dad down the old ladder.

"Lights," Dad said, clicking on his light and ducking inside the old tunnel."

"Not too fast," Carol said. "Let me check out the timbers. We don't want this caving in on us."

Dad stopped and Carol eased around him, shining her flashlight on the beams and old support timbers. It was clear to even my eye that whoever had built this had made it to last.

Not one ounce of dirt was in sight. The ceiling, walls, and floors were all covered completely by wood after a few feet inside the entrance. Carol could stand up straight in the tunnel, but both Dad and I had to duck.

"Wow!" Carol said. "I've never seen anything like this. No reason to build all this unless you planned on living in here."

"This place gets stranger and stranger," I said.

Dad agreed and pointed his light down the tunnel. It curved to the left about twenty feet ahead. With Carol in the lead we worked our way underground along the wooden corridor, Carol walking slowly and cautiously, testing each step. Dad and I bent over, following her.

We must have gone a good hundred yards, with two turns and a slight downward angle before we hit another tunnel.

"Main tunnel," Carol said. She pointed her light back up the incline. "This heads right in the direction of the meadow."

In the main tunnel I could stand up completely without even coming close to the high ceiling and my back was very glad that I could. But on top of the backache

I was starting to get a real uneasy feeling about this place. The main tunnel was also completely enclosed by wood and every twenty feet there was an old lantern hanging on a peg from a support beam. Someone had spent a huge amount of time and money in here. And not recently. I shined my light around the wider main tunnel.

"Carol. Any reason they would shore this up like this?"

"Not if this was a regular gold mine. No." She shined her light at the wood planks of the floor. "No rails or any other way to get the gold ore out of here. And there is no reason to have a gold mine shaft this wide and big. My guess is that if this was a gold mine, then it was expanded and the flooring and walls were put in after the mining was finished."

"Why would anyone do that?" Dad asked.

Carol shrugged. "Never heard of it before," she said. "But I imagine the answer is down there." She pointed the flashlight down the tunnel. "Maybe someone really did live here."

"You as creeped out by this place as I am?" I asked.

Both Dad and Carol nodded. Then Carol led the way, again going slow and cautious.

About two hundred feet later we found the answer to our question. The mine shaft ran smack into a solid metal wall. The tunnel branched both left and right, following the curve of the metal off in both directions.

"What the hell is this?" Dad said, rubbing his hand along the metal. "It's manufactured. Why . . . ?"

Carol and I both were running our hands along the smooth gray metal. It felt cold and polished to my touch, like the hood of a car. And the curve into the distance in both directions was exact, with no markings or anything else. "Carol?" I asked, "How far underground would you think we are?"

Carol kept running her hand over the surface of the metal, as if not really believing that it was there. I didn't believe it either. After a moment she looked over at me and pointed upward. "In that direction I would say a good thousand plus feet." She pointed at an angle back along the main tunnel. "In that direction more like five hundred."

I looked off in both directions. "Why would someone build this down here? And for what reason?"

Carol walked a few feet to the right, running her hand along the metal. "You might want to consider that they found this here while digging for gold."

Dad turned and walked away from the metal, back up the tunnel, then turned around and sat down on the wood planking, facing the metal wall. "Not possible," he said. "That would make this, whatever it is, over a million years old. These are young mountains around here, but not that young."

Carol nodded. "At this depth it would be at least that old. Maybe much more."

We stood there in silence, our flashlight beams glued to the metal surface. My mind was just not accepting what I was seeing. None of this could be true. None of it. My grandpa had been a crazy old man. And in the later years his laugh had driven me nuts. For some reason he had built this down here and all we had to do was keep exploring until we found out why. "Dad, let's keep going." I pointed to the right. "Might be some answers."

Dad nodded slowly and climbed back to his feet.

PLAYING IN THE STREET

This time I led the way. Not a seam in the metal, nothing, as we slowly curved down and to the left. For a short time I thought we were just going to end up circling around and ending back up at the junction of the main tunnel.

But then I found the open air lock.

And there was no longer any doubt as to what we had found.

No wonder Grandpa had joined the Lost Wheelbarrow Mine Association to keep the mine hidden. This discovery would blow the lid off the current world, let alone the world of 1915. Of that there was no doubt.

Moscow, Idaho. October 21, 2025

I carefully placed my boots in the exact same footprints as I always had as I started down the street. Nothing had changed in the months since I had been here. Of course, it never did. This street was frozen in time, locked in death by my family's stupidity.

The gray dust made no noise through my protective suit and in front of my parents' house I stopped and looked around. I could imagine the times when we used to play football in the street. I could remember the laughter and the fun. I had always played receiver, so I got to duck in and out of the parked cars, trying to get free to catch the pass. I usually did. I was always good at football.

Those summer and fall days were full of cut grass smells and the tastes of carnivals. Life back then seemed to have no problems and no worries. Now I had finally returned to that point. It is lucky that Carol has been dead all these years. She would call me self-pitying. She would be right.

My parents and everyone in Moscow and the surrounding area were killed when Dad's team tried to start up the simplest power system in the buried ship. Now no children would ever play in these streets again.

I stood on my parents' front steps and tried to remember the laughter.

Berkeley, California. July 10, 1999.
I stood in front of the television, my mouth open, staring.

"Over a hundred square miles," the CNN announcer said, "of Northern Idaho has been evacuated. The gray cloud causing the deaths has slowly settled over the Moscow, Idaho area. No reason for the cloud has been uncovered, but the theory that a small mountain to the north of Moscow has erupted is not true. We will keep you updated as more information comes in."

"Dad? Mom?" Carol put her arm around me, holding me while crying. I couldn't cry. I was too much in shock.

I just kept staring at the television, not really believing what I knew must have happened.

The day we found the buried spaceship, Carol and Dad and I had sat inside the control room in the alien chairs. Just as Grandpa and the men before him, we decided that the world wasn't ready for this discovery. We decided that Grandpa and the old Wheelbarrow Association had been right. This ship needed to stay secret for a while. Or at the very least we would bring outsiders in slowly.

Dad had taken charge and within a week had brought in a trusted friend who was a professor of physics at Cal Tech. Then over the next few years the Wheelbarrow Association, as we called ourselves, gained more and more members as Dad put together a private research team made up of some of the best scientists in the nation to study the ship.

They made slow headway, filing patents on what they did figure out how to work, and being careful to document every step they took.

Carol and I were married the following year and both of us kept going to school and working around the ship in the summers. After a few years we even came to feel comfortable with knowing there was an alien ship buried under Moscow Mountain. It became a part of our lives. I took a job at the University of California, Berkeley, doing research in electrical engineering, mostly along lines we were uncovering in the ship. Carol finished her doctorate in geology and was teaching across the bay.

We spent the summers in Moscow.

Life for all of us was good. Settled. Until the research team decided to start one of the ship's power systems. For years nothing that crazy had been suggested. That summer I spent time on the ship arguing against trying to power anything up. I argued that the systems the aliens were using were not completely understood yet. I argued that there was a real reason this ship was here that we didn't understand and that reason might have to do with a malfunction in the power systems. We didn't know what might happen.

But Dad and his team said it was right to try, all safety precautions would be taken, and everything would be done by the book.

Dad and his friends didn't say what book.

I helped with the early stages, hoping against hope that I could talk them out of trying anything. But all the research and all the exacting detailed studies went so smoothly that eventually, when school started, Carol and I went back to California.

Every night I talked to Dad and some of the other scientists. And three times that fall I went back up to try to stop the testing. But I had no luck. From what Dad told me on the phone the night before they were killed, everything still seemed just fine. Powering up the smallest power system seemed to be progressing as planned and he was excited about finally getting into some of the data banks on the ship. I was supposed to call him and be on the phone when the test started in case they needed me for anything.

But, of course, something went wrong. Terribly wrong.

Carol and I were eating breakfast when we heard the news of what they were calling an explosion in Northern Idaho during the night. I had been expecting a call from Dad about the test being postponed for one reason or another. I was sure there would be small problems that would stop the power-up for a few more weeks. But I guess I was wrong.

At first the news sources thought that Moscow Mountain had blown itself apart in a volcanic eruption sometime around three in the morning. But Moscow Mountain was still there and could be photographed from a distance. And there had been no seismic activity that night to show an explosion.

Carol and I knew what had happened. The ship had gone through a melt-down of some sort or another. The test Dad and the rest had wanted to try had not been scheduled to start until later in the morning. Dad was still in bed, at home, with Mom, when the accident occurred.

After staring at the news reports for most of the morning, I finally stood and went to the phone.

Carol moved up beside me and touched my shoulder lightly as I dialed the phone to finally tell the world about the alien spaceship in the Lost Wheelbarrow Mine.

Of course, at that point it was way too late.

Moscow, Idaho. October 21, 2025

I looked down the gray-coated street. Maybe the ghosts of all the dead children were still playing there. Maybe after today I would be able to see them, hear their laughter. It would be nice to see laughter on this street again.

The gray dust under my feet was the same color as I remembered the hull of the ship. A vast cloud of gray dust, probably material from the hull, had poured out of the northern side of the mountain.

In the end it was lucky that there was very little wind. The cloud of gray dust settled silently in the night over the small city of Moscow, Idaho and killed everyone in that city instantly. Most in their sleep.

The specialists say that if there had been a wind it could have been much worse, taking out Missoula and other cities east.

By the next morning the dust had quit spewing from the side of the mountain and it rained. A simple fall rain that turned the gray dust into something harder than concrete, gluing death to everything it touched.

Exploration teams eventually entered the mountain and the old mine and found what was left, a melted mass of grayness in a huge empty hole in the ground.

They explored that hole for a while, until it became clear there was nothing to gain. Then they left and sealed off the area. Left the dead frozen in their sleep. Set up guards to keep the world out.

There was nothing else the world could do.

No one lives within a hundred mile radius of Moscow, Idaho, now.

And no one will for centuries.

I took one last look at the street, hoping to see children playing there. Then I turned into the house. Carefully placing my feet in my footprints from my very first visit I climbed the stairs to my parents' room.

For only a moment I thought about going down to my old room, to the safety it offered. But then turned and went into their room.

"Hi, Mom. Hi, Dad," I said, but my voice echoed around inside my protective suit. "I'd like to pretend it's Christmas morning. Can I join you?"

Without waiting for an answer I strode across the unmarked dust on the floor around their bed.

I unzipped my suit, took off my helmet, and took a deep breath. The air smelled dry and stale and I felt my eyelids getting heavy.

Quickly I jumped onto the bed and then lay down beside Mom. I didn't look at them because I didn't want to know if I had disturbed the scene.

I took another deep breath and let it slowly out. For a moment I thought I could smell Grandpa's pipe smoke and hear his cackling, crazy laughter.

For some reason that made me smile.

I took one last deep breath.

Outside, beyond the window, I heard the sounds of children laughing and playing in the street.

THE APOCALYPSE QUATRAIN

by Robert Weinberg

Century X, #74

At the end of the year of the great seventh number
It will appear at the time of the games of sacrifice
Not far from the great age of the Millennium
When the buried shall come forth from their tombs

Someone was knocking on the door. Loudly. Groggily, Sidney Taine rolled over in bed and glanced at the clock of his nightstand. It was four a.m. Not the usual time for visitors. Forcing himself awake, Taine pulled on his robe and headed for the door. The pounding continued, relentless and unceasing.

Cautiously, Taine peered out the peephole into the hallway. As a private detective specializing in cases too bizarre, too unusual for other investigators to handle, he had made more than his share of enemies. It never hurt to be extra careful, though it seemed doubtful that anyone seeking revenge would announce his presence by knocking.

Two big, burly men in trench coats stood in the corridor. Taine didn't recognize either of them, but he knew their type instantly. Government agents.

"You gentlemen looking for me?" he asked, opening the door.

"Sidney Taine?" replied the taller of the two.

"That's me," said the detective.

"Your government needs you, Mr. Taine," said the other man, pulling out his wallet and flashing an identification card. Taine hardly bothered looking at it. There was no reason for deception. "Would you please get dressed? Immediately."

"I take it the government can't wait till morning," said Taine. He wasn't surprised when the agent shook his head. "Come on in. It will take me a few minutes to put on some clothes."

"Dress warm," advised the first man. "It's pretty damned cold where you're going."

The agent wasn't exaggerating. Three hours later, Taine climbed out of an air force jet onto a landing strip in the middle of nowhere. A howling wind roared off the desolate, empty plains. The cold hit Taine like a hammer, chilling him to the bone. He guessed he was somewhere in the Dakotas, but if someone told him it was actually the ancient Norse hell, he would not have disagreed.

A half-dozen men in army uniforms escorted him to the only buildings in sight, a handful of concrete huts that barely broke the surface of the prairie. Taine wasn't surprised to discover that there was nothing inside the blockhouses other than elevators leading beneath the surface. Wordlessly, the soldiers put him in one, and pressed the down button. The forty seconds it took at high speed to reach the bottom told the detective all he needed to know about how big and how important a base was buried beneath the frozen ground. It was obviously very big and very important.

A familiar figure waited for him when the elevator

door opened to a bustling underground complex. "General Parker," said Taine, smiling. "I should have guessed you were behind this abduction."

"Good to see you again, Taine," said Parker, advancing with hand outstretched. "Sorry for all the mystery. We required a man of your talents and there wasn't time for long explanations. So we sent out the hounds. Thank God they found you."

A short, stocky man with bright red cheeks and thick mane of shockingly white hair, Parker was the army's top man in the Midwest. Taine had met him the year before when the general's son disappeared under very unusual circumstances. The detective's unique grounding in the occult had enabled him to find the boy when all others failed. From his initial remarks, Parker had evidently not forgotten Taine's special skills.

They shook hands. The general's grip was as firm as ever, but his arm trembled either from fatigue or worry. Taine suspected it was a combination of both. Something important was going on that frightened the officer, and Parker was not a man who scared easily.

"Come with me," said the general. "The others are waiting for us in the conference room. Did you eat breakfast? I can have some food sent over from the mess hall."

"Black coffee will be fine," said Taine. "Exactly what is this place, General? With the Soviet Union gone, I thought secret bases like this no longer existed."

Parker smiled briefly as they walked down a long, white corridor. Dozens of men and women, in both uniforms and civilian clothing, hurried past them, rushing from place to place like rats in a gigantic maze.

"You're at the hub of the North American Early Defense System, Taine. It's a self-contained fortress with links to all the major missile and chemical weapon networks on the continent. There's a similar base located a few miles outside of Washington, D.C. As envisioned by its creators, one or the other stronghold is where the major battles of the next war were to be fought and won. Fortunately, that prospect no longer seems probable.

"Officially, this base no longer exists. All our records indicate that it, and the one in Washington, were dismantled shortly after the implementation of various treaties signed during the past ten years. We lied, of course, as did the Russians. Neither of us fooled the other. The only difference was that now they've retired from the game. We're the only player left. But there're plenty of others on the sidelines waiting to deal themselves in.

"The Cold War may be over, Taine, but that doesn't mean we can relax our defenses. World conditions are more volatile than when the Soviets were the only perceived threat. There're too many unfriendly nations with nuclear weapons capabilities. Communism might be dead, but it's been replaced by rabid nationalism and religious fanaticism. To be frank, I'm not sure the Cold War wasn't preferable to what we're faced with in its place."

The general ushered the detective into a large meeting room. A dozen men sitting at a U-shaped table sat there waiting for their arrival. Parker walked to an empty chair at the front of the room and motioned for Taine to take the seat next to him. As soon as the detective slid into place, an orderly brought him a cup of black coffee. Parker insisted on efficiency. Taine knew that if the general specifically wanted him here, there had to be a good reason. Which meant that it involved his knowledge of the supernatural and the occult.

"Gentlemen, we are ready to begin," said Parker. "Mr. Taine is here at my invitation. I have dealt with him before and know something of his unique skills. He may be our only hope in understanding what is taking place the past few days. Please speak freely to him. We don't have much time left. Dr. Silas, will you begin?"

Silas, a tall shadow of a man, completely bald, wearing glasses with lenses the thickness of pop bottle glass, rose to his feet. He did not look happy. None of the men at the table appeared cheerful. They were grim and, after a few seconds of contemplation, Taine realized, apprehensive. As if they were waiting for a bomb to explode. On a base of this importance, the thought was a frightening one.

"Yesterday afternoon, during a routine random camera scan of high-level technicians serving the NAEDS mainframe computer, a programmer was observed feeding unauthorized information into the machine's memory banks. When confronted by security personnel, the man, Alan Wetherby, reacted violently and had to be subdued by force. Fortunately, he was not injured and several hours later we were able to question him. He made no attempt to hide what he had done and later examinations using truth drugs confirmed everything he told us. Actually, he seemed quite proud of his accomplishments."

Though it was quite cool in the meeting room, Dr. Silas wiped off beads of sweat dripping down his forehead. "Wetherby, we discovered when investigating his background, had experienced a number of personal and emotional disasters during the past few years. His mother and father died in a car crash; his wife left him for another man; and his only child, a daughter, died from a drug overdose. Under such intense pressure, he turned not to religion, which he thought was a sham, but instead to mysticism. Primarily, he found comfort in the obscure prophecies of the famous sixteenth century physician and seer, Michel de Nostradamus."

Taine grimaced. "He wasn't. . . ."

"Unfortunately, yes, he was," answered Dr. Silas. "For the past three months, Mr. Wetherby secretly fed the prophecies of Nostradamus into the NAEDS Base Computer. As far as we can tell, he managed to enter all but the last few quatrains into the mainframe's memory core."

"Why wasn't he caught earlier?" asked Taine.

"Good question," replied Silas. "I've repeated it a thousand times myself. I don't have an answer, though. Outwardly, Wetherby acted perfectly normal. He worked on the NAEDS project for more than ten years and had the highest security clearance. Until he was apprehended, entirely by accident, there was no reason to be suspicious of him. Needless to say, we are revising our psychological screening tests. But, in this case, the damage is already done."

"Thank you, Doctor," said General Parker, nodding the man back to his seat. "Major Watkins, would you continue?"

Watkins spoke in quiet, measured tones, but fear echoed in his every word.

"My department handles computer repairs and debugging. As soon as we understood what Wetherby had done, my men attempted to retrieve and eliminate the extraneous data from the core. It was then that we learned the full extent of our problem."

Watkins paused, taking a deep breath, as if about to plunge into a lake of ice water. The room was deathly silent as he continued.

"The NAEDS computer resisted all efforts to tamper with the core memory. Wetherby entered the prophecies as Class 1 priority transmissions. That code classified the documents as wartime security information. The mainframe thus treated the prophecies as fact, not fancy.

"At the mention of Nostradamus, the computer, following standard defense procedures, immediately went on full alert, isolating its functions from any outside interference. Since that time, it has proceeded with actions we can only deem extremely dangerous to our national well-being. We can still communicate with the machine, but it refuses to answer any of our questions. Instead, it continues to print out four lines of verse I am told forms one of the quatrains."

Watkins passed a sheet of paper up to Taine. The detective scanned the page. Someone had scribbled on the top of the sheet, *Century X, Quatrain* 74.

At the end of the year of the great seventh number
It will appear at the time of the games of sacrifice
Not far from the great age of the Millennium
When the buried shall come forth from their tombs

The blood drained out of Taine's face as he read the passage. Now he understood why the general and his staff were so worried. They were staring at the end of the world and wanted him to tell them that it wasn't true.

"What actually can the computer do?" Taine asked, wanting to make sure he wasn't assuming too much.

"The NAEDS computer is designed to wage all-out war in case of an enemy attack. If, as it seems to be the case, the machine believes that we are involved in a war, it is capable of launching physical and chemical retaliation against the aggressors, wherever they may be in the world."

"Can't the president . . . ?"

"The NAEDS mainframe was conceived," said Watkins, "as being our country's final line of defense if the president and congress were unable to act. Meaning, in the simplest terms, that they had been wiped out in the first enemy assault. It is a fully functional, stand-alone, defensive battle system, probably the most advanced computer network ever constructed. And, as best we can determine, it is insane."

"The quatrain, Taine," said General Parker. "You're familiar with it?"

"Yes," said the detective, rising to his feet. He raised his voice loud enough so that everyone in the room could hear him. There was no reason to hide the bad news. "It's known among students of the occult as 'The Apocalypse Quatrain.' "

Taine paused, deciding what to say next. The direct approach, he concluded, was best. "Nostradamus wrote his prophecies in no particular order, but most scholars agree if they were arranged in sequence, this particular one would be very close to the end. It describes the coming of Armageddon."

THE APOCALYPSE QUATRAIN

"The language seems pretty obscure," said the General. "Would the verse make any sense to the NAEDS mainframe?"

"That depends on how sophisticated a library the computer possesses and whether it can access the necessary information," said Taine. "From what Major Watkins stated, I suspect I know the answer to both queries."

"One of the prime functions of the NAEDS systems is logical analysis of information from a variety of sources," declared the Major glumly. "Its memory bank contains the contents of the entire Library of Congress."

"Which, I feel certain," said Taine, "includes the *Bible,* and therefore, The Book of Revelation. Since most scholars feel that book provided Nostradamus' inspiration for this verse, I feel we must assume the meaning of the verse is quite clear to the computer. And, from what you have told me, it is acting on that information."

"Please explain," said General Parker, his voice a whisper of dread.

"At the end of the year of the great seventh number, " said Taine, "does not refer to a specific date but instead is a direct reference to the Book of Revelation. Seven appears throughout the text—there are seven stars, seven angels, seven trumpets, seven plagues, seven seals, seven vials of wrath. The most important grouping to us is the seven plagues—including earthquakes, pestilence, wars, and such—which would all occur in one year, signifying the coming Apocalypse. Considering recent history, that year is right now.

"It will appear at the time of the games of sacri-

fice," continued Taine, "refers to a period of many wars. Need I mention the outbreaks of fighting in Europe, Asia, and elsewhere?"

The room was deathly silent as he recited the next line. *"Not far from the great age of the Millenium.* We are only a few years away from the new millennium."

Taine's voice echoed hollow in the chamber. "The last line presents the inevitable conclusion. *When the buried shall come forth from their tombs.* Revelations again, with the dead returning to life at the Last Judgment."

"Or worse," said General Parker. "When we took our atomic missiles off line as per treaty agreements, we listed them as 'dead and buried.' Their silos soon became known as 'the tombs.' From what you have said and our own observations, it appears that the NAEDS is attempting to fulfill the quatrain's prophecy. It is preparing the dead to go out from their tombs. And bring about mankind's final apocalypse."

"You've informed the President?" asked Taine.

"He knows," said Parker. "He knows that the plotting of a lunatic believer in the prophecies of a sixteenth century astrologer threaten the entire world with nuclear destruction. But there's nothing he can do other than wait. And pray."

"Can't you shut off the computer's power supply? Or disconnect the weapons systems from it?"

"Don't you think we've tried all the obvious choices?" replied Parker angrily. He cooled off in seconds. "NAEDS is constructed to survive a major enemy assault. The computer mainframe has its own power source and is virtually invulnerable to a frontal attack. We could disable it and cut it off from the outside world in a week. But we don't have a week. According to our latest projections, the rearmed missile systems will be at full readiness in two more hours."

"Their targets?" asked Taine.

"Hundreds of locations in Europe and Asia," said Parker. "Every trouble spot in the past two centuries, and that covers just about all the major cities on both continents. We haven't been able to pinpoint each one, but if even a small percentage of the nuclear weapons explode, half the world will become a radioactive wasteland."

"Then there's only one question left to be answered," said Taine. "Why am I here? I'm not a military man or computer expert. How can I help?"

An attractive young woman rose to her feet. "We're hoping, Mr. Taine, that you can shut down the NAEDS computer on your own. Actually, we're praying. None of our other plans have worked. You're our last chance."

"Ms. Smythe is our resident computer guru," said General Parker. "She understands the NAEDS mainframe better than anyone. Her proposal is a longshot, but at this stage of the game, considering the stakes, I'm willing to gamble."

"What do you want me to do?" asked Taine.

"My scheme," said Ms. Smythe, "calls for someone who is extremely quick-witted, firmly grounded in mysticism and the occult, and can twist the truth to fit his own purposes. General Parker assures me that you fit the bill."

Taine smiled. "Close enough."

Ms. Smythe didn't smile back. "Everything hinges

on the fact that we can still communicate with the NAEDS mainframe. The machine listens to us but refuses to believe that it is acting on erroneous information. The machine accepts the prophecies as truth. We can't change that. However, since the quatrains are so ambiguous, we're hoping that we can—you can—convince the computer that there is more than one logical interpretation of the verse."

"What will that accomplish?"

"One of the basic differences between man and machine, Mr. Taine, is that humans have the capability of accepting variable truths. In other words, we recognize that specific circumstances or facts do not always lead to the same conclusion. The laws of logic, of cause and effect, cannot be applied to human behavior."

A slight smile creased Ms. Smythe's lips. "We are creatures of emotion as well as logic. That is not the case with a computer. In its universe, if A implies B and B implies C, then A must imply C. Every question has one answer, and one answer alone. The laws of mathematics and logic are fundamental and unyielding.

"Working with world events or battle scenarios, the mainframe can balance factors, evaluate possibilities, and come up with the most likely situation. However, we aren't dealing with actual happenings, but with the words of a man dead for centuries. The computer has settled on one specific meaning to the verse. We want you to provide it with another."

"I think I see where you're heading," said Taine. "If I can convince the mainframe that its analysis of the quatrain is not the only logical explanation, that multiple solutions exist, the machine will be faced with a situation outside its frame of reference."

Ms. Smythe nodded. "Which, in theory, should throw its logic circuits into an unending memory loop, freezing the machine."

"In theory?" repeated Taine.

"We've never dealt with an insane computer before," said Ms. Smythe. "Nor one that believes in the prophecies of Nostradamus."

"Can you do it, Taine?" asked General Parker, his features grim. "Can you?"

The detective shrugged. "I wish the machine had picked another quatrain. Coming up with an alternate meaning is going to be a challenge. Especially considering the amount of time left. But I don't see that I have much choice. No choice at all."

Drawing in a deep breath, Taine opened his eyes and looked around. He stood on the edge of a huge stone cliff, a thousand feet above a raging, stormy sea. Monstrous waves, hundreds of feet high, crashed into the rock with incredible fury. Something immense and blood red, but otherwise vague, stirred in the center of the maelstrom.

Above him, immense crimson-tinted gray clouds swirled about angrily, stirred by powerful winds that ripped and tore at his clothing. Barely visible in their heart was a mighty throne covered with emerald light. Before it, burned seven torches of fire. Taine noted that no one sat in the great chair. Evidently, even the NAEDS computer had difficulty conceptualizing God.

Lightning flashed and thunder roared, and the world shook with the sound of hoofbeats. Four gigantic horsemen approached, riding through the dark sky. The detective nodded as if in confirmation of his expectations.

"Remember," he whispered to himself, "this isn't real. It's merely a computer simulation. I'm sitting inside a communications booth at the NAEDS base, hooked up directly to the mainframe by Virtual Reality software. It's the normal method base personnel use to conduct business with the machine. Only now, instead of talking to the simulation of a helpful office manager, I'm dealing with the computer's new persona." Mentally, he footnoted his last thought. "The *insane* computer's new persona."

The riders circled Taine, each of them the size of a small battleship. The first rode a pure white horse and carried a bow. He was the conqueror, and Taine expected he would speak for the group. The second, mounted on a red horse, carried a sword and brought war. The third, sitting on a black steed, carried a balance. The fourth rider, skeletal and clothed in a black robe, was Death, armed with a scythe, on a pale horse.

Taine knew them as the Four Horsemen of the Apocalypse, as described in Revelations. The chair in the heavens was the Throne of God, while the monster stirring in the sea was the Great Beast. Judging by the visible signs and portents, Taine concluded that the computer considered these moments the prelude to Armageddon. He adjusted his plans accordingly.

In his left ear, Ms. Smythe's voice whispered, "Thirty minutes to estimated missile launch, Taine." The miniature radio receiver was his only link to the real world.

"Who are you, mortal?" asked the white rider, his

booming voice echoing through the night. "Why have you come here?"

"My name is Daniel," said Taine, the name of the most famous prophet of the Old Testament, whose visions helped shape Revelations. "I come seeking the truth."

"What truth?" asked the white rider, modulating its voice so that it was no louder than normal speech.

According to most occult researchers, in a later section of Revelations, a rider on a white horse represented Christ resurrected. The implications of the computer's use of that figure as its spokesman disturbed Taine. Quite possibly, the machine considered itself the instrument of God's will on Earth. It was not a comforting thought.

Taine closed his eyes for a second, marshaling his thoughts. Everything hinged on the next exchange with the computer. His unwavering gaze fixed on the white rider, the detective declared, "I search for understanding, for wisdom. What is the meaning of the number of the beast?"

"It is a human number," answered the white rider, the words coming directly from Revelations. "Its number is 666."

Inwardly, Taine breathed a sigh of relief. The dialogue had begun. None of the computer experts, including Ms. Smythe, knew for sure whether the mainframe in its battle alert mode would continue to answer all questions directed at it. With that difficulty resolved, the detective could now proceed with his planned sabotage of the machine.

"The number is 666," repeated Taine. "That confuses me. What then is the great seventh number?"

"The dawning of the apocalypse," said the white rider. "It is the time of seven seals, the seven angels, the seven gold bowls filled with the wrath of God, and the Beast with Seven Heads."

Taine smiled. The machine was drawing its information directly from Revelations. Considering the contradictory and obscure nature of that book, it was a dangerous practice—one that Taine fully intended to exploit.

"I don't understand," said Taine. "Nostradamus spoke of the year of the great seventh number accomplished and said that *it* will appear. How can a time appear?"

The white rider hesitated before answering. "Nostradamus wrote in vague generalities and terms," the machine finally declared. "He was often poetic in speech."

"The seventh number," continued Taine, pressing his advantage. "Why didn't Nostradamus merely say seven if he meant that number. Isn't it likely that he was referring instead to the early Arabic practice of examining the whole numbers starting not with one but with zero? In that manner, all possible integers can be formed using combinations of single digits."

"It is possible," said the white rider, frowning.

"Using that assumption," said Taine, "the seventh *number* would actually be six. The great seventh number thus becomes six multiplied. The year of the Great Seventh Number accomplished would therefore mean the year of Number 666. And since that is how the Great Beast is named in Revelations, *it* would clearly refer to the arrival of the Great Beast on Earth."

Taine realized his rationalization of the numbers was

quite unorthodox. Still, he felt confident the computer would accept his reasoning. Especially since binary, the heart of all computer language, was based on the use of zero as the first number.

Below, in the ocean, the thing at the heart of the maelstrom gained substance and shape. Though still partially hidden by the waters, the monster now had four heads. Taine didn't need a closer look to know that the creature possessed attributes of a leopard, bear, lion, and a dragon. Or that one of its heads seemed to bear marks of a mortal wound that had healed. It was the Great Beast of the Apocalypse. The computer had revised its scenery.

"Isn't the Great Beast another name for Satan?" asked Taine. "Wasn't Satan, the father of lies, thrown into the sea where he rose again as the Beast?"

"That is correct," answered the computer, not realizing it had advanced another foot forward into Taine's trap.

"Another question puzzles me," said the detective. "What are games of sacrifice?"

"War," answered the second rider, the bearer of the sword. "Men at war conduct games of sacrifice."

"War?" repeated Taine, sounding dubious. "No man considers war a game. Doesn't the word *games* refer to pleasurable occupations?"

He paused dramatically, to reinforce his point. "Isn't man's greatest pleasure, sex, often called a game—the game of love? Is it possible that the games of slaughter refers instead to sex leading to death."

The second rider shook his head. "That does not compute. Why would anyone engage in pleasurable behavior leading to extinction?"

"Nostradamus knew the answer," said Taine.

In his ear, Ms. Smythe's voice whispered, "Ten minutes and counting, Taine. Hopefully, you're making progress."

Using Virtual Reality to communicate directly to the computer cut Taine off completely with the outside world. General Parker, Ms. Smythe, and the rest had no idea how he was progressing. And there was no way he could tell them. Obviously, his conversation so far had not caused the mainframe to delay the missile launching.

"Explain your remark," said the white rider.

"When the *buried* shall come forth from their *tombs,*" said Taine, emphasizing the two words. "Nostradamus phrased his quatrains very carefully. He didn't say the dead would return to life, as in the Last Judgment. Instead, he spoke of the buried coming out of their tombs. The prophet wasn't describing some imaginary event. He was describing an actual event, something he witnessed himself. During his lifetime, men wrapped themselves up in shrouds and dwelled in their tombs. They were the buried who entered and departed their tombs."

Taine turned and pointed to the third rider, the one holding the balance. "You know who I mean. Don't you? They were your children."

The rider of the black horse nodded. "Nostradamus lived during the time of the Black Death. In the plague years, many victims acted in just such a manner."

"A plague," said Taine. "The last line of the quatrain refers to a plague, not to the resurrection of the dead."

He spun around and confronted the white rider, now only a few feet away. In the blink of an eye, the four horsemen had shrunk down to mortal size. Below, the seas no longer churned, and the heavens above were silent.

"Five minutes," whispered Ms. Smythe, sounding desperate.

"Century Ten, Verse 74, is not concerned with the end of the world," declared Taine hurriedly, knowing he was running out of time. "Instead, it predicts the coming of the plague in the years leading up to the millennium, at the time of the Great Seventh Number accomplished. A plague we are experiencing right now. A plague brought about by sex that leads to death. A plague whose history is hidden in lies and deceit. A plague spread by behavior considered by Fundamentalist Christians to be fostered by Satan, the Great Beast. *A plague called AIDS.*"

The riders were gone. As was their world. Taine stood facing a man who looked quite a bit like General Parker. They were in a meeting room similar to the one the detective had left an hour earlier.

"AIDS?" said the computer. "But ... but ..."

Blackness.

After a moment, Taine realized the Virtual Reality Helmet was no longer functioning. In his ear, a very subdued Ms. Smythe declared, "All mainframe systems shut down nineteen seconds ago. Missile systems are frozen. Congratulations, Mr. Taine. You did it. With nearly one minute to spare."

Much later, Taine, Ms. Smythe, whose first name turned out to be Pamela, and General Parker celebrated saving the world with the best meal possible at the NAEDS Base. Which, considering the importance of the installation and some of its visitors, was quite spectacular. During the course of the meal, the detective described in detail his encounter with the computer.

"Amazing," said the General, when Taine finished speaking. "To think that you were able to save the world by connecting the horror of AIDS to Nostradamus' prediction."

Taine chuckled. "Not really. It was the first thing that came to mind. If I hadn't thought of AIDS, I would have found something else that worked. Given enough time, I could have produced a dozen different meanings for the verse. My only problem was producing enough evidence quickly to convince the computer. That was the real challenge.

"Prophecy is a wonderful scam, General. It has nothing to do with actually predicting the future. The trick is to make a statement so vague, so nonspecific that it could mean a hundred different things.

"Fortune-tellers do it all the time. A gypsy tells her gullible client she will meet a tall, dark stranger in the near future. The seeress would never dare be more definite than that. *Near* could be next week, next month, even next year. Tall and dark are equally vague. The validity of the prediction relies entirely on the victim's perceptions. Sooner or later, she has to encounter someone matching the correct description. And remember with awe the gypsy soothsayer's words."

"But Nostradamus . . ." began the General.

". . . was only slightly more specific than my hypothetical gypsy woman," said Taine. "His predictions were worded in such a manner that any one of them could have a dozen different meanings. Before World War Two, nearly a hundred of the quatrains described Napoleon's conquests. During and after the war, occultists claimed the same verses dealt with Hitler. Recently, a few enterprising souls connected the identical lines with Saddam Hussein."

The detective shook his head. "The game never ends."

Pamela Smythe smiled, leaned over, and patted Taine on the cheek. "True but not true. Prophecy is a sham, but it often does come to pass. The predictions themselves can alter the future. Wetherby's actions, feeding the quatrains into the mainframe, prove it.

"Think of what would have happened if you hadn't been able to shut down the NAEDS computer. The missile attack would have been launched, bringing about an end of civilization, perhaps of all life on our planet. To me, that sounds like the final apocalypse. Which means that everything in the verse as you originally described it to us would have taken place. Exactly as the Frenchman stated."

Taine nodded. "You're right. I can almost hear Nostradamus laughing at us from the grave. Armageddon would have occurred, brought about by the very verse predicting it. It would have been the seer's most amazing triumph." Taine paused, as if awed by the notion. "Hundreds of years after his death, Nostradamus would have been responsible for the greatest self-fulfilling prophecy of all time."